Dr. Fife's
KETO
COOKERY

Nutritious and Delicious Ketogenic Recipes for Healthy Living

Bruce Fife, ND

P B

Piccadilly Books, Ltd.
Colorado Springs, CO

The information herein is not intended to diagnose, treat, cure, or prevent any disease. The author/publisher claim no responsibility to any person or entity for any liability, loss, or damage caused or alleged to be caused directly or indirectly as a result of the use, application, or interpretation of the information presented herein.

Piccadilly Books, Ltd.
P.O. Box 25203
Colorado Springs, CO 80936, USA
info@piccadillybooks.com
www.piccadillybooks.com

Library of Congress Cataloging-in-Publication Data
Names: Fife, Bruce, 1952- author.
Title: Dr. Fife's keto cookery : nutritious and delicious ketogenic recipes
  for healthy living / by Bruce Fife, ND.
Description: Colorado Springs, CO : Piccadilly Books, Ltd., [2016] |
Includes
  index.
Identifiers: LCCN 2016007816 | ISBN 9780941599979 (trade pbk.)
Subjects: LCSH: Ketogenic diet. | Reducing diets--Recipes. | LCGFT:
Cookbooks.
Classification: LCC RC374.K46 F54 2016 | DDC 641.5/6383--dc23 LC
record available at http://lccn.loc.gov/2016007816

Printed in the USA

Table of Contents

Introduction

The Ketogenic Diet

A ketogenic diet is one that shifts the body into ketosis—a metabolic state in which the body burns fat as its primary source of fuel instead of glucose (sugar). When you are at this point, you are said to be in ketosis. Because this form of ketosis is induced by the types of foods eaten, it is often referred to as nutritional ketosis.

The ketogenic diet is basically a very low-carbohydrate, high-fat, moderate-protein diet. The therapeutic effect comes from the strict limit on carbohydrate and the liberal use of fat, with just enough protein to meet daily requirements.

The health benefits of a ketogenic diet are many. The diet was originally developed as a therapeutic tool in the 1920s specifically to treat epilepsy. Today, the ketogenic diet is the only treatment that has proven successful in reversing epilepsy, even in the most serious, drug-resistant cases. Over the years, the diet has been successful in the treatment of many other brain disorders such as Alzheimer's, Parkinson's, ALS, autism, and traumatic brain injury.

Dietary fat is a key component of the ketogenic diet constituting between 60 to 90 percent of daily calories. Such a high percentage of fat has led some doctors to question the safety of such a diet. For many years it was assumed that fat, particularly saturated fat, promoted heart disease. The ketogenic diet has been used therapeutically for nearly a century. Thousands of patients have used this diet successfully, and in some cases for many years, without any serious adverse effects. In fact, not only is it not harmful, but it appears to improve all the parameters doctors commonly measure to evaluate a patient's health. Blood cholesterol levels go down; HDL cholesterol, the so-called good cholesterol that is believed to protect against heart disease and stroke, goes up; blood triglycerides (a risk factor for heart attack) decreases; high blood pressure comes down; blood sugars normalize; brain function improves; systemic inflammation decreases; excess weight comes off; energy levels increase; physical performance and endurance are enhanced; digestive function works better; the health of the entire body improves. As a result, many health problems improve or disappear entirely.

The Purpose of This Book

Eating a ketogenic diet is simple, but it does take a change in eating habits and a shift in the way meals are prepared. Most people turn to the Internet for recipes. This could be a big mistake! Don't get me wrong, the Internet is a very useful tool and you can find a lot good information there, but it is also a source of much misinformation, especially when it comes to diet and health. The Internet is the first place most people go when looking for ketogenic recipes. Unfortunately, a large number of these so-called ketogenic recipes are not really healthy or even ketogenic. They are loaded with carbohydrate, sweeteners, unhealthy fats, and other questionable ingredients.

Many people posting these recipes assume that ketogenic is the same thing as low-carb. Not so! All ketogenic recipes are low-carb, but not all low-carb recipes are ketogenic. I have found that many of the so-called ketogenic recipes on the Internet are not truly ketogenic. Using these recipes will only hamper your efforts to achieve nutritional ketosis and slow your progress. If you are taking up a ketogenic diet for therapeutic reasons, you need to make sure the recipes you are using are actually ketogenic, otherwise your results and your progress will be disappointing.

With the growing popularity of the keto lifestyle, ketogenic recipes abound. You can easily find hundreds of recipes not only on the Internet, but in books and magazines as well. Many of them sound delicious, like keto cupcakes or keto ice cream…really? Is there such a thing?

People looking for ketogenic recipes generally just assume that any recipe that is labeled "ketogenic" or "low-carb" is actually ketogenic. Nothing could be further from the truth. The term "low-carb" is relative. For example, a single slice of ordinary chocolate cake may supply 50 grams of carbohydrate. A low-carb version of the same size piece of cake may supply a slightly lower 40 grams of carbohydrate. Forty grams is a lot of carbs when you are on a ketogenic diet in which your total carbohydrate allotment for an entire day may be only 20 or 30 grams. But since 40 grams is lower than 50 grams, the cake is labeled as being "low-carb." And many low-carbers wonder why they don't lose weight eating these pseudo low-carb foods!

In order to make low-carb and ketogenic foods taste as sweet and tempting as full-carb versions, low-calorie artificial sweeteners of all types are added, generally aspartame or Splenda. Many people still fear fats, especially saturated fats, so they make their recipes low in fat or use margarine or vegetable oils in place of healthy saturated fats.

It can be frustrating sorting through all the so-called low-carb and ketogenic recipes to find those that are truly ketogenic, as well as healthy. That is what led me to write this book. I wanted to provide "real" ketogenic recipes using healthy ingredients. This book contains all of my favorite ketogenic recipes that I have accumulated and developed over the years. These recipes focus on fresh, whole, natural foods, without chemical additives, harmful fats, or synthetic sweeteners. No gluten or grains are used in any of the recipes. Simplicity was also a goal. Some keto recipes require hours to prepare. Not here. These recipes are generally quick and simple, yet extraordinarily delicious. The ingredients are all common and readily available. It can be frustrating when you see a fantastic dish, but when you try to make it you find that it requires galangal, kaffir lime leaves, or prik kee noo. These ingredients may be common in Thailand, but not other places. Many exotic herbs and spices can be ordered through the Internet, but who wants to pay $10 to ship a $5 spice? The ingredients in this book are all readily available at most grocery stores.

The recipes in this book, for the most part, use real food, not canned, bottled, frozen, or packed foods. The exceptions are generally condiments such as pickles and mustard. Each recipe is limited to no more than 15 grams of carbohydrate per serving, and generally is much less. Accompanying each recipe is a breakdown of the grams of fat, carbohydrate, and protein as well as total calories per serving. Unlike the typical ½ cup servings used in other recipe books, the serving sizes in this book are generally three to four times that much. One serving of a main dish would constitute an entire meal for one person. Regardless of how large a serving size in this book may be, each serving contains less than 15 grams of carbs.

Achieving Nutritional Ketosis

Nutritional ketosis is generally achieved by consuming 60 to 90 percent of calories as fat, 15 to 20 percent as protein, and 0 to 15 percent as carbs. Each meal does not have to have these exact proportions, but the total daily intake should fall within these bounds. Note that carbohydrate consumption is severely limited; this is vital for the production of ketones. Your body only makes ketones when your blood sugar is low. Eating carbohydrate raises blood sugar. Therefore, carbohydrate consumption must be kept to a minimum.

Trying to figure the percentages of all these nutrients that are consumed at each meal during the day can be cumbersome. You really don't need to do any calculations for the recipes in this book. An easier way to determine if a meal is ketogenic is to simply limit the amount of carbs eaten and make sure you get an ample amount of fat. To get into and maintain a state of nutritional ketosis you should limit your net carbohydrate consumption to under about 40 grams per day, with no more than 15 grams coming from any one meal. "Net" carbohydrate is defined as total carbohydrate minus fiber (fiber is classified as a carb but provides no calories and does not adversely affect blood ketone levels).

Protein should also be limited to about 60 to 90 grams daily depending on your size and level of physical activity. A bigger person, or someone who is physically active, would need more protein than a smaller or less active person. These numbers are provided for you at the end of each recipe. If you want to keep track of what you are eating, all you need to do is to add up your daily grams of carbohydrate and protein.

With a few exceptions, most of the recipes have an adequate amount of fat to make them ketogenic, so you don't need to keep track of the amount of fat you eat at each meal. Those recipes with lower fat counts should be combined with other higher fat recipes. For example, a steak by itself normally does not supply enough fat to be ketogenic, so it should be combined with one or more of the high-fat salad or vegetable dishes that would boost total fat consumption to ketogenic levels. I call these "keto friendly" foods because they are very low-cab and can easily be incorporated into a ketogenic diet.

Fats and Oils

One of the foundations of the ketogenic diet is fat. Dietary fat provides the building blocks for ketones. You must eat an ample amount of fat for the body to switch from burning glucose to burning fat.

Coconut oil is used as the primary fat in most of the recipes in this book. The reason for this is that coconut oil is a good cooking oil, highly stable under normal cooking temperatures, and tastes good. However, the primary reason it is commonly used in ketogenic diets is because it is more ketogenic than most other types of fat. Coconut oil is easily converted into ketones and will quickly boost blood ketone levels far more than other fats.

Some fats are healthier than others. Although the recipes may suggest a certain type of fat, you can generally substitute any type of fat you desire. Choose fats from the "Recommended Fats" category below. All of these oils are safe for food preparation. Steer away from the "Non-Recommended Fats" and never use them in your cooking or meal preparation.

For cooking and baking, coconut oil, palm oil, palm shortening, red palm oil, palm kernel oil, and animal fats are the best to use. Since coconut oil is more ketogenic than other fats, I like to use it whenever I can. I like all of the vitamins (beta-carotene, vitamin E, lycopene, etc.) that are found in red palm oil, and I enjoy the taste of butter, lard, and beef tallow. Lard and beef tallow have good non-sticking properties, making them useful for frying. For these reasons, I use all these fats in cooking and often combine them to take advantage of each of their properties.

Olive oil, macadamia nut oil, avocado oil, butter, ghee, and MCT oil are better reserved for moderate- to low-temperature cooking and for baking and non-cooking purposes such as spreads, salad dressings, and beverages.

Recommended Fats	Non-Recommended Fats
Coconut oil	Corn oil
Palm oil/palm fruit oil	Safflower oil
Palm shortening	Sunflower oil
Red palm oil	Soybean oil
Palm kernel oil	Cottonseed oil
Extra light olive oil	Canola oil
Extra virgin olive oil	Peanut oil
Macadamia nut oil	Walnut oil
Avocado oil	Pumpkin seed oil
Animal fats (lard, tallow, duck fat, etc.)	Grapeseed oil
Butter	Margarine
Ghee	Shortening
MCT oil	Hydrogenated vegetable oils

Meats

On a ketogenic diet you can eat all types of fresh meats—beef, pork, lamb, buffalo, venison, fish, shellfish, poultry, and game meats. Preferably meat should come from organically raised, grass-fed animals that have not be subjected to hormones and antibiotics. Wild-caught fish is recommended over farm-raised. Fatty cuts of meat are preferred over lean cuts. Leave the skin on poultry and eat it along with the meat. It is often the tastiest part.

Processed meats that contain nitrates, nitrites, MSG, or sugar should be avoided. This includes most lunch and processed meats like hot dogs, sausage, bacon, and ham. However, meats processed with only herbs and spices added are fine. Read the ingredient labels. If they don't contain chemical additives or sugar, they are likely okay to use. If they contain only a small amount of sugar you may still use them if you take into account the sugar and add it to your total carbohydrate allotment for the day. Look at the Nutrition Facts panel on the label for the sugar content.

Health food stores and many conventional stores now carry sugar-free, nitrite-free ham, bacon, and other processed meats. Another source of bacon is fresh side, also known as pork belly. It is simply uncured bacon. Have the butcher cut it into bacon-sized strips and use it like you would any other type of bacon.

A ketogenic diet is not a high-protein or high-meat diet. It is an adequate-protein diet. Some people assume that if carbohydrate is restricted and fat is allowed without restriction, then protein, since it is also not a carbohydrate, is also allowed without limit. Not so. The problem with protein is that the body can convert about half of the protein you eat into glucose, which raises blood sugar levels and blocks ketone production. Therefore, eating too much protein can be counterproductive.

As a general rule of thumb, you should limit your protein intake to 1 gram of protein for every kilogram of body weight (or ½ gram of protein for every pound of body weight). This is your "ideal" body weight, not your weight if you are overweight. If your proper body weight is 75 kilograms (165 lbs), you should eat about 75 grams of protein each day. If you are an athlete or are very physically active, you can increase that amount by 10 or 20 grams.

One of the biggest mistakes people make when they try to go keto is eating too much protein. The recipes in this book have restricted the protein content to be suitable with a ketogenic diet. Protein content per serving is listed at the end of each recipe. In this book, you will find a number of recipes for steaks, roasts, and whole poultry. Serving sizes for meat recipes should be limited as described above and be combined with ketogenic vegetable and salad dishes to balance out the meal and provide an adequate amount of fat.

Vegetables and Fruits

On a healthy ketogenic diet you will probably eat more vegetables than you have in your entire life, which is one of the reasons why this diet is so beneficial. Besides fat, the bulk of your diet should consist of low-carb vegetables. You will be eating more vegetables than meat. A ketogenic diet can also be referred to as a vegetable-based diet.

When you remove from your diet all the grains, high-carb vegetables and fruits, and sweets that are normally consumed, you need to replace these calories with another type of food to provide you with the bulk, nutrients, and calories you need to accompany the fat you eat. Low-carb vegetables fill this need. You can accurately describe a ketogenic diet as a very low-carbohydrate, high-fat, moderate-protein, vegetable-based diet.

Since carbohydrate consumption must be restricted to less than 40 grams a day, all high-carb produce is best eliminated. These include all grains, starchy vegetables, and most fruits. A limited amount of nuts, seeds, and low-carb fruits can be eaten.

Berries have the lowest carbohydrate content of all the fruits. Blackberries, raspberries, boysenberries, gooseberries, and strawberries are relatively low in carbohydrate. One handful contains about 3 to 4 grams of carbs. Blueberries have a slightly higher carb content, but they are still fairly low compared to most other fruits. You can actually eat most any type of fresh fruit on a ketogenic diet, you just need to limit the amount you eat to stay under 15 grams per meal. Some fruits are very high in carbs, so this would amount to a very small portion. Some of the recipes in this book use a small amount of fruit. The amount, however, must be kept small to maintain ketosis. Dried fruits, such as prunes and raisins, should not be eaten when on a ketogenic diet, as the dehydration process concentrates the sugars and makes these foods very rich in carbohydrate.

Sugar and Sweeteners

There are no sugars, natural or synthetic, used in the recipes in this book. In order to keep carbohydrate levels low enough to get into ketosis and stay there, you need to eliminate all sweet foods and sweeteners.

Perhaps the biggest stumbling block to achieving and maintaining nutritional ketosis is sugar addiction. Since sugar is pure carbohydrate, it is completely incompatible with a ketogenic diet. In order to avoid the detrimental effects of sugar, people have turned to artificial sweeteners and sugar substitutes that are essentially carbohydrate-free. This way, people can enjoy the sweet treats they've always loved without all the carbs.

The problem with these low-carb and no-carb sugar replacements is that they are really no better than sugar. For one thing, they feed sugar addiction and keep it alive even if you are on a low-carb diet, which increases the temptation to cheat and to ultimately fail at the diet. Even more troubling, however, is that all sugar substitutes are anti-ketogenic and make getting into and maintaining nutritional ketosis very difficult.

All sugars and sugar substitutes affect blood sugar and/or ketone levels. Artificial sweeteners like aspartame and Splenda also have negative effects on health in general and promote weight gain and metabolic problems. Sugar alcohols, such as xylitol and erythritol, are often used to sweeten so-called ketogenic desserts, syrups, candies, and treats. People assume that since sugar alcohols provide no appreciable calories, they are safe to use in a ketogenic diet. Not so. People have been knocked out of ketosis simply by brushing their teeth with xylitol-containing toothpaste.

The same goes for stevia. Too often I've seen people knocked out of ketosis after eating what would otherwise have been a ketogenic snack or beverage that contained a few drops of liquid stevia. This isn't just a brief dip in ketone levels. This effect can persist for an entire day or more even when a strict ketogenic diet is maintained. It's amazing what just a tiny amount of erythritol or stevia can have on blood ketone levels. For this reason, there is no such thing as a ketogenic dessert that is sweetened with any form of artificial sweetener or sugar substitute. And eating such foods will only hamper your success with the ketogenic diet. If you are on a ketogenic diet for therapeutic reasons, eating foods with any type of sweetener will interfere with the beneficial effects of the diet and prevent you from achieving your desired results.

I have written a detailed report describing the effects of sugar substitutes on health and why they are incompatible with a ketogenic diet. If you are interested in learning more about this topic, go to http://cocoketodiet.com/?page_id=623.

Sauces and Gravies

Sauces and gravies enhance the taste of meats, fish, poultry, and especially vegetables. It is amazing how a little sauce can turn otherwise bland vegetables into culinary heroes. Most children, and adults too for that matter, view vegetables as boring or even yucky. The reason they think this way is because most parents, in order to serve their families "healthy" meals, cut out all sources of fat. Fats give foods flavor and enhance their taste. Consequently, vegetables tend to be prepared by steaming or boiling and are served with little more than a dash of salt and pepper—boring! Most vegetables taste dull when prepared this way. However, if you can add fats in the form of butter, sauces, and gravies, vegetables take on new life and become absolutely delicious! Even the most finicky eaters will eat their vegetables when they are prepared this way.

One of the major benefits of using sauces and gravies, for those on low-carb and ketogenic diets, is that they provide an excellent means to significantly increase fat intake. Most sauces and gravies are fat based. A tablespoon of sauce may contain 8 to 10 grams of fat. Just a few tablespoons of sauce can turn an otherwise low-fat meal into a fully ketogenic one.

What is the difference between *sauce* and *gravy*? Sauce gets its base flavor from some combination of butter, cream, milk, stock, cheese, or herbs and is usually served with vegetables, fish, and poultry. Gravy, on the other hand, derives its flavor from meat drippings and is served with the meat or its accompaniments.

When meats are roasted or pan fried, their drippings leave a browned "glaze" in the pan. This glaze appears as stray burnt bits of meat and fat that stick to the bottom of the pan. It's this glaze that gives gravy its delicious flavor. Gravy is made by deglazing the pan by adding water and boiling it on the stovetop. As the water is gently boiled and stirred, the glaze partially dissolves and mixes with the boiling liquid. The addition of seasonings and a thickener completes the job.

Starches and Flours

The biggest drawback to sauces and gravies for those who are following a ketogenic diet is that most of them require some type of thickening agent, and traditional thickeners are rich in starch—a carbohydrate. The most common thickeners are wheat flour and corn starch. If you only need a small amount of thickener, the number of carbs supplied by these thickeners may be very small and have little impact on a low-carb or ketogenic diet. Regular white (wheat) flour, for instance, contains 6 grams of carbs per tablespoon. Two tablespoons of white flour (12 g of carbs) is needed to thicken 1 cup (240 ml) of liquid. A ¼ cup (60 ml) serving would contain 3 grams of carbohydrate.

Corn starch has a little higher starch or carbohydrate content, 7 grams per tablespoon, but it has a greater thickening effect than white flour. Only ½ tablespoon can thicken 1 cup of liquid. A ¼ cup serving would contain slightly less than 1 gram of carbohydrate. Such a small amount can easily be incorporated into a ketogenic diet.

Wheat and corn are both grains. Many people try to avoid grains for various reasons. Some people are gluten-intolerant and must avoid wheat completely. Other popular non-grain thickeners are tapioca and arrowroot flours, which come from the roots of the cassava and arrowroot plants, respectively. They, too, get their thickening power from starch and supply about the same amount of carbohydrate as corn starch. As long as you only use a tablespoon or so for thickening, you can still keep your total carbohydrate intake within the limits of a ketogenic diet.

Flours and starches need to be mixed with a small portion of cold water, cream, or milk before combining them with the hot sauce or gravy, otherwise they form lumps. Once you have mixed the flour with a cold liquid, stir the mixture into the hot sauce to thicken.

Water-Soluble Gums and Seeds

It you want a thickener that supplies no carbs at all, you can use some of the various water-soluble vegetable gums, such as guar gum, agar, and xanthan gum. These gums absorb water to form a gel. They are often used as thickeners and stabilizers in commercial products. You can buy them for home use. They are popular in Asian cooking.

There are also commercial low-carb products that are usually a mixture of vegetable gums. One example is Thicken Thin Not/Starch Thickener, which is made from guar, xanthan, carob, and acacia gums. There are many others.

Some seeds are rich in water-soluble vegetable gums and can be used as thickeners such as flaxseed, chia seed, and psyllium seed husks. Psyllium has been used for decades as a dietary supplement to treat digestive problems such as constipation, diarrhea, and irritable bowel syndrome. It has a long history of safe use. Unlike flaxseed and chia seed, it blends into the sauce and becomes invisible. All of the gums create sauces with a gelatinous texture that some people find unappetizing. I prefer xanthan, as it creates a fairly uniform sauce without being too gelatinous. It is available online, in health food stores, and in some grocery stores.

Before adding gums to sauces, you should mix them into a little oil or melted butter first, then stir the mixture into the sauce. This will prevent lumps from forming. A little can go a long way; just ½ teaspoon of xanthan gum can thicken 1 cup of liquid, so go slow and add just a small amount at a time to thicken. Both xanthan gum and psyllium start to thicken as soon as they are exposed to moisture, so they will thicken cold liquids as well as hot. When added to a hot liquid, gums gradually thicken the sauce. They generally take a little longer to thicken sauces than do starches and flours.

Nut Flours

Nut flours, like almond and coconut flours, are often used in low-carb cooking as a replacement for other, higher-carb flours for making baked goods. While they work well for this purpose, they are not suitable as thickening agents. They do not contain enough starch or soluble fiber to adequately thicken liquids.

Cream

Dairy cream can be used in some recipes as a thickener. If cream makes up a significant portion of the recipe, slow simmering can cause it to thicken as moisture evaporates. However, you cannot add a little cream to a dish and get it to thicken. The dish must have a high proportion of cream for this to happen.

You need real dairy cream for thickening. Most milk and cream substitutes, such as almond, soy, and coconut milks, will not thicken well.

Egg Yolks

Egg yolks can also be used to thicken sauces. It takes about 2 egg yolks to thicken 1 cup of liquid. Using egg yolks to thicken sauces needs to be done very carefully. Beat egg yolks with a fork until uniform in color, then blend it with a small portion of hot sauce. You need to combine a little of the hot sauce with the yolks to heat them slightly, otherwise the egg yolk will curdle. Now, stir the egg yolk mixture into the rest of the hot sauce. For best results, cook and stir egg-thickened sauces over lowest heat or in the top of a double boiler over simmering, not boiling, water. Cook and stir only until sauce is thickened and there is no raw egg taste.

Thickener	Net grams Carbs/Tbs	Amount needed to thicken 1 cup (240 ml) of liquid*
Arrowroot flour	7	½ Tbs (8 g)
Corn starch	7	½ Tbs (8 g)
Tapioca flour	7	½ Tbs (8 g)
White flour	6	2 Tbs (16 g)
Xanthan gum	0	½ teaspoon
Guar gum	0	½ teaspoon
Psyllium powder	0	½ teaspoon
Egg yolk	0.5 (1 yolk)	2 yolks

*Liquid refers to water, broth, and milk. For cream, you need about half as much thickener.

Basic Brown Gravy

Gravy is made by deglazing or dissolving the meat drippings that form the brownish glaze on the bottom of the pan when cooking meat and poultry. This is what gives gravy its flavor.

Before you cook the meat, you need to consider the type of roasting pan you use. It must be both oven and stovetop safe, as you will be making the gravy in the same pan. Glass roasting pans may not be suitable. Instead use stainless steel or enamel-covered cookware that can endure the heat on the stovetop. Gravy can also be made from the drippings left after cooking meat in a skillet on the stovetop.

After the meat has been cooked, most cooks tend to remove the majority of the fat that is left behind. The reason for this is to reduce the fat content of the gravy and to allow the flour or starch to mix more evenly into the gravy. Excess fat will separate from the gravy. However, one of the goals of a ketogenic diet is to add fat to the meal. So unless there is an excessive amount of fat, it is best to use it all when making gravy and not worry too much if any of the fat separates, just mix it in and enjoy it.

The amount of meat drippings will vary greatly depending on the size and type of meat cooked. To get an accurate measure of the amount of drippings you have, pour them into a measuring cup. Depending on the amount of drippings you started with, add enough water (or meat, bone, or vegetable broth) to make an equal half cup measurement, such as 1 cup, 1½ cup, or 2 cups of liquid. You want to know the amount of liquid you have so that you can accurately judge how much thickener to use. Pour the liquid back into the baking pan, put the pan on the stovetop burner, and bring the liquid to a gentle boil. Stir with a wooden spoon or wire whisk to break up and dissolve the glaze. Add salt and black pepper to taste and ½ to 1 tablespoon (5 to 10 g) minced yellow onion per cup of gravy.

If you are using tapioca flour or arrowroot flour as the thickening agent, measure out ½ tablespoon (4 g) for every cup of gravy in the pan. Combine each ½ tablespoon (8 g) of thickener with at least 1 tablespoon (15 ml) of cold water. Stir it into the hot gravy and continue stirring until thickened. For instance, if you have 2 cups (480 ml) of gravy, combine 1 tablespoon (16 g) of thickener with 2 tablespoons (30 ml) of cool water.

If you are using guar or xanthan gum as the thickener, measure out ½ teaspoon for every cup (240 ml) of gravy in the pan. Combine each ½ teaspoon of xanthan gum with 1 tablespoon (14 g) of melted butter. Stir the mixture into the hot gravy and continue stirring until the gravy thickens. Gums require more time to thicken than starches and flours.

Yield varies depending on the amount of drippings and water used. Protein content per ¼ cup serving will be negligible; fat content too variable to determine precisely, but typically ranges from 10 to 15 grams per serving; net carb content from tapioca or arrowroot would be about 1 gram per serving and nearly zero grams per serving if you use guar or xanthan gum.

Variations:
Giblet Gravy

Giblet gravy makes a tasty accompaniment to poultry. Giblets refer to the liver, heart, gizzard, and neck of turkey and other poultry. Put the raw giblets into 2 cups (480 ml) of water and simmer for about 30 minutes. Remove the giblets from the broth, but reserve the broth. Finely chop the heart and gizzard, and if you like the liver, chop it, as well. Debone the neck and discard the bone.

Make Brown Gravy according to directions. Omit the water and use the broth from the giblets. Add chopped giblets, ½ teaspoon dried sage, and ½ teaspoon dried thyme to the gravy before thickening.

White Gravy

White gravy goes very well with poultry or cooked vegetables. White gravy can be made from meat drippings using the same method above, however, replace the water with cream and make as directed above. Add a little ground sage and powdered rosemary with the salt and black pepper. Taste the gravy and adjust seasonings to your preference.

Herb Gravy

The type of herbs you use will depend on the type of meat you are cooking. Make the Brown Gravy as directed, but simmer the following herbs into the hot meat juices for a few minutes before blending in the thickening agent. Beef: ½ teaspoon savory, thyme, and/or marjoram. Lamb or veal: 1 teaspoon tarragon or mint and/or ½ teaspoon ground rosemary. Pork and poultry: ½ teaspoon sage and/or thyme.

White Onion Gravy

Make the White Gravy as directed above, but before adding the thickener sauté ¼ cup (40 g) chopped yellow onion in 1 tablespoon (14 g) butter for every cup (240 ml) of gravy. Cook until the onion starts to brown. Add onion and butter mixture to the gravy with the salt and pepper. Omit the sage and rosemary and add ⅛ teaspoon dried thyme for every cup of gravy.

Mushroom Gravy

Make the Brown or the White Gravy as directed above, but when you add the salt and pepper, also add ½ cup (35 g) of chopped mushrooms and an additional ½ tablespoon (5 g) diced yellow onions to each cup (240 ml) of gravy.

Sausage Gravy

This is a wonderful all-purpose gravy that will enhance the flavor of all types of cooked vegetables and meats.

2 tablespoons (28 g) butter
4 ounces (115 g) sausage or ground pork
¼ cup (40 g) minced yellow onion
½ cup (120 ml) heavy cream or coconut milk
½ cup (120 ml) chicken broth
⅛ teaspoon salt
⅛ teaspoon freshly ground black pepper
¼ teaspoon dried thyme

¼ teaspoon dried ground rosemary
1 teaspoon tapioca or arrowroot flour*
2 tablespoons (30 ml) cool water

Heat butter in saucepan to medium heat. Add pork and onion and cook for about 10 minutes stirring occasionally, until meat and onions begin to brown. Add cream, chicken broth, salt, black pepper, thyme, and rosemary, and simmer for about 5 minutes, stirring occasionally, to allow flavors to blend. Mix tapioca flour into 2 tablespoons (30 ml) of cool water and stir into hot mixture. Stir constantly until sauce thickens. After the sauce thickens, remove from heat to prevent scorching the bottom of the pan.

*This recipe can be made using guar or xanthan gum in place of tapioca flour. Make the recipe above as directed, but mix ¼ teaspoon of xanthan gum with 1 tablespoon (14 g) of melted butter. Stir the xanthan gum–butter mixture into the hot sauce and stir constantly until thickened, about 8 minutes.

Yield: 5 servings, ¼ cup (60 ml) each
Per serving, using tapioca flour: 14.5 g fat; 2 g net carbs; 7 g protein; 166 calories
Per serving, using xanthan gum: 16.5 g fat; 1 g net carbs; 7 g protein; 180 calories

Fiesta Gravy
Follow the directions for making Sausage Gravy, but after adding the thickener, add ¼ cup (65 g) salsa and ¼ cup (30 g) shredded sharp cheddar cheese.

Yield: 6 servings, ¼ cup (60 ml) each
Per serving, using tapioca flour: 13.5 g fat; 2 g net carbs; 7.5 g protein; 159 calories
Per serving, using xanthan gum: 15.5 g fat; 1 g net carbs; 7.5 g protein; 173 calories

Chunky Chicken Gravy
This is a good way to use leftover chicken. Tastes good over cooked vegetables or mashed cauliflower.

6 tablespoons (84 g) butter
¼ cup (40 g) diced yellow onion
¼ cup (30 g) diced celery

¼ cup (20 g) diced mushrooms
1 cup (140 g) finely chopped, cooked chicken
2 cups (480 ml) chicken broth
½ teaspoon salt
¼ teaspoon black pepper
½ teaspoon thyme
1½ tablespoons (12 g) tapioca flour or arrowroot flour*
½ cup (120 ml) cream or coconut milk

Heat butter in a large saucepan over medium heat. Sauté onion and celery until soft. Add mushrooms, chicken, chicken broth, salt, pepper, and thyme, and simmer for about 10 minutes. Blend tapioca flour with cream and stir into hot mixture, stirring continuously until thickened.

*This recipe can be made using guar or xanthan gum in place of tapioca flour. Make the recipe above as directed, but sauté onions in 5 tablespoons (75 g) butter, add the cream to the gravy with the broth, and mix 1 teaspoon of xanthan gum with 1 tablespoon (14 g) of melted butter. Stir the xanthan gum–butter mixture into the hot gravy and stir constantly until thickened, about 8 minutes.

Yield: 4 servings, 1 cup (240 ml) each
Per serving, using tapioca flour: 31 g fat; 4 g net carbs; 13.5 g protein; 349 calories
Per serving, using xanthan gum: 31 g fat; 2 g net carbs; 13.5 g protein; 341 calories

Velouté Sauce

This is one of the five classic French mother sauces from which many daughter sauces are derived. It is a broth-based sauce using chicken, beef, veal, pork, or fish broth. Traditionally thickened by a flour-based roux, this low-carb version is thickened with low-carb friendly thickeners.

¼ cup (40 g) minced yellow onion
6 tablespoons (90 g) butter
¼ cup (20 g) minced mushrooms
2 cups (480 ml) chicken, beef, or fish broth
¼ teaspoon salt
Dash white pepper
¼ to ½ teaspoon herbs*
1 tablespoon (8 g) tapioca or arrowroot flour**

Sauté onion in butter until tender, about 5 minutes. Add mushrooms and continue cooking until onions turn golden brown, about 5 minutes. Add 1½ cups (360 ml) broth, salt, pepper, and herbs, and simmer for about 15 minutes. Blend tapioca flour with ½ cup (120 ml) of cold broth and stir into hot mixture, stirring constantly until thickened.

*For chicken or turkey broth, use sage, rosemary, or thyme. For beef broth, use savory, thyme, or marjoram. For lamb or veal broth use tarragon, rosemary, or sage. For fish use marjoram, dill, thyme, curry, or parsley.

**This recipe can be made using guar or xanthan gum in place of tapioca flour. Make the recipe above as directed, but sauté onions in 5 tablespoons (75 g) butter and mix ½ teaspoon of xanthan gum with 1 tablespoon (14 g) of melted butter. Stir the xanthan gum–butter mixture into the hot sauce and stir constantly until thickened, about 8 minutes.

Yield: 10 servings, ¼ cup (60 ml) each
Per serving, using tapioca flour: 7.5 g fat; 1.5 g net carbs; 1 g protein; 77 calories
Per serving, using xanthan gum: 7.5 g fat; 0.5 g net carbs; 1 g protein; 173 calories

Basic White Sauce

This is a low-carb version of the classic Béchamel sauce, one of the five classic French sauces. It is a basic white sauce that goes with just about anything. It can be used as a base to make a variety of other sauces.

4 tablespoons (120 g) butter
¼ cup (40 g) minced yellow onion
½ cup (120 ml) cream or coconut milk
½ cup (120 ml) chicken broth
¼ teaspoon salt
⅛ teaspoon white pepper
¼ teaspoon dried thyme
1 teaspoon tapioca or arrowroot flour*
2 tablespoons (30 ml) water

Heat butter in saucepan to medium heat and sauté onion until it begins to brown. Reduce heat to low. Add cream, chicken broth, salt, pepper, and thyme, and simmer, stirring frequently, for about 6 to 8 minutes for flavors to blend. Mix tapioca flour with water and stir it into the hot cream sauce. Stir constantly until sauce thickens. Taste and adjust salt and pepper to preference.

*This recipe can be made using xanthan gum in place of tapioca flour. Make the recipe above as directed, but sauté onions in 3 tablespoons (90 g) butter instead of 4 and mix ¼ teaspoon of xanthan gum with 1 tablespoon (14 g) of butter. Stir the xanthan gum and butter mixture into the hot sauce and stir constantly until thickened.

Yield: 5 servings, ¼ cup (60 ml) each
Per serving, using tapioca flour: 28 g fat; 2 g net carbs; 1 g protein; 264 calories
Per serving, using xanthan gum: 28 g fat; 1 g net carbs; 1 g protein; 260 calories

Variations:
Anchovy Sauce
Make Basic White Sauce as directed, but omit the salt, replace chicken broth with fish broth, and add 4 teaspoons of anchovy paste and a dash of cayenne pepper. Goes well with fish or cooked vegetables.

Yield: 5 servings, ¼ cup (60 ml) each
Per serving, using tapioca flour: 34 g fat; 2 g net carbs; 1.5 g protein; 320 calories
Per serving, using xanthan gum: 34 g fat; 1 g net carbs; 1.5 g protein; 316 calories

Caper Sauce
Make Basic White Sauce as directed, but omit the salt. Just before serving, stir in ¼ cup (34 g) coarsely chopped capers and ½ tablespoon (8 g) lemon juice. Goes well with fish.

Yield: 5 servings, ¼ cup (60 ml) each
Per serving, using tapioca flour: 28.5 g fat; 2 g net carbs; 1.5 g protein; 270 calories
Per serving, using xanthan gum: 28.5 g fat; 1 g net carbs; 1.5 g protein; 266 calories

Horseradish Sauce

Make Basic White Sauce as directed, then mix in 2 tablespoons (30 g) prepared horseradish and ⅛ teaspoon dry mustard blended with 2 tablespoons cream, and heat 2 to 3 minutes. Goes well with beef or lamb.

Yield: 5 servings, ¼ cup (60 ml) each
Per serving, using tapioca flour: 30 g fat; 2.5 g net carbs; 1 g protein; 284 calories
Per serving, using xanthan gum: 30 g fat; 1.5 g net carbs; 1 g protein; 280 calories

Mornay Sauce

This is a delicate cheese sauce that goes well with seafood, poultry, eggs, or vegetables. Prepare Basic White Sauce as directed. On low heat, add ¼ cup (20 g) each of grated Parmesan and Gruyere cheese, and stir until melted.

Yield: 5 servings, ¼ cup (60 ml) each
Per serving, using tapioca flour: 30 g fat; 2 g net carbs; 3.5 g protein; 292 calories
Per serving, using xanthan gum: 30 g fat; 1 g net carbs; 3.5 g protein; 288 calories

Shrimp Sauce

Make Basic White Sauce as directed, but omit the salt, replace chicken broth with fish broth, and add ¼ teaspoon fish sauce and ½ cup (60 g) minced shrimp. Tastes good over eggs or vegetables.

Yield: 6 servings, ¼ cup (60 ml) each
Per serving, using tapioca flour: 23 g fat; 1.5 g net carbs; 3 g protein; 225 calories
Per serving, using xanthan gum: 23 g fat; 0.5 g net carbs; 3 g protein; 221 calories

Sour Cream Sauce

Make Basic White Sauce as directed, but reduce the cream to ¼ cup (60 ml). After the sauce has thickened, make sure heat is on a low setting and stir in ½ cup (115 g) sour cream. Do not allow the sauce to boil.

Yield: 5 servings, ¼ cup (60 ml) each
Per serving, using tapioca flour: 28 g fat; 2 g net carbs; 1 g protein; 264 calories

Per serving, using xanthan gum: 28 g fat; 1 g net carbs; 1 g protein; 260 calories

Creamy Mushroom Sauce

Make Basic White Sauce as directed, but add 1 cup (70 g) chopped button or Portobello mushrooms with the cream.

Yield: 6 servings, ¼ cup (60 ml) each
Per serving, using tapioca flour: 23 g fat; 2 g net carbs; 1 g protein; 219 calories
Per serving, using xanthan gum: 23 g fat; 1 g net carbs; 1 g protein; 215 calories

Mustard Sauce

Make Basic White Sauce as directed, but add ¼ cup (44 g) prepared mustard with the cream. Goes well with cooked vegetables and eggs.

Yield: 6 servings, ¼ cup (60 ml) each
Per serving, using tapioca flour: 23 g fat; 2 g net carbs; 1 g protein; 219 calories
Per serving, using xanthan gum: 23 g fat; 1 g net carbs; 1 g protein; 215 calories

Ham Sauce

Make Basic White Sauce as directed, but add ½ cup (75 g) diced sugar-free and nitrite-free ham to the onions as they are being sautéed. Stir in ½ teaspoon dry mustard with the cream. Good over cooked vegetables and eggs.

Yield: 6 servings, ¼ cup (60 ml) each
Per serving, using tapioca flour: 24 g fat; 1.5 g net carbs; 3 g protein; 234 calories
Per serving, using xanthan gum: 24 g fat; 0.5 g net carbs; 3 g protein; 230 calories

Cheese Sauce

This is a simple and delicious cheese sauce that can be poured over any type of cooked meat or vegetable. Each ¼ cup (60 ml) serving delivers 20 grams of fat, making this sauce an excellent means by which to boost the fat content of a variety of meals. This recipe uses sharp cheddar cheese, but you can use other types of cheese for a variety of flavors.

3 tablespoons (45 g) butter
1 cup (240 ml) cream
1 cup (115 g) shredded sharp cheddar cheese
⅛ teaspoon salt
2 teaspoons tapioca or arrowroot flour*
¼ cup (60 ml) water

Heat butter and cream in a saucepan over low heat. Stir in cheese and salt and simmer, stirring until cheese melts. Blend tapioca flour into the water and pour into the hot mixture. Stir constantly until sauce thickens, about 4 to 5 minutes. Goes well over cooked broccoli, cauliflower, zucchini, eggplant, mushrooms, green beans, asparagus, Brussels sprouts, and meats.

*This recipe can be made using guar or xanthan gum in place of tapioca flour. Make the recipe above as directed, but omit the water and mix ½ teaspoon of xanthan gum into 1 tablespoon (14 g) of melted butter. Stir the xanthan gum–butter mixture into the hot sauce and stir constantly until thickened, about 8 minutes.

Yield: 8 servings, ¼ cup (60 ml) each
Per serving, using tapioca flour: 20 g fat; 1.5 g net carbs; 4 g protein; 202 calories
Per serving, using xanthan gum: 21 g fat; 0.5 g net carbs; 4 g protein; 207 calories

Variations:
Salsa Cheese Sauce
Make Cheese Sauce as directed, but add ½ cup (130 g) salsa with the cream.

Yield: 10 servings, ¼ cup (60 ml) each
Per serving, using tapioca flour: 16 g fat; 2 g net carbs; 3.5 g protein; 166 calories
Per serving, using xanthan gum: 16 g fat; 1 g net carbs; 3.5 g protein; 162 calories

Jalapeño Cheese Sauce
Make Cheese Sauce as directed, but add 2 tablespoons (18 g) chopped jalapeño peppers.

Yield: 8 servings, ¼ cup (60 ml) each
Per serving, using tapioca flour: 20 g fat; 1.5 g net carbs; 4 g protein; 202 calories
Per serving, using xanthan gum: 21 g fat; 0.5 g net carbs; 4 g protein; 207 calories

Garlic Cheese Sauce
Make Cheese Sauce as directed, but add 2 small or 1 large crushed clove of garlic with the cream.

Yield: 8 servings, ¼ cup (60 ml) each
Per serving, using tapioca flour: 20 g fat; 1.5 g net carbs; 4 g protein; 202 calories
Per serving, using xanthan gum: 21 g fat; 0.5 g net carbs; 4 g protein; 207 calories

Mushroom Onion Cheese Sauce
Sauté ½ cup (35 g) chopped mushrooms and ¼ cup (40 g) minced yellow onion in the butter until vegetables are soft. Combine tapioca flour, salt, and cream and stir into the mushroom mixture. Delete water. Replace cheddar cheese with ½ cup (60 g) shredded Monterey Jack and ¼ cup (30 g) shredded Parmesan cheese. Add cheeses to hot mixture and stir constantly until melted.

Yield: 8 servings, ¼ cup (60 ml) each

Per serving, using tapioca flour: 20 g fat; 2.5 g net carbs; 4 g protein; 206 calories

Per serving, using xanthan gum: 21 g fat; 1.5 g net carbs; 4 g protein; 202 calories

Espagnole Sauce

This is a low-carb version of Espagnole sauce, which is one of the five mother sauces used in French cooking. The thickening comes from the pureed vegetables.

4 strips sugar-free, nitrite-free bacon, cooked crisp and crumbled
2 tablespoons (28 g) butter
1 medium yellow onion, finely chopped
1 medium carrot, finely chopped
1 stalk celery, finely chopped
2 cups (480 ml) beef or bone broth (pages 78 and 79)
2 cloves garlic, minced
½ teaspoon dried thyme
¼ teaspoon dried marjoram
½ teaspoon dried oregano
¼ teaspoon salt
½ bay leaf
¼ cup (60 g) tomato sauce
2 tablespoons (30 ml) lemon juice

Cook bacon in a large skillet until crisp. Remove bacon, crumble, and set aside. Keep bacon drippings in the pan, add butter, and sauté onion, carrot, and celery for about 10 to 12 minutes, until they start to turn brown.

Add beef broth, bacon, garlic, thyme, marjoram, oregano, salt, and bay leaf, cover and simmer for 30 minutes. Remove bay leaf and puree sauce in a food processor. Pour puree back into the skillet, and stir in tomato sauce and lemon juice. Heat to a simmer, remove from the heat, and serve over cooked vegetables and meats.

You can store leftover sauce in an airtight container in the refrigerator for a few days. It is good to keep on hand, so if you are short on time it will only take a few minutes to transform ordinary vegetables into something special.

Yield: 6 servings (½ cup/120 g each)
Per serving: 10 g fat; 3.5 g net carbs; 7 g protein; 132 calories

Espagnole Sauce.

Variations:
Diable Sauce
Make Espagnole Sauce as directed, but omit the lemon juice and add 2 tablespoons (30 ml) Worcestershire sauce and 1 tablespoon (15 ml) red wine vinegar.

Yield: 6 servings (½ cup/120 g each)
Per serving:10 g fat; 3.5 g net carbs; 7 g protein; 132 calories

Piquante Sauce
Make Espagnole Sauce as directed, but add ½ cup (120 g) finely chopped dill pickle and 2 tablespoons (8 g) minced parsley.

Yield: 6 servings (½ cup/120 g each)
Per serving: 10 g fat; 4 g net carbs; 7 g protein; 134 calories

Herb Sauce
This sauce blends beef broth and butter with a variety of the most popular herbs.

¼ cup (60 g) butter
½ cup (80 g) minced onion

2 cups (480 ml) beef broth, divided
¼ teaspoon dried marjoram
¼ teaspoon dried thyme
¼ teaspoon dried savory
¼ teaspoon dried sage
¼ teaspoon dried basil
⅛ teaspoon ground nutmeg
⅛ teaspoon black pepper
⅛ teaspoon salt
1 tablespoon (8 g) tapioca or arrowroot flour*
1 tablespoon (15 ml) lemon juice
1 teaspoon fresh minced tarragon or ¼ teaspoon dried tarragon
1 teaspoon fresh minced chervil or ¼ teaspoon dried chervil

Heat butter in a medium-size saucepan and sauté onion until it begins to turn brown, about 8 to 10 minutes. Add 1½ cups (360 ml) broth, marjoram, thyme, savory, sage, basil, nutmeg, black pepper, and salt, and simmer for about 5 minutes. Blend tapioca flour into the remaining ½ cup (60 ml) of broth, and stir it into the sauce, stirring constantly until thickened. Mix in lemon juice, tarragon, and chervil. Remove from heat and serve.

*This recipe can be made using xanthan gum in place of tapioca flour. Make the recipe above as directed, but sauté onions in 3 tablespoons (90 g) butter instead of 4 and mix ¼ teaspoon of xanthan gum with 1 tablespoon (14 g) of butter. Stir the xanthan gum–butter mixture into the hot sauce and stir constantly until thickened.

Yield: 8 servings, ¼ cup (60 ml) each
Per serving using tapioca flour: 6.5 g fat; 2.5 g net carbs; 1.5 g protein; 74 calories
Per serving using xanthan gum: 8 g fat; 1.5 g net carbs; 1.5 g protein; 84 calories

Red Pepper Sauce
This is makes an excellent substitute for spaghetti sauce.

4 tablespoons (56 g) coconut or red palm oil
8 ounces (226 g) ground beef
1 medium yellow onion, finely chopped
2 stalks celery, finely chopped

2 cloves garlic, minced
2 medium red bell peppers, chopped
1 cups (240 ml) beef or bone broth (pages 78 and 79)
½ cup (120 g) tomato sauce
½ teaspoon dried thyme
½ teaspoon dried oregano
½ teaspoon dried basil
½ teaspoon dried rosemary
½ teaspoon salt
¼ teaspoon black pepper
¼ cup (20 g) Parmesan cheese (optional)

Heat oil in a large skillet over medium heat. Cook ground beef, breaking it into small pieces, until browned. Remove the beef from the skillet and set aside, keep the oil in the skillet.

Sauté onion, celery, garlic, and red bell peppers for about 12 minutes, or until they are tender and start to turn brown. Add beef broth, tomato sauce, thyme, oregano, basil, rosemary, salt, and black pepper, and simmer for 30 minutes. Remove from the heat and let cool slightly. Puree sauce in a food processor or blender. Pour puree back into the skillet along with the cooked beef to reheat. Stir in Parmesan cheese and remove from heat. Serve over cooked vegetables, eggs, or meat.

Yield: 6 servings (½ cup/120 g each)
Per serving: 12.5 g fat; 4 g net carbs; 13 g protein; 180 calories

Hollandaise Sauce

Hollandaise Sauce uses egg yolks as its thickening agent. Egg-based sauces can be tricky to make, but if you keep in mind that too much heat will curdle the sauce, you should be successful. You will use a double boiler and cook the sauce over simmering, not boiling, water. As soon as the sauce thickens, remove it from the heat.

4 egg yolks
1 tablespoon (15 ml) heavy cream or coconut milk
½ cup (120 g) butter, softened
¼ teaspoon salt
Dash white pepper
1 tablespoon (15 ml) lemon juice

Hollandaise Sauce over salmon salad.

Beat egg yolks until creamy and lemon colored. Mix in cream and pour into the top of a double boiler over gently simmering water. Heat, stirring constantly, for 2 to 3 minutes, until warm, but not hot. Stir in half of the butter; add the other half of the butter after the previous butter is well blended in. Cook and stir for 2 to 3 minutes, until sauce thickens enough to coat the back of a spoon. Move double boiler off of burner and stir in salt, pepper, and lemon juice. Serve over eggs, seafood, or cooked vegetables.

Curdling is a common problem when too much heat is used. If this happens to you, don't throw the sauce away. It can still be saved. Add 2 tablespoons (30 ml) boiling water and beat vigorously until smooth.

Yield: 4 servings, ¼ cup (60 ml) each
Per serving: 30 g fat; 0.5 g net carbs; 3 g protein; 284 calories

Variations:
Figaro Sauce

Prepare Hollandaise Sauce as directed, but blend in ⅓ cup (78 g) of tomato sauce and 1 tablespoon minced parsley or cilantro, and heat and stir over barely simmering water for 2 to 3 minutes. Goes well with seafood.

Yield: 4 servings, ¼ cup (60 ml) each
Per serving: 30 g fat; 1.5 g net carbs; 3 g protein; 288 calories

Mustard Hollandaise Sauce

Prepare Hollandaise Sauce as directed but blend in ½ teaspoon dry mustard with lemon juice before adding to the sauce. Goes well with cooked vegetables, eggs, and fish.

Yield: 4 servings, ¼ cup (60 ml) each
Per serving: 30 g fat; 0.5 g net carbs; 3 g protein; 284 calories

Avgolemono Sauce

This is a traditional Greek egg-based sauce. Tastes good with asparagus, broccoli, and artichokes.

1¼ cups (300 ml) chicken broth
Dash nutmeg
3 egg yolks, lightly beaten
3 tablespoons (45 ml) lemon juice
Salt
Black pepper

Heat broth and nutmeg in the top of a double boiler over simmering, not boiling, water. Blend about ½ cup (120 ml) of the heated broth into the egg yolks. Pour egg yolk mixture into the rest of the broth, stirring constantly until thickened. Remove from heat and stir in lemon juice 1 tablespoon (15 ml) at a time. Add salt and pepper to taste.

Yield: 6 servings, ¼ cup (60 ml) each
Per serving: 2.5 g fat; 0.5 g net carbs; 2.5 g protein; 34 calories

Green Chili Sauce

This sauce can be poured over cooked vegetables or meats. Tastes great over scrambled eggs.

¼ cup (56 g) bacon drippings or coconut oil
½ cup (75 g) diced pork or sugar-free and nitrite-free ham
½ medium onion, chopped
2 cloves garlic, minced
1½ cups (360 ml) pork or chicken broth, divided
1 can (10 ounce/280 g) green chilies or 1 cup (120 g) chopped roasted
    green chilies

¼ teaspoon dried oregano
¼ teaspoon ground cumin
¼ teaspoon salt
1 tablespoon (8 g) tapioca or arrowroot flour*

Heat bacon drippings in a medium saucepan and sauté pork and onion until the onion becomes soft, about 5 minutes. Add garlic and cook 2 minutes, until garlic becomes fragrant. Stir in 1 cup (240 ml) broth, chilies, oregano, cumin, and salt, and simmer for about 15 minutes. Blend tapioca flour into ½ cup (120 ml) broth, pour into hot mixture, and stir constantly until thickened.

*This recipe can be made using guar or xanthan gum in place of tapioca flour. Make the recipe above as directed, but mix ¼ teaspoon of xanthan gum with 1 tablespoon (14 g) of melted butter. Stir the xanthan gum–butter mixture into the hot sauce and stir constantly until thickened, about 8 minutes.

Yield: 8 servings, ¼ cup (60 ml) each
Per serving, using tapioca flour: 8 g fat; 3 g net carbs; 3.5 g protein; 98 calories
Per serving, using xanthan gum: 9.5 g fat; 2 g net carbs; 3.5 g protein; 107 calories

Cocktail Sauce

Cocktail sauce is ordinarily used as a dipping sauce, but it makes an excellent salad dressing as well. Most commercial cocktail sauces are loaded with this sugar. This version is sugar-free and tastes great. The horseradish flavor is on the mild side in this recipe, if you like more of a bite, add an extra teaspoon of horseradish.

8 ounces (220 g) tomato sauce
4 teaspoons fresh lemon juice
¼ teaspoon salt
2 teaspoons prepared horseradish
2 teaspoons hot sauce

In a small bowl, thoroughly mix together all of the ingredients. Use immediately, or put into an airtight container and store in the refrigerator. It will stay fresh for about two weeks.

Yield: about 1¼ cups (280 g)
Per tablespoon (14 g): 0 g fat; 0.5 g net carbs; 0 g protein; 2 calories

Alfredo Sauce

This is a great cheesy sauce for meats, eggs, and vegetables.

¼ cup (56 g) butter
1¼ cups (295 ml) heavy cream
½ cup (50 g) grated Parmesan cheese
¼ cup (25 g) grated Pecorino Romano cheese
⅛ teaspoon fresh ground black pepper

Melt butter in a medium saucepan over medium heat. Add cream and simmer until reduced to 1 cup, about 8 minutes. Remove from heat and stir in cheeses and black pepper. Stir until melted. Serve hot.

Yield: 4 servings
Per serving: 38 g fat; 2 g net carbs; 7.5 g protein; 380 calories

Tartar Sauce

1 cup (225 g) mayonnaise (pages 37-40)
3 scallions, minced
1 tablespoon (4 g) minced parsley
1 tablespoon (4 g) minced fresh tarragon
¼ cup (60 g) minced dill pickle
2 tablespoons (17 g) capers
1 teaspoon Dijon mustard
1 tablespoon (15 ml) red wine vinegar

Mix all ingredients, cover, and chill for 2 to 3 hours. Serve with seafood.

Yield: about 1¼ cups (280 g)
Per tablespoon (14 g): 8.5 g fat; 0.5 g net carbs; 0 g protein; 78 calories

Creamy Horseradish Sauce

½ cup (120 ml) cream
½ cup (115 g) mayonnaise (pages 37-40)
2 tablespoons (30 g) prepared horseradish
1 tablespoon (15 ml) lemon juice
1 tablespoon (6 g) lemon zest

Gradually beat cream into mayonnaise until smooth. Stir in horseradish, lemon juice, and lemon zest. Chill for ½ hours and serve with cold beef, lamb, or pork.

Yield: about 1 cup (112 g)
Per tablespoon (14 g): 4.5 g fat; 0 g net carbs; 0 g protein; 40 calories

Sour Cream Bacon Sauce

1 cup (230 g) sour cream
4 strips sugar-free, nitrite-free bacon, cooked crisp and crumbled
2 tablespoons melted bacon drippings

Mix sour cream with crumbled bacon and bacon drippings. Goes well over seafood and cooked and raw vegetables.

Yield: about 1 cup (112 g)
Per tablespoon (14 g): 6.5 g fat; 0.5 g net carbs; 2 g protein; 68 calories

Sour Cream Cheese Sauce

¼ cup (60 ml) heavy cream
1 cup (115 g) shredded sharp cheddar cheese
⅛ teaspoon onion powder
1 cup (230 g) sour cream

Combine cream, cheese, and onion powder in the top of a double boiler. Over simmering water, melt the cheese and blend the ingredients. Once smooth, stir in sour cream and remove from heat. Goes well with cooked or raw vegetables.

Yield: about 1¾ cups (390 g)
Per tablespoon (14 g): 4 g fat; 0.5 g net carbs; 1 g protein; 42 calories

Salads and Dressings

This chapter is divided into three sections: Low-Carb Salad Dressings, Dinner Salads, and Side Salads. Low-Carb Salad Dressings include different types of mayonnaise, which can be used as is or combined with other ingredients to make other types of salad dressings. Most of the salad dressings are oil- or cream-based.

Dinner Salads are large salads that make a complete meal. Most of these recipes make 2 to 4 servings, and each serving constitutes an entire meal. However, you can make half a recipe or cut the serving size down to make these recipes a side dish.

The Side Salads are smaller in size and can be used for a small meal or combined with a main dish. Side Salads go well with steaks, chops, roasts, and other meat and fish dishes.

Salads, in general, are very well suited to adjustments and experimentation. You can alter the types and amounts of the ingredients listed in these recipes to suit your own personal tastes and preferences. You can also make the serving sizes larger or smaller depending on your appetite or the number of people you are planning to feed. Feel free to modify these recipes as you see fit.

LOW-CARB SALAD DRESSINGS

Tossed green salads make a good addition to any low-carb or ketogenic diet and when combined with an oil-based dressing can supply a sufficient amount of fat in a single meal. Salads can be made with a number of ingredients and dressings that can give you a variety of tastes and flavors. Don't limit yourself to the common iceberg lettuce—try butterhead lettuce, red leaf, romaine, and other varieties. Vegetables that go well with salads include cucumber, bell peppers, banana peppers, tomatoes, avocado, parsley, onion, shallots, scallions, radishes, jicama, parsley, cilantro, watercress, sprouts, celery, celery root (celeriac), bok choy (Chinese cabbage), napa cabbage, red and green cabbage, broccoli, cauliflower, spinach, chard, kale, carrots, Jerusalem artichoke, sauerkraut, chicory, endive, and snow peas. Salads don't always have to include lettuce. You can make a variety of lettuce-free salads with all of these vegetables.

Toppings add spark to salads. Low-carb toppings include hard-boiled eggs, ham, crumbled bacon, beef, chicken, turkey, pork, fish (salmon, sardines, etc.), crab, shrimp, nori, hard cheeses (cheddar, Monterey, Munster, etc.), soft cheeses (feta, cottage, etc.), nuts, olives, and pork rinds.

The dressing is perhaps the most important part of the salad. It is what makes the salad stand out and gives the other ingredients zing. Most commercially prepared dressings are made using a base of soybean or canola oils and often include sugar, high fructose corn syrup, MSG, and other undesirable additives. Many of them are promoted as low-calorie or low-fat, but few are low-carb. A better choice is a homemade low-carb salad dressing using healthier ingredients. The following are a few such recipes.

Mayonnaise

Most vegetable oils can be used to make mayonnaise. Olive oil produces a mayonnaise that is far healthier than the type you get in the store that is made from polyunsaturated oils. Extra virgin olive oil, however, gives mayonnaise a very strong olive oil flavor that can overpower the foods it is combined with. Another type of oil called "extra light" olive oil, has a mild flavor and makes excellent mayonnaise.

2 egg yolks
2 tablespoons (30 ml) apple cider vinegar
1 teaspoon prepared mustard
¼ teaspoon paprika
½ teaspoon salt
1 cup (240 ml) extra light olive oil, separated

Have all ingredients at room temperature before beginning. Combine egg yolks, vinegar, mustard, paprika, salt, and ¼ cup (60 ml) oil in blender or food processor. Blend for about 60 seconds. While machine is running, pour in the remaining oil *very slowly*, drop by drop at first and gradually building to a fine, steady stream. The secret to making good mayonnaise is to add the oil in slowly. Mayonnaise will thicken as the oil is added. Taste and adjust seasonings as needed. Store the mayonnaise in an airtight container in the refrigerator. It will keep in the refrigerator for several weeks.

Yield: about 20 tablespoons (280 g)
Per tablespoon (14 g): 10.5 g fat; 0 g net carb; 0 g protein; 94 calories

Coconut Mayonnaise

Make the Mayonnaise recipe as directed above, but replace ½ cup of the extra light olive oil with ½ cup coconut oil. Make sure the coconut oil is liquid and at room temperature before using. You can use either expeller pressed coconut oil or virgin coconut oil for making mayonnaise. The virgin coconut oil will give the mayonnaise a slight coconut taste. The expeller pressed coconut oil is more refined and has no coconut flavor.

You can make mayonnaise using only coconut oil, without any olive oil, but you must use it all immediately. Because coconut oil hardens when chilled, if you store the mayonnaise in the refrigerator it will harden and become generally unusable. Mixing the oils allows the mayonnaise to remain soft and creamy when chilled.

Yield: about 20 tablespoons (280 g)
Per tablespoon (14 g): 10.5 g fat; 0 g net carb; 0 g protein; 94 calories

Mediterranean Mayonnaise

This mayonnaise is made with a mixture of extra virgin and extra light olive oils. The extra virgin olive oil gives the olive, or Mediterranean, flavor to the mayonnaise. You can make mayonnaise using all extra virgin olive oil, but the olive flavor can become overpowering. This half/half mixture provides just enough of the olive oil taste to flavor the mayonnaise but not dominate it.

  2 egg yolks
  2 tablespoons (30 ml) apple cider vinegar or lemon juice
  1 teaspoon prepared mustard
  ¼ teaspoon paprika
  ½ teaspoon salt
  ½ cup (120 ml) extra virgin olive oil, divided
  ½ cup (120 ml) extra light olive oil

Have all ingredients at room temperature before beginning. Combine egg yolks, vinegar, mustard, paprika, salt, and ¼ cup (60 ml) extra virgin olive oil in blender or food processor. Blend for about 60 seconds. While machine is running, pour in the remaining extra virgin and the extra light olive oils *very slowly*, drop by drop at first and gradually building to a fine, steady stream.

The secret to making good mayonnaise is to add the oil in slowly. Mayonnaise will thicken as the oil is added. Taste and adjust seasonings as needed. Store the mayonnaise in an airtight container in the refrigerator. It will keep in the refrigerator for several weeks.

Yield: about 20 tablespoons (280 g)
Per tablespoon (14 g): 10.5 g fat; 0 g net carb; 0 g protein; 94 calories

Leslie's Fiesta Coconut Mayo

This is one of my wife's (Leslie) favorite mayonnaise recipes. All ingredients should be at room temperature before beginning. To quickly warm up eggs that have been stored in the refrigerator, you can immerse them in very warm water for about 10 minutes before breaking them into the food processor bowl. Use this mayonnaise in any recipe that calls for mayonnaise.

2 egg yolks
1 whole egg
Juice from 2 lemons
2 teaspoons Dijon mustard
¾ teaspoon salt
Pinch of white pepper
¼ cup (12 g) minced fresh chives
½ cup (8 g) minced fresh cilantro

¼ cup (60 ml) extra virgin olive oil
⅔ cup (160 ml) extra light olive oil
1 cup (235 ml) expeller pressed coconut oil

Put the egg yolks, egg, lemon juice, mustard, salt, white pepper, chives, cilantro, and extra virgin olive oil in the bowl of the food processor or blender; process for about 10 seconds until blended.

With the food processor running continuously, pour in the extra light olive oil very slowly, in drops at first, to start the emulsion process. As the oil blends into the mixture, you can gradually increase the flow to a very thin, steady stream. The secret to making good mayonnaise is to add the oil very slowly. Finally, add the coconut oil in a slow, steady stream. As you do so, the mayonnaise should begin to thicken. Once it has thickened, transfer the mayonnaise to a jar or glass container with an airtight lid and store in the refrigerator.

Yield: about 2 cups (450 g)
Per tablespoon (14 g): 10.5 g fat; 0 g net carb; 0 g protein; 94 calories

Vinegar and Coconut Oil Dressing

¼ cup (60 ml) coconut oil, melted*
¼ cup (60 ml) extra light olive oil
2 tablespoons (30 ml) water
¼ cup (60 ml) apple cider vinegar
⅛ teaspoon salt
⅛ teaspoon white pepper

Put all ingredients into a Mason jar or similar container. Cover and shake vigorously until well blended. Let stand at room temperature until ready to use. This dressing can be stored in the cupboard for several days without refrigeration. If the dressing is to be stored for more than a week, however, put it into the refrigerator. When chilled, the oil will tend to solidify. To liquefy, take it out of the refrigerator at least 1 hour before using.

*You may also use MCT oil in place of coconut oil. If desired, you may replace both coconut and extra light olive oils with an equal amount of extra virgin olive oil.

Yield: 14 tablespoons (200 g)
Per tablespoon (14 g): 7.7 g fat; 0 g net carb; 0 g protein; 67 calories

Herb Mayonnaise

This dressing tastes good served with fish and shellfish or as a dressing on vegetable salads. You can make this recipe using one of the recipes above as the base.

½ cup (32 g) minced parsley
⅓ cup (28 g) minced watercress
2 tablespoons (6 g) minced chives
1 tablespoon (4 g) minced fresh dill
1¼ cups (285 g) mayonnaise (pages 37-40)
1 teaspoon lemon juice
¼ teaspoon salt
2 to 3 drops hot sauce

Mix all ingredients well, cover, and refrigerate for several hours.

Yield: about 1½ cups (336 g)
Per tablespoon (14 g): 9 g fat; 0 g net carb; 0 g protein; 81 calories

Asian Almond Dressing

½ cup (110 g) coconut oil
¼ cup (25 g) slivered almonds
1 tablespoon (15 ml) extra light olive oil
2 tablespoons (30 ml) tamari sauce
1 tablespoon (15 ml) apple cider vinegar
¼ teaspoon ground ginger
¼ teaspoon salt

Put coconut oil in small saucepan. At medium to low heat, sauté slivered almonds until lightly browned. Remove from heat and let cool to room temperature. Stir into the almonds the remaining ingredients. As the dressing sits, the oil will separate to the top and the almonds will sink to the bottom. Stir just before using. Spoon dressing onto salad, making sure to include the almonds. Dressing may be stored in cupboard for several days without refrigeration. If it is to be stored for more than a week, however, put it into the refrigerator.

Yield: 14 tablespoons (200 g)
Per tablespoon (14 g): 9.5 g fat; 0.5 g net carb; 0.5 g protein; 89.5 calories

Vinaigrette

¼ cup (60 ml) red or white wine vinegar
¼ teaspoon salt
⅛ teaspoon white pepper
¾ cup (180 ml) extra virgin olive oil

In a bowl, mix vinegar, salt, and pepper with a fork. Add oil and mix vigorously until well blended.

Yield: 1 cup (224 g)
Per tablespoon (14 g): 10.7 g fat; 0 g net carb; 0 g protein; 92 calories

Garlic Herb Dressing

2 cloves garlic, peeled and crushed
1 teaspoon tarragon
1 teaspoon marjoram
1 teaspoon dry mustard
½ teaspoon salt
¼ teaspoon black pepper
½ cup (120 ml) extra virgin olive oil
¼ cup (60 ml) red or white wine vinegar

Put all of the ingredients in a pint Mason jar or similar container. Screw on lid and shake contents to mix. Let stand at room temperature at least 1 hour. Shake again just before using.

Yield: 6 tablespoons (84 g)
Per tablespoon (14 g): 7.1 g fat; 0 g net carb; 0 g protein; 62 calories

Ranch Dressing

This dressing is made using sour cream. It tastes best freshly made, so the recipe below uses small portions so there are little or no leftovers.

3 tablespoons (45 g) sour cream
1 tablespoon (15 ml) heavy cream
½ teaspoon diced onion
⅛ teaspoon dill
⅛ teaspoon salt
Dash black pepper

Mix all of the ingredients together and serve on a salad.

Yield: 4 tablespoons (56 g)
Per tablespoon (14 g): 3.8 g fat; 0.6 g net carb; 0.4 g protein; 37 calories

Sour Cream Lemon Dressing

½ cup (115 g) sour cream
1 tablespoon (15 g) lemon juice
1 tablespoon (4 g) chopped parsley
½ teaspoon salt
½ teaspoon dried dill weed
¼ teaspoon freshly ground black pepper
1 small clove garlic, crushed

Mix all of the ingredients, and store in the refrigerator until ready to use.

Yield: about 10 tablespoons (140 g)
Per tablespoon (14 g): 2.5 g fat; 0.5 g net carb; 0.5 g protein; 26 calories

Sesame Seed Dressing

½ cup (110 g) coconut oil, melted
1 cup (240 ml) extra virgin olive oil*
½ medium red onion, chopped
2 cloves garlic, minced
2½ tablespoons (40 ml) soy sauce
2½ tablespoons (40 ml) fresh lemon juice
¼ cup (24 g) sesame seeds, toasted

Thoroughly mix all of the ingredients in a blender, except the sesame seeds. Blend, then stir in sesame seeds. Pour into jar with lid, and chill before serving.

*You may use any liquid oil, such as extra light olive oil, MCT oil, macadamia oil, etc. An oil that remains liquid when poured over a cold salad is needed to dilute the coconut oil so that the dressing doesn't harden when combined with the cold salad greens.

Yield: 2 cups (450 ml)
Per tablespoon (14 g): 10 g fat; 0.5 g net carb; 0 g protein; 92 calories

Oregano Dressing

½ cup (120 ml) extra virgin olive oil
⅓ cup (80 ml) wine vinegar
1½ teaspoons salt
1½ teaspoons dried oregano

Put all of the ingredients in a jar with a tightly covered lid. Shake to mix. Store in the refrigerator.

Yield: about 13 tablespoons (180 ml)
Per tablespoon (14 g): 8.5 g fat; 0 g net carb; 0 g protein; 76.5 calories

Tomato Cucumber Dressing

½ cup (115 g) mayonnaise (pages 37-40)
1 medium tomato, finely chopped
½ medium cucumber, finely chopped

½ teaspoon salt
¼ teaspoon dried sage leaves

Thoroughly mix all of the ingredients together. Store in the refrigerator in an airtight container.

Yield 1 cup (224 g)
Per tablespoon (14 g): 7 g fat; 0 g net carb; 0 g protein; 63 calories

Thousand Island Dressing

1 cup (225 g) mayonnaise (pages 37-40)
6 tablespoons (90 g) tomato sauce or low-carb ketchup
¼ cup (60 g) pickle relish or chopped dill pickle
1 tablespoon (10 g) minced red onion
1 tablespoon (15 ml) lemon juice
1 teaspoon hot sauce
¼ teaspoon salt

Using a whisk, blend all ingredients together. Cover and store in the refrigerator until ready to use.

Yield: 1½ cups (360 g)
Per tablespoon (14 g): 7 g fat; 1 g net carb; 0 g protein; 67 calories

Russian Dressing

1 tablespoon (10 g) minced red onion
1 cup (225 g) mayonnaise (pages 37-40)
¼ cup (70 g) chili or hot sauce
1 teaspoon prepared horseradish
¼ teaspoon Worcestershire sauce
½ teaspoon paprika

Using a whisk, blend all ingredients together. Cover and store in the refrigerator until ready to use.

Yield: 1¼ cup (300 g)
Per tablespoon (14 g): 8.5 g fat; 0 g net carb; 0 g protein; 76 calories

French Dressing

>   1 cup (240 ml) extra virgin olive oil
>   ¼ cup (60 ml) apple cider vinegar
>   ¼ cup (60 ml) lemon juice
>   1 teaspoon salt
>   ½ teaspoon dry mustard
>   ½ teaspoon paprika

Thoroughly mix all of the ingredients together. A convenient way to do this is to put all the ingredients into a tightly covered jar and shake vigorously. Store in the refrigerator. Shake before serving.

Yield: about 1½ cups (336 g)
Per tablespoon (14 g): 9 g fat; 0 g net carb; 0 g protein; 81 calories

Cilantro Lime Dressing

>   1 cup (16 g) loosely packed cilantro
>   ½ cup (115 g) plain Greek yogurt
>   2 cloves garlic
>   Juice of 1 lime
>   Pinch of salt
>   ¼ cup (60 ml) olive oil
>   2 tablespoons (30 ml) apple cider vinegar

Combine cilantro, yogurt, garlic, lime juice, and salt in the bowl of a food processor. With the processor running, add olive oil and vinegar in a slow stream until emulsified. Store in an air-tight container in the refrigerator.

Yield: about 19 tablespoons (270 g)
Per tablespoon (14 g): 3.5 g fat; 0.5 g net carb; 0.5 g protein; 35.5 calories

Green Goddess Dressing

This dressing was invented in the 1920s by a chef at the Palace Hotel in San Francisco to commemorate actor George Arliss and his play "The Green Goddess." A key ingredient is anchovies or anchovy paste. It is the magic that gives the dressing its memorable flavor.

1 cup (225 g) mayonnaise (pages 37-40)
½ cup (115 g) sour cream
⅓ cup (5 g) chopped parsley
3 tablespoons (9 g) chopped chives
3 tablespoons (42 g) anchovy paste or finely chopped anchovy fillets
3 tablespoons (45 ml) tarragon or wine vinegar
1 tablespoon (15 ml) lemon juice
¼ teaspoon salt
⅛ teaspoon black pepper

Mix all ingredients and refrigerate.

Yield: about 2 cups (450 g)
Per tablespoon (14 g): 8 g fat; 0 g net carb; 0 g protein; 72 calories

Blue Cheese Dressing

¾ cup (90 g) crumbled blue cheese, separated
3 ounces (85 g) cream cheese, softened
½ cup (115 g) mayonnaise (pages 37-40)
⅓ cup (80 ml) heavy cream

Separate ⅓ cup (40 g) of blue cheese and set aside. Take the remaining blue cheese and combine it with the cream cheese and beat it with an electric beater on low speed. Add mayonnaise and cream and beat on medium speed until creamy. Stir in reserved blue cheese. Cover and refrigerate for at least 3 hours.

Yield: about 26 tablespoons (370 g)
Per tablespoon (14 g): 5.5 g fat; 0 g net carb; 1 g protein; 53 calories

Creamy Onion Dressing

1 cup (230 g) mayonnaise (pages 37-40)
½ cup (120 ml) cream or coconut milk
2 scallions, finely chipped

Mix all ingredients, cover, and refrigerate for at least 4 hours.

Yield: about 1½ cups (370 g)
Per tablespoon (14 g): 9 g fat; 0 g net carb; 0 g protein; 81 calories

Buttermilk Dressing

¾ cup (175 g) mayonnaise (pages 37-40)
½ cup (120 ml) buttermilk
1 teaspoon dried parsley flakes
½ teaspoon instant minced onion
1 clove garlic, crushed
½ teaspoon salt
Dash of freshly ground black pepper

Mix all ingredients and refrigerate at least 2 hours. Stir before serving.

Yield: about 1¼ cups (280 g)
Per tablespoon (14 g): 6.5 g fat; 0.5 g net carb; 0 g protein; 60 calories

DINNER SALADS

Garden Salad

1 cup (70 g) shredded cabbage
½ green bell pepper, cut in julienne strips
1 medium carrot, shredded
2 scallions, chipped
1 stalk celery, chopped
½ medium cucumber, sliced
4 radishes, thinly sliced
½ small white turnip, shredded
½ cup (50 g) chopped cauliflower
French Dressing (page 46)

Prepare vegetables and put into the refrigerator for at least 2 hours. Serve with French Dressing. The ingredients in this salad have little fat, so you will need to add an adequate amount of dressing to boost the fat content.

Yield: serves 2
Per serving without dressing: 0.5 g fat; 9.5 g net carb; 2.5 g protein; 52 calories

Caesar Salad

These directions make enough to provide a full meal for two or a side salad for 4 or more people.

1 clove garlic, diced
8 anchovy or sardine fillets, cut up
⅓ cup (80 ml) extra virgin olive oil
1 teaspoon Worcestershire sauce
Juice of 1 lemon
½ teaspoon salt
¼ teaspoon dry mustard
¼ teaspoon freshly ground black pepper
8 romaine lettuce leaves torn into bite-size pieces
2 hard-boiled eggs, sliced
¼ cup (20 g) grated Parmesan cheese
8 pork rinds (croutons)

To make the dressing, mix together in a small bowl the garlic, anchovies, oil, Worcestershire sauce, lemon juice, salt, mustard, and pepper. In a large bowl, toss dressing with the lettuce. Top with sliced eggs, cheese, and pork rinds.

Yield: serves 2
Per serving: 48 g fat; 2.5 g net carb; 18 g protein; 514 calories

Olympian Salad

8 romaine lettuce leaves, torn into bite-size pieces
4 radishes, sliced
½ medium cucumber, sliced
2 scallions, chopped
10 pitted black olives
¼ cup (35 g) feta cheese
1 can (3.75 oz/106 g) sardines, drained
Oregano Dressing (page 44)

Combine lettuce, radishes, cucumber, scallions, olives, and feta cheese in a bowl. Add dressing to taste.

Yield: serves 2
Per serving without dressing: 12.5 g fat; 6.5 g net carb; 16.5 g protein; 204 calories

Mashed Avocado Salad

2 avocados, cut up
¼ cup (60 g) sour cream
2 tablespoons (30 ml) extra virgin olive oil
2 scallions, chopped
1 tablespoon (15 ml) lime juice
1 teaspoon salt
½ teaspoon celery seed
¼ teaspoon hot sauce
1 medium tomato, chopped
½ cup (8 g) chopped cilantro
6 cups (120 g) lettuce leaves, torn in bite-size pieces
2 ounces (60 g) cheddar cheese, shredded

Mash avocados with a fork. Add sour cream, olive oil, scallions, lime juice, salt, celery seed, and hot sauce, and beat until creamy. Toss avocado mixture with tomato, cilantro, and lettuce leaves. Serve topped with shredded cheese.

Yield: serves 2
Per serving: 70 g fat; 9.5 g net carb; 13.5 g protein; 722 calories

Florentine Salad

1 clove garlic, crushed
⅓ cup (80 ml) extra virgin olive oil
¼ cup (60 ml) wine vinegar
¼ teaspoon salt
⅛ teaspoon fresh ground black pepper
12 ounces (340 g) fresh spinach, torn into bite-size pieces
6 strips sugar-free, nitrite-free bacon, cooked crisp and crumbled
1 hard-boiled egg, sliced

Let garlic stand in oil for at least 1 hour to infuse the flavor into the oil. Discard the garlic. Add vinegar, salt, and pepper to the oil. Toss the oil with the spinach and bacon. Top with sliced egg.

Yield: serves 2
Per serving: 64 g fat; 4 g net carb; 28.5 g protein; 706 calories

Artichoke Salad

2 cooked artichoke hearts, cut into bite-size pieces
6 cups (120 g) salad greens
½ cup (60 g) chopped cucumber
10 pitted black olives
4 strips sugar-free, nitrite-free bacon, cooked crisp and crumbled
Sour Cream Lemon Dressing (page 43)

Toss together artichoke hearts, salad greens, cucumber, olives, and bacon. Mix in salad dressing.

Yield: serves 2
Per serving without dressing: 18.5 g fat; 11 g net carb; 20 g protein; 290 calories

Wilted Spinach Salad with Bacon

10 ounces (280 g) fresh spinach
6 strips sugar-free, nitrite-free bacon
½ medium red onion, sliced

½ cup (120 ml) wine vinegar
2 tablespoons (30 ml) tomato sauce
½ teaspoon salt
⅛ teaspoon black pepper

Wash and dry spinach and place in a salad bowl. In a skillet, cook bacon until crisp, remove, and set aside. Reserve the bacon droppings in the skillet. Stir-fry the onion slices in the bacon drippings until tender. Add remaining ingredients and continue cooking, and stirring, for 3 to 4 minutes. Remove from heat and pour the hot mixture over spinach and toss well. Add crumbled bacon, toss again, and serve.

Yield: serves 2
Per serving: 32 g fat; 7 g net carb; 25 g protein; 416 calories

Strawberry Salad

⅓ cup (36 g) sliced almonds, toasted
6 cups (120 g) lettuce, torn into bite-size pieces
1 medium stalk celery, sliced
½ red bell pepper, chopped
2 scallions, chopped
¾ cup (128 g) sliced strawberries
¼ cup (60 ml) wine vinegar
¼ cup (60 ml) extra virgin olive oil

Toast almonds in oven at 350° F (180° C) for about 6 minutes or until lightly browned. Remove from oven and let cool to room temperature. Mix together lettuce, celery, bell pepper, scallions, strawberries, vinegar, and oil. Top with toasted almonds.

Yield: serves 2
Per serving: 37.5 g fat; 10.5 g net carb; 5.5 g protein; 401 calories

Bacon Cauliflower Salad

6 cups (120 g) romaine lettuce, torn into bite-size pieces
1 cup (100 g) chopped cauliflower
½ avocado, sliced

½ cup (75 g) julienne sliced or shredded daikon radish
2 scallions, chopped
¼ cup (60 g) mayonnaise (pages 37-40)
¼ cup (60 g) sour cream
¼ teaspoon dried dill weed
Freshly ground black pepper to taste
2 ounces (56 g) cheese, shredded
6 strips sugar-free, nitrite-free bacon, cooked crisp and crumbled

Combine lettuce, cauliflower, avocado, daikon radish, and scallions. In a separate bowl, stir together the mayonnaise, sour cream, dill, and black pepper. Fold the dressing into the vegetables and top with cheese and bacon.

Yield: serves 2
Per serving: 66 g fat; 8 g net carb; 33 g protein; 758 calories

Taco Salad

If you like tacos, then you will love this salad. It has everything except the taco shell.

2 tablespoons (28 g) coconut oil
8 ounces (225 g) ground beef
½ green bell pepper, chopped
½ medium onion, chopped
½ teaspoon chili powder
½ teaspoon cumin
½ teaspoon paprika
¼ teaspoon salt
Tabasco sauce or other hot sauce to taste
6 cups (120 g) shredded lettuce
1 avocado, sliced
1 medium tomato, chopped
¼ cup (4 g) chopped cilantro
½ cup (58 g) shredded cheese
½ cup (115 g) sour cream

Heat oil in a skillet, add ground beef, bell pepper, onion, chili powder, cumin, paprika, and salt. Cook until the meat is browned and vegetables soft. Stir in Tabasco sauce, then remove from heat and set aside to cool. Combine lettuce, avocado, tomato, and cilantro, and divide evenly onto two serving plates. Pour the warm (not hot) meat mixture, including the oil, over the fresh vegetables. Top with shredded cheese and sour cream.

Yield: serves 2
Per serving: 57.5 g fat; 11 g net carb; 46.5 g protein; 747 calories

Cucumber Cottage Cheese Salad

4 romaine lettuce leaves, torn into bite-size pieces
1 medium cucumber, sliced and quartered
4 radishes, thinly sliced
2 scallions, chopped
1 cup (225 g) cottage cheese
½ cup (115 g) sour cream
2 tablespoons (30 ml) extra virgin olive oil
1 tablespoon (15 ml) tarragon vinegar
¼ teaspoon salt
¼ teaspoon black pepper

Combine lettuce, cucumber, radishes, and scallions, and set aside. In a separate bowl, mix cottage cheese, sour cream, olive oil, vinegar, salt, and black pepper. Stir dressing into the vegetables.

Yield: 2 servings
Per serving: 28.5 g fat; 12.5 g net carb; 18.5 g protein; 380 calories

Asian Chicken Salad

¼ cup (30 g) sliced almonds, toasted
2 chicken breasts, cooked and cut into bite-size pieces
6 cups (120 g) lettuce, torn into bite-size pieces
½ red bell pepper, chopped
2 scallions, chopped
1 medium carrot, cut into julienne strips
1 cup (70 g) shredded cabbage
Asian Almond Dressing (page 41)

Toast almonds in oven at 350° F (180° C) for about 6 minutes or until lightly browned. Remove from oven and set aside to cool. In a salad bowl, combine chicken, lettuce, bell pepper, scallions, carrot, cabbage, and toasted almonds. Add Asian Almond Dressing and toss.

Yield: 2 servings
Per serving without dressing: 18 g fat; 8 g net carb; 45 g protein; 374 calories

Japanese Shrimp Salad

6 cups (120 g) lettuce, torn into bite-size pieces
1 cup (90 g) shredded or sliced red cabbage
½ medium cucumber, cut in julienne strips
½ cup (75 g) shredded daikon radish
2 scallions, chopped
1 medium carrot, shredded
½ cup (100 g) cooked baby shrimp
Asian Almond Dressing (page 41)

Toss vegetables and shrimp in a salad bowl. Serve with Asian Almond Dressing. Garnish with small red chili peppers and parsley if desired.

Yield: 2 servings
Per serving without dressing: 0.5 g fat; 10 g net carb; 11.5 g protein; 90 calories

Spaghetti Salad

The spaghetti in this recipe has no noodles, but it does have a rich, tasty sauce. The sauce is poured over a bed of fresh salad greens. Combining spaghetti -like sauce with salad greens may sound a little unusual, and it is, but it makes a delicious "dressing" for an otherwise ordinary tossed salad.

Make a tossed salad like you normally would using any of the fresh vegetables from the following list:

Lettuce	Shredded carrot	Broccoli
Spinach	Avocado	Celery
Kale	Cabbage	Cilantro
Cucumber	Bell pepper	Watercress
Cauliflower	Parsley	Daikon radish

Combine the vegetables in a bowl. Make the Red Pepper Sauce recipe on page 29 and allow it to cool slightly so it doesn't wilt the lettuce. Pour the sauce over the tossed salad and top with 1 ounce (28 g) of shredded cheese. A dollop of sour cream makes it surprisingly delicious!

Per ½ cup (120 g) serving of sauce only: 12.5 g fat; 4 g net carbs; 13 g protein; 180 calories

Per serving (2 cups/110 g) of salad greens: 0 g fat; 3.5 g net carb; 2.5 g protein; 23 calories

Shrimp, Egg, and Avocado Salad

The flavor will be best if shrimp and eggs are cooked and still slightly warm when mixed into the salad.

½ cup (115 g) mayonnaise (pages 37-40)
¼ cup (56 g) French Dressing (page 46)
Dash of cayenne pepper
½ teaspoon anchovy paste (optional)
2 tablespoons minced chives or 2 scallions, chopped
1 medium stalk celery, chopped
1 cup (120 g) chopped cucumber
1 avocado, chopped
3 hard-boiled eggs, peeled and coarsely chopped
1 pound (550 g) cooked, shelled, shrimp

Mix mayonnaise, French Dressing, cayenne pepper, anchovy paste (or a dash of salt if anchovy paste is not used), and chives. Cover and chill for 2 to 3 hours. Stir in celery, cucumber, and avocado. Just before serving, add freshly cooked eggs and shrimp and toss very gently.

Yield: 4 servings
Per serving: 35 g fat; 5 g net carb; 37 g protein; 483 calories

Shrimp Salad with Cocktail Sauce Dressing

6 ounces (170 g) precooked shrimp
6 cups (120 g) shredded lettuce
1 medium tomato, cut in 8 wedges
2 scallions, chopped
1 cup (60 g) sliced cucumber
½ green bell pepper, chopped
1 medium stalk celery, chopped
2 tablespoons (28 g) mayonnaise (pages 37-40)
¼ cup (60 g) Cocktail Sauce (page 33)

In a medium bowl, toss together cooked shrimp, lettuce, tomato, scallions, cucumber, bell pepper, and celery. To make the dressing, mix together mayonnaise and cocktail sauce. Put salad in serving bowls and top with dressing.

If desired, you can increase the fat content of this salad by adding 1 to 2 tablespoons (15 to 30 ml) of extra virgin olive oil or 4 to 6 strips of crumbled bacon.

Yield: serves 2
Per serving without dressing: 12 g fat; 9.5 g net carb; 21 g protein; 230 calories

Chicken Salad

1 cup (140 g) diced cold cooked chicken
½ cup (50 g) celery, chopped
2 scallions, chopped
¼ green bell pepper, chopped
½ avocado, sliced
2 tablespoons (2 g) chopped cilantro

1 tablespoon (9 g) minced pimiento
⅓ cup (115 g) mayonnaise (pages 37-40)
2 tablespoons (30 ml) French Dressing (page 46)
¼ teaspoon salt
⅛ teaspoon black pepper

In a salad bowl toss chicken, celery, scallions, bell pepper, avocado, and cilantro. In a separate bowl, mix pimiento, mayonnaise, French Dressing, salt, and black pepper. Add the dressing to the vegetables and toss.

Yield: 2 servings
Per serving without dressing: 37.5 g fat; 3 g net carb; 22.5 g protein; 439 calories

Strawberry Salmon Salad

6 ounces (170 g) cooked salmon
½ avocado, chopped
½ cup (85 g) sliced strawberries
1 cup (120 g) sliced cucumber
6 cups (120 g) romaine lettuce, torn into bite-size pieces
½ cup (75 g) feta cheese
¼ cup (28 g) slivered or sliced almonds
2 tablespoons (30 ml) raspberry vinegar

In a salad bowl, combine salmon, avocado, strawberries, cucumber, lettuce, feta cheese, and almonds. Add raspberry vinegar and toss.

Yield: serves 2
Per serving: 28 g fat; 9.5 g net carb; 26.5 g protein; 396 calories

Crab Louis Salad

12 ounces (340 g) cooked crabmeat or imitation crabmeat
4 medium tomatoes, cut into wedges
4 hard-boiled eggs, cut into wedges
18 black olives, pitted
6 cups (120 g) salad greens, torn into bite-size pieces
Louis Dressing (below)

Louis Dressing:
¾ cup (210 g) chili sauce
½ cup (115 g) mayonnaise (pages 37-40)
1 teaspoon instant minced onion
¼ teaspoon Worcestershire sauce

To make the salad, arrange the crabmeat, tomato wedges, egg wedges, and olives on the salad greens. Cover with Louis Dressing.

To make the dressing, mix all ingredients. Cover and refrigerate until ready to pour on the salad.

Yield: about 4 servings
Per serving: 29.5 g fat; 7.5 g net carb; 27.5 g protein; 405 calories

Peach Salmon Salad

¼ cup (56 g) mayonnaise (pages 37-40)
1 tablespoon (15 ml) extra virgin olive oil
6 cups (180 g) fresh spinach, torn into bite-size pieces
2 medium stalks celery, chopped
¼ cup (4 g) chopped cilantro
3 scallions, chopped
6 ounces (170 g) cooked salmon
¾ cup (127 g) diced peaches
¼ cup (28 g) chopped pecans

Mix mayonnaise and olive oil together to make the dressing. Toss dressing with spinach, celery, cilantro, and scallions. Top with flaked salmon, peaches, and pecans, and serve.

Yield: serves 2
Per serving: 44 g fat; 8.5 g net carb; 22 g protein; 518 calories

Turkey Bacon Club Salad

6 cups (120 g) shredded lettuce, torn into bite-size pieces
2 ounces (56 g) cheese, shredded
1 large tomato, cut into thin wedges
2 scallions, chopped

4 ounces (110 g) cooked turkey, cut into bite-size pieces
1 cup (60 g) sliced cucumber
¼ green bell pepper, chopped
Dressing*
6 slices sugar-free, nitrite-free bacon, cooked crisp and crumbled

In a salad bowl, combine lettuce, cheese, tomato, scallions, turkey, cucumber, and green bell pepper. Add dressing to taste and top with crumbled bacon.

*Serve with one of the following dressings: Vinaigrette, Ranch, Garlic Herb, Cilantro Lime (pages 42-46).

Yield: serves 2
Per serving without dressing: 36 g fat; 7 g net carb; 46 g protein; 536 calories

Shrimp Artichoke Salad

6 cups (120 g) mixed leafy greens (lettuce, spinach, cabbage, kale, etc.)
1 large tomato, cut into 8 wedges
2 canned or freshly cooked artichoke hearts, chopped
6 ounces (170 g) cooked baby shrimp
2 hard-boiled eggs, sliced
Russian Dressing (page 45)

Divide salad greens evenly on two serving plates. Place an equal amount of tomato wedges, artichoke hearts, shrimp, and egg slices on each plate. Top with Russian Dressing and serve.

Yield: 2 servings
Per serving without dressing: 6.5 g fat; 14 g net carb; 31 g protein; 238 calories

Avocado Crab Salad

6 cups (120 g) mixed leafy greens (lettuce, spinach, cabbage, kale, etc.)
1 avocado, sliced
5 ounces (135 g) crabmeat

2 hard-boiled eggs, sliced
1 medium tomato, cut into 8 wedges
2 scallions, chopped
Thousand Island Dressing (page 45)

Divide leafy greens evenly on two serving plates. Place an equal amount of avocado slices, crabmeat, egg slices, tomato wedges, and chopped scallions over the greens on each plate. Top with Thousand Island Dressing and serve.

Yield: 2 servings
Per serving without dressing: 19.5 g fat; 15.5 g net carb; 22 g protein; 325 calories

Salmon Salad

You can use either salmon or tuna or for this salad.

1 can (7 ounces/200 g) salmon or tuna or other fresh cooked fish
1 tablespoon (15 ml) lemon juice
½ cup (60 g) mayonnaise (pages 37-40)
¼ teaspoon celery seed
¼ teaspoon salt
⅛ teaspoon freshly ground black pepper
¼ medium red onion, chopped
2 tablespoons (8 g) minced parsley
4 cups (80 g) lettuce leaves, torn into bite-size pieces
1 medium cucumber, chopped
¼ red bell pepper, chopped
1 medium tomato, cut into wedges
Dash of paprika

In a small bowl, mix salmon, lemon juice, mayonnaise, celery seed, salt, and black pepper. Fold in onion and parsley and set aside. In a salad bowl, combine lettuce, cucumber, and bell pepper. Toss vegetables with the dressing. Garnish with tomato wedges and a dash of paprika.

Yield: 2 servings
Per serving: 57.5 g fat; 9 g net carb; 22 g protein; 551 calories

Smoked Salmon Salad with Cheese

This salad tastes best using smoked salmon. However, if you don't have smoked salmon, you can use leftover cooked or canned salmon.

1 tablespoon (15 ml) lemon juice
¼ cup (30 g) mayonnaise (pages 37-40)
¼ cup (30 g) sour cream
¼ teaspoon salt
⅛ teaspoon freshly ground black pepper
6 cups (120 g) lettuce leaves, torn into bite-size pieces
2 scallions, chopped
2 tablespoons (2 g) minced cilantro
1 medium stalk celery, chopped
½ green bell pepper, chopped
½ cup (58 g) cheddar cheese, shredded
1 tablespoon (8 g) capers
7 ounces (200 g) cooked salmon

In a small bowl, mix lemon juice, mayonnaise, sour cream, salt, and black pepper, and set aside. In a salad bowl, combine lettuce, scallions, cilantro, celery, bell pepper, cheddar cheese, and capers. Toss salad with dressing, and then stir in flaked salmon.

Yield: 2 servings
Per serving: 40 g fat; 5.5 g net carb; 29 g protein; 498 calories

Ham and Cheese Salad

4 cups (60 g) lettuce, torn into bite-size pieces
1 cup (150 g) cooked ham, cubed
½ cup (58 g) shredded cheddar cheese
2 hard-boiled eggs, peeled and coarsely chopped
¼ cup (40 g) chopped green bell pepper
2 scallions, chopped
½ large dill pickle, finely chopped
¼ cup (60 g) mayonnaise (pages 37-40)
½ tablespoon (7 g) lemon juice
½ tablespoon (7 g) heavy cream
½ teaspoon Worcestershire sauce
¼ teaspoon prepared yellow mustard

In a bowl, toss lettuce, ham, cheese, eggs, bell pepper, scallions, and pickle. In a separate bowl, mix mayonnaise, lemon juice, cream, Worcestershire sauce, and mustard until well blended. Just before serving mix the dressing into the salad.

Yield: 2 servings
Per serving: 41.5 g fat; 6 g net carb; 26 g protein; 501 calories

Ham and Egg Salad

4 hard-boiled eggs, peeled and chopped
½ cup (75 g) cooked ham, diced
4 cups (60 g) lettuce, torn into bite-size pieces
2 tablespoons (15 g) dill pickle, diced
2 scallions, chopped
½ cup (60 g) diced celery
1 tablespoon (4 g) diced parsley
¼ teaspoon salt
⅛ teaspoon black pepper
¼ cup (60 g) mayonnaise (pages 37-40)
½ teaspoon Dijon mustard
1 tablespoon (15 ml) extra virgin olive oil

In a bowl, toss eggs, ham, lettuce, pickle, scallions, celery, and parsley. In a separate bowl, mix salt, pepper, mayonnaise, mustard, and olive oil until well blended. Just before serving mix the dressing into the salad.

Yield: 2 servings
Per serving: 40.5 g fat; 4 g net carb; 18.5 g protein; 454 calories

Green Bean and Bacon Salad

10 ounces (280 g) cooked green beans
4 scallions, chopped
¼ cup (60 ml) extra virgin olive oil
2 tablespoons (30 ml) apple cider vinegar
¼ teaspoon salt
⅛ teaspoon black pepper
2 hard-boiled eggs, chopped

2 tablespoons (28 g) mayonnaise (pages 37-40)
1 teaspoon apple cider vinegar
½ teaspoon prepared mustard
⅛ teaspoon salt
6 strips sugar-free, nitrite-free bacon, cooked crisp and crumbled
4 romaine lettuce leaves
Paprika

In a bowl, combine green beans, scallions, olive oil, 2 tablespoons (30 ml) apple cider vinegar, ¼ teaspoon salt, and black pepper, and set aside. In another bowl, mix eggs, mayonnaise, 1 teaspoon apple cider vinegar, mustard, and ⅛ teaspoon salt. Each mixture can be made in advance and kept in the refrigerator for up to 24 hours until ready to serve.

Just before serving, drain the bean mixture, if needed. Add the bacon and toss. Arrange lettuce leaves on 2 salad plates and scoop equal portions of the bean mixture and egg mixture onto each plate. Garnish with paprika and serve.

Yield: 2 servings
Per serving: 67 g fat; 8 g net carb; 30 g protein; 755 calories

SIDE SALADS

Coleslaw

1 tablespoons (14 g) sour cream
1 tablespoon (14 g) mayonnaise (pages 37-40)
1 teaspoon apple cider vinegar
⅛ teaspoon salt
⅛ teaspoon dry mustard
2 cups (110 g) shredded cabbage
1 medium carrot, shredded
¼ green or red bell pepper, cut in julienne strips
2 tablespoons (14 g) slivered almonds, toasted

To make the dressing, mix sour cream, mayonnaise, vinegar, salt, and mustard in a small bowl. In a larger bowl, mix cabbage, carrot, bell pepper, and almonds. Stir in dressing.

Yield: serves 2
Per serving: 10 g fat; 5.5 g net carb; 2.5 g protein; 122 calories

Kohlrabi Slaw

½ avocado
¼ cup (60 ml) extra virgin olive oil
2 tablespoons (30 ml) apple cider vinegar
⅓ cup (77 g) sour cream
½ teaspoon salt
1½ tablespoons (6 g) minced tarragon
2 tablespoons (8 g) minced parsley
1 tablespoon (3 g) chopped chives
Fresh ground black pepper
4 medium kohlrabies
2 medium carrots

To make the dressing, peel and slice avocado. Combine with olive oil, vinegar, sour cream, and salt in a food processor and puree until smooth. Stir in tarragon, parsley, and chives. Taste for salt and black pepper and season to your preference.

Peel kohlrabies and carrots and cut into julienne strips. Toss with enough dressing to coat and serve.

Yield: serves 4
Per serving: 23 g fat; 7 g net carb; 3 g protein; 247 calories

Sauerkraut Slaw

2 cups (280 g) sauerkraut
2 medium stalks celery, chopped
1 small red bell pepper, chopped
1 scallion, chopped
½ cup (115 g) sour cream
½ teaspoon celery seed

Mix all of the ingredients. Cover and refrigerate for at least 24 hours, stirring occasionally.

This salad has only a moderate amount of fat. Serve as a complement to something that is higher in fat, such as bacon, sausage, or marbled steak.

Yield: serves 2
Per serving: 12.5 g fat; 8 g net carb; 4.5 g protein; 162 calories

Cabbage Apple Slaw

4 cups (280 g) shredded cabbage
2 medium carrots, shredded
½ cup (75 g) diced apple
¼ cup (28 g) chopped pecans, lightly toasted
6 tablespoons (84 g) mayonnaise (pages 37-40)
1 tablespoon (15 ml) rice or coconut vinegar
2 teaspoons soy sauce
¼ teaspoon salt

In a medium-size bowl, combine cabbage, carrots, apple, and pecans. To toast pecans, put them in an oven safe dish and bake them at 325° F (170° C) for about 6 minutes. Watch carefully because they burn easily. In a separate bowl, using a whisk, blend together mayonnaise, vinegar, soy sauce, and salt. Stir the dressing into the cabbage mixture.

Yield: serves 4
Per serving: 12 g fat; 12 g net carb; 2 g protein; 164 calories

Red Cabbage Salad

This is a good salad to make beforehand and keep in the refrigerator. The flavors blend over time. Tastes just as good, if not better, the second day.

½ medium head red cabbage
⅓ cup (80 ml) wine cider vinegar
½ small red bell pepper, chopped
½ cup (60 ml) extra virgin olive oil
1 scallion, chopped
1 teaspoon salt
½ teaspoon celery seed
½ teaspoon dry mustard
¼ teaspoon black pepper

Mix all of the ingredients together. Cover and refrigerate for 3 hours before serving. Drain just before serving.

Yield: serves 4
Per serving: 14.5 g fat; 4.5 g net carb; 1.5 g protein; 154 calories

Cucumber Dill Salad

This is a very simple and quick salad that makes a good vegetable accompaniment to a meat dish.

½ cup (120 g) sour cream
1 small clove garlic, crushed
¼ teaspoon dried dill weed
¼ teaspoon salt
1 large or 2 small cucumbers, thinly sliced
Snipped parsley or cilantro (optinal)

Mix sour cream, garlic, dill, and salt. Stir in sliced cucumber. Garnish with snipped parsley or cilantro if desired.

Yield: 2 servings
Per serving: 13 g fat; 11 g net carb; 4 g protein; 177 calories

Tomato Cucumber Salad

1 large tomato, chopped
½ medium cucumber, sliced and halved
½ red bell pepper, chopped
2 scallions, chopped

Salt and black pepper
Dressing (Vinaigrette, Garlic Herb, Vinegar and Coconut Oil)

Combine the vegetables in a bowl, add salt and pepper to taste, and toss with salad dressing.

Yield: 2 servings
Per serving without dressing: 0.5 g fat; 7 g net carb; 2 g protein; 40 calories

Stuffed Tomatoes
This recipe makes a great vegetable side dish to a high-fat meal.

6 medium tomatoes
2 ounces (60 g) cooked baby shrimp
1 small cucumber, chopped
⅓ cup (75 g) mayonnaise (pages 37-40)
1 clove garlic, crushed
1 tablespoon (4 g) parsley, chopped
Dash of salt
Hot sauce to taste (optional)
Lettuce leaves

Remove the stem ends from the tomatoes. Cut the tomatoes in half and remove the pulp. Drain the pulp and put aside. Place the tomato shells, cut side down, on paper towels and refrigerate for at least 2 hours.

Chop reserved tomato pulp and drain liquid. Stir in shrimp, cucumber, mayonnaise, garlic, parsley, salt, and hot sauce. Cover and refrigerate for at least 2 hours.

Just before serving, arrange each tomato shell on a leaf of lettuce. Fill the tomatoes with the shrimp mixture. Garnish with small sprig of parsley.

Yield: 12 stuffed tomato halves
Per serving: 4.5 g fat; 2.5 g net carb; 2 g protein; 58 calories

Salmon Gelatin Salad

Sour Cream Sauce (below)
1 envelope unflavored gelatin
¼ cup cold water

¾ cup boiling water

2 tablespoons (30 ml) lemon juice

1½ teaspoons apple cider vinegar

1 teaspoon salt

1 medium stalk celery, chopped

⅓ cup (40 g) chopped cucumber

10 thin slices of cucumber

1 can (15½ oz/440 g) salmon, drained and flaked

Leafy salad greens (lettuce, spinach, cabbage, kale, etc.)

Sour Cream Sauce:

¼ cup plus 2 tablespoons (90 g) sour cream

½ small green pepper, finely chopped

1 teaspoon chopped parsley

1 teaspoon, chopped chives

¼ teaspoon salt

Dash of pepper

To make the sour cream sauce, mix all ingredients together and refrigerate until ready to serve.

To make the salad, mix gelatin in cold water to soften. Gradually pour in boiling water and stir until gelatin is dissolved. Stir in lemon juice, vinegar, and salt, and set aside.

Mix celery and chopped cucumber. Arrange the sliced cucumber on the bottom of a 4 cup (1 liter) gelatin mold. On top of the sliced cucumber, layer half of the salmon, the celery-cucumber mixture, and the remaining salmon. Pour gelatin on top of the salmon. Refrigerate until set, about 3 hours.

Unmold the gelled salmon on top of salad greens. Serve with Sour Cream Sauce.

Yield: about 4 servings
Per serving: 11.5 g fat; 3 g net carb; 24 g protein; 211 calories

Lettuce Wedges with Crumbled Bacon

6 strips sugar-free, nitrite-free bacon, cooked crisp and crumbled

8 ounces (225 g) cream cheese

1 tablespoon (14 g) mayonnaise (pages 37-40)

2 scallions, chopped

½ cup (55 g) shredded carrot

1 medium tomato, finely chopped and drained
¼ teaspoon salt
Hot sauce to taste
½ medium-size head iceberg lettuce, cut in half
Thousand Island or French Dressing (page 46)

Cook bacon and set aside. Mix cream cheese and mayonnaise until well blended. Mix in scallions, carrot, tomato, salt and hot sauce. Cut lettuce into 4 equal-size wedges. Place lettuce wedges on individual serving plates. Scoop cream cheese mixture on top of each wedge, add Thousand Island or French Dressing, and top with crumbled bacon.

Yield: 4 servings
Per serving without dressing: 34 g fat; 4 g net carb; 15 g protein; 382 calories

Cauliflower Salad (Mock Potato Salad)

What's summer without a potato salad? Here is a low-carb version made with cauliflower that tastes remarkably similar to the old favorite.

1 medium head cauliflower, chopped into bite-size pieces
2 medium stalks celery, chopped
¼ cup (40 g) finely chopped red onion
1 whole dill pickle, chopped
1 cup (225 g) mayonnaise (pages 37-40)
2 teaspoons prepared mustard
1 tablespoon (15 ml) apple cider vinegar

1 tablespoon (4 g) chopped fresh dill or 1 teaspoon dried dill
Salt and freshly ground black pepper to taste

Place cauliflower in a large pot of water. Bring the water to a boil, lower the heat, and simmer for 15 to 20 minutes or until the cauliflower is tender. Drain the cauliflower and set aside to cool to room temperature.

Combine celery, onion, pickle, mayonnaise, mustard, vinegar, and dill, and mix thoroughly. Stir in cauliflower, and add salt and black pepper to taste.

Yield: 5 servings of about 8 ounces (225 g) each
Per serving: 31 g fat; 4.5 g net carb; 3.5 g protein; 311 calories

Ham and Cauliflower Salad

This is a mock potato salad loaded with ham, eggs, and vegetables; hearty enough to make an entire meal.

1 medium head cauliflower, chopped into bite-size pieces
4 ounces (110 g) ham, cut into ½-inch (1-cm) cubes
2 medium stalks celery, chopped
¼ cup (40 g) finely chopped red onion
1 whole dill pickle, chopped
¼ cup (4 g) chopped cilantro
1 cup (225 g) mayonnaise (pages 37-40)
2 teaspoons prepared mustard
1 tablespoon (15 ml) apple cider vinegar
1 tablespoon (4 g) chopped fresh dill
Salt and freshly ground black pepper to taste
2 hard-boiled eggs, cut into thin slices
10 cherry tomatoes

Place cauliflower in a large pot of water. Bring the water to a boil, lower the heat, and simmer for 15 to 20 minutes or until the cauliflower is tender. Drain the cauliflower and set aside to cool to room temperature.

Combine ham, celery, onion, pickle, cilantro, mayonnaise, mustard, vinegar, and dill, and mix thoroughly. Stir in cauliflower, and add salt and black pepper to taste. Top with egg slices and cherry tomatoes.

Yield: 6 servings of about 8 ounces (225 g) each
Per serving: 31 g fat; 5 g net carb; 7.5 g protein; 329 calories

Cucumbers with Sour Cream Sauce

¾ cup (175 g) sour cream
1 tablespoon (15 ml) tarragon vinegar
1 tablespoon (15 ml) lemon juice
1 tablespoon (4 g) minced fresh dill
¼ teaspoon salt
⅛ teaspoon black pepper
2 medium cucumbers, sliced

To make the sauce, blend the sour cream, vinegar, lemon juice, dill, salt, and pepper. Add cucumbers and toss to coat.

Yield: 4 servings
Per serving: 9.5 g fat; 7 g net carb; 2.5 g protein; 123 calories

Celery Victor

8 stalks celery, leaves removed
1½ cups (355 g) beef broth
½ cup (112 g) French Dressing (page 46)
1 small bunch watercress or lettuce
¼ teaspoon salt
⅛ teaspoon black pepper
1 tablespoon (4 g) minced parsley
1 can (4 oz/106 g) sardines
1 large tomato, cut in 8 wedges
8 black olives
4 tablespoons (60 ml) extra virgin olive oil

Cut celery stalks in 3-inch (7-cm) lengths and simmer, covered, in broth until tender, about 20 minutes. Remove the celery and save the broth for another recipe. Toss the celery with French dressing, cover, and marinate in the refrigerator at least 4 hours, but can be marinated overnight. Serve celery on bed of watercress or lettuce on individual salad plates. Sprinkle with salt and pepper, garnish with parsley, sardines, tomato wedges, and olives. Pour a tablespoon (15 ml) of olive oil over each salad.

Yield: 4 servings
Per serving: 36 g fat; 2 g net carb; 7 g protein; 360 calories

Green Bean Salad

This salad goes especially well with pork, ham, or lamb.

12 ounces (340 g) green beans, boiled and drained
½ small red onion, sliced thin
Dressing (below)

Dressing:
1 tablespoon (1 g) chopped cilantro
1 small clove garlic, crushed
1 teaspoon Dijon mustard
¼ teaspoon salt
¼ cup (60 ml) extra virgin olive oil
2 tablespoons (30 ml) wine or rice vinegar
½ tablespoon (7 g) tomato sauce

Place cooked green beans and sliced onion in a salad bowl. To make the dressing, combine all of the dressing ingredients. Pour dressing over green beans and onions and toss. Cover and let stand at room temperature for about 1 hour. Toss again just before serving.

Yield: 2 servings
Per serving: 28 g fat; 8 g net carb; 3.5 g protein; 298 calories

Asparagus with Curry Dressing

1 pound (450 g) cooked asparagus
½ cup (110 g) French Dressing (page 46)
6 lettuce leaves
Curry Dressing (below)
1 pimiento, drained and cut in ¼-inch (1-cm) strips

Curry Dressing:
¼ cup (115 g) mayonnaise (pages 37-40)
1 tablespoon (14 g) sour cream
½ teaspoon curry powder
½ teaspoon lemon juice

Steam asparagus until tender. Remove from heat and let cool. Cover asparagus with French Dressing and marinate in the refrigerator for 3 to 4 hours, turning occasionally. Just before serving, make Curry Dressing by combining all of the dressing ingredients. Drain the French Dressing off of the asparagus (the dressing can be used for another salad). Place asparagus on lettuce leaves and cover with Curry Dressing. Top with strips of pimiento.

Yield: 2 servings
Per serving: 23 g fat; 7 g net carb; 6.5 g protein; 261 calories

Bacon Avocado Cups

This recipe is so simple, but so good. It makes a great high-fat accompaniment to any meal, or you can make an entire meal with 1 avocado.

2 avocados
4 strips sugar-free, nitrite-free bacon, cooked crisp and crumbled
3 tablespoons (42 g) butter
1 teaspoon minced garlic
1 tablespoon (15 ml) balsamic vinegar

Cut avocados in half lengthwise and remove the pits. Fill each avocado cavity with crumbled bacon using one piece of bacon per avocado half. In a small saucepan over low heat, melt the butter. Add garlic and cook until fragrant, about 2 minutes. Add balsamic vinegar and remove from heat. Drizzle over the avocado halves and serve.

Yield: 4 avocado halves
Per serving: 36 g fat; 2.5 g net carb; 9 g protein; 370 calories

Vegetable Vinaigrette

This salad is made with a choice of cooked vegetables. You may use any one or more of the following:

Artichoke hearts	Daikon radish
Asparagus	Fennel
Broccoli	Green or wax beans
Cauliflower	Hearts of palm
Celery	Leeks
Celeriac (celery root)	Turnips

The quantity you use will depend on how many vegetables you use and how many servings you plan to make.

Cook the vegetables by steaming or boiling until tender. Arrange the vegetables in a shallow bowl and generously coat with French Dressing (page 46). Cover and marinate in the refrigerator for several hours or overnight, turning occasionally so vegetables are evenly coated with dressing. Serve chilled on a bed of lettuce.

Fat content can be estimated by the amount of dressing used. Yield and other nutritional values vary too greatly for any meaningful count.

Avocado, Bacon, and Egg Salad

This is a quick and easy salad for breakfast, lunch, or dinner.

1 avocado, chopped
4 hard-boiled eggs, peeled and sliced
1 medium tomato, chopped
2 tablespoons (30 ml) lemon juice
6 strips sugar-free, nitrite-free bacon, cooked crisp and crumbled
2 tablespoons (2 g) minced cilantro
Salt
Freshly ground black pepper

Combine avocado, eggs, tomato, lemon juice, bacon, and cilantro in a bowl. Toss and add salt and black pepper to taste.

Yield: 2 servings
Per serving: 52.5 g fat; 7 g net carb; 35 g protein; 640 calories

Soups and Stews

I love soups and stews. They are incredibly easy to make and go very well with ketogenic diets. You can easily adjust the ingredients to boost the fat content. It is often difficult to prepare foods that have enough fat to make them ketogenic. Soups allow you a very palatable way to add as much fat as you need. And if you need more fat in your diet, just add more to the soup. A little soup can make 2, 3, or 4 tablespoons (28 to 42 g) of fat taste delicious.

BROTHS

Broths provide a flavorful base for soups, stews, sauces, curries, casseroles, and other dishes. Broths bring added nutrients, flavor, and richness to a meal. They can be made in quantity ahead of time and stored in the freezer for later use. Broths will stay good frozen for over a year. If you make a large pot, you can then freeze it in individual 1 to 4 cup (250 to 1,000 ml) portions for easy use later.

Broths can be made from any type of meat—beef, pork, lamb, chicken, turkey, duck, fish, or shellfish—the process is basically the same. Broths are generally made from the cheapest cuts of meat with bones, such as the shank or knuckles, and from leftovers after the more choice pieces of meat have been removed from the bone or eaten. Meat scraps, bones, and cartilage also make good broth.

Homemade broths are superior to store-bought; they have a richer flavor without any preservatives, flavor enhancers, or other chemical additives.

Homemade broths tend to contain a higher percentage of fat, which should not be removed but consumed with the broth.

Chicken Broth

You can make chicken broth from a whole bird or from the leftovers after eating a whole chicken. You can often buy wings and backs at a significantly lower cost and use that in place of a whole bird. The following recipe is for a whole bird or wings and backs. If you are using just the leftover bones and scraps, skip the first part and simmer with herbs and vegetables for 2 to 6 hours.

    1 whole chicken, including giblets
    2 quarts (2 liters) water
    1 bay leaf
    6 peppercorns
    1 medium yellow onion, quartered
    1 medium carrot, cut in 1-inch (2.5-cm) lengths
    1 stalk medium celery, cut in 1-inch (2.5-cm) lengths
    1½ teaspoons salt

Place chicken, bay leaf, and peppercorns in a large kettle or slow cooker, cover, and simmer for 2 to 2½ hours. Lift the bird from the broth and cool.

Remove the meat from the bones and save for use in recipes calling for cooked chicken. Return all the bones, cartilage, and skin to the pot. Add the remaining ingredients and continue to simmer for 2 to 6 hours. Check the water level occasionally as it simmers. If needed, add a little more water.

Remove the pot from the heat and let cool. Strain to separate out the broth. Store in multiple small airtight containers. If you are not going to use the broth within the next 24 hours or so, store it in the freezer.

Yield: varies
Per 1 cup serving yields approximately: 3 g fat; 0.5 g net carbs; 4 g protein; 45 calories

Beef, Pork, and Lamb Broth

These broths are made basically the same way as chicken broth. Use cheap cuts of bone-in meat, such as hocks. You could also use tougher cuts of meat, such as the brisket, short plate, and flank.

4 to 5 pounds (1.8 to 2 kg) meat, bones, and cartilage
1 large yellow onion, coarsely chopped
2 leeks, coarsely chopped
2 medium carrots, cut in 1-inch (2.5-cm) lengths
2 stalks medium celery, cut in 1-inch (2.5-cm) lengths
5 quarts (5 L) water
6 peppercorns
2 bay leaves
2 to 3 sprigs parsley
1 tablespoon salt

Combine all ingredients in a large kettle, cover, and simmer for 4 to 5 hours. Check pot occasionally and add more water if needed. Skim off any scum that may form on top and discard. Do not skim off the fat. Remove from heat and let cool. Meat can be trimmed off the bones and saved for use in recipes that call for cooked meat. Strain the broth to remove the solids. If you are not going to use it within 24 hours, store broth in small 1 to 2 cup (250 to 500 ml) portions in airtight containers and freeze.

Yield: varies
Per 1 cup serving yields approximately: 3 g fat; 0.5 g net carbs; 4 g protein; 45 calories

Fish Broth

Fish broth is made from fish bones, heads, trimmings, and shellfish shells.

2 quarts (2 L) water
1 pound (450 g) fish bones and trimmings
1 tablespoon salt

Put all of the ingredients in a stockpot or kettle, cover, and simmer for 1½ hours. Remove from heat and let cool. Strain the broth through a sieve to separate out all the solids. If not used within 24 hours, store in the freezer.

Yield: varies
Per 1 cup serving yields approximately: 3 g fat; 0.5 g net carbs; 4 g protein; 45 calories

Bone Broth

Bone broths are made from bones, cartilage, and any little scraps of meat and fat clinging to the bones. The broth can be made from the leftover carcass of a roasted chicken or turkey or the remains of a roast or ribs. You can also buy fresh bones from the butcher. When making bone broth, vinegar is added to the water to help dissolve and pull out minerals, making the broth an excellent source of calcium, magnesium, phosphorous, and other minerals necessary for good bone health.

Put bones in a kettle or slow cooker and add enough water to cover by about 3 inches (7 cm). Add 2 tablespoons (30 ml) of apple cider vinegar for every quart (liter) of water used. Heat the water to a simmer, cover, and cook for 36 to 48 hours. If desired, halfway through the cooking process you can add some chopped carrots, celery, onion, salt, and black pepper. Skim off and discard any scum that forms on top of the broth. Add more water if needed while cooking to keep the bones covered.

Remove from heat and let cool. Strain through a sieve to remove the solids. Do not discard the fat or any little pieces of meat; return them to the broth. Make sure to remove all the marrow from the bones and add it back into the broth. If not used within a couple of days, store in the freezer. Will stay good frozen for up to a year.

> *Yield: varies*
> *Per 1 cup serving yields approximately: 2 g fat; 0.5 g net carbs; 3 g protein; 32 calories*

SOUP RECIPES

Sausage Borscht

Borscht is a traditional Ukrainian beet stew. It is always made using beets, but can include a variety of other vegetables. It is often meatless, but in this version we add sausage and replace some of the beets with cabbage. You can use beet tops in place of the cabbage if you like, or use a mixture of each. The result is a thick, hearty, delicious stew. Each 2 cup serving supplies 23 grams of fat. You can easily increase the fat content of the stew by adding butter or more sour cream.

    5 cups (1.2 liter) beef broth or water
    2 medium beets, shredded or chopped
    1 medium onion, chopped
    8 ounces (225 g) sausage
    1 cup (100 g) chopped fennel or celery
    3 cups (270 g) chopped cabbage or beet tops
    ½ teaspoon celery seed
    1 teaspoon dill weed
    Salt and pepper
    Sour cream

Bring beef broth to a boil. Add beets, onion, sausage, and fennel, reduce heat and simmer for about 10 minutes. Add cabbage, celery seed, and dill;

simmer for 30 minutes. Add salt and pepper to taste. Remove from heat and let cool slightly. Serve warm with a dollop of sour cream.

Yield: Serves 4
Per serving: 23 g fat; 10.5 g net carbs; 17.5 g protein; 332 calories

Traditional Borscht

Borscht is an excellent way to use less expensive cuts of meat. The long stewing process tenderizes even the toughest cuts. This version uses ham hocks to make the soup base, but you can also use stew meat, meaty bones, beef shank, flank or skirt steak, or brisket. The leftover bone from a bone-in ham makes excellent stock.

1½ to 2 pounds (0.7-1 kg) ham hocks
112 ounces or 14 cups (3.3 liters) water
1 medium onion, chopped
3 stalks celery, chopped
2 cups (220 g) beets, cut in julienne strips*
1 medium carrot, chopped
3 cups (270 g) cabbage, chopped
1 teaspoon dill weed
½ teaspoon salt
¼ teaspoon black pepper
Juice from 1 lemon (about 2 tablespoons/30 ml)
Sour cream

Put the ham hocks and water in a large pot, bring it to boiling, reduce heat, cover, and simmer for about 4 hours. Some of the water will evaporate during the cooking process. Add onion, celery, beets, and carrot; cover and continue to simmer for 1½ to 2 hours or until all of the vegetables are soft. Remove the ham hocks, trim off all meat and cut to bite-size pieces, and discard the bones. Return the meat to the pot and add the cabbage, dill weed, salt, and black pepper; cover and simmer for 20 to 30 minutes or until the cabbage is soft. Add lemon juice and remove from heat. Serve with a dollop of sour cream.

*Julienne strips are thin strips about ⅛-inch (3-mm) thick.

Yield: Serves 6
Per serving: 26 g fat; 7 g net carbs; 15 g protein; 322 calories

Tomato Borscht

Borscht is made using a variety of ingredients. This version uses stewed tomatoes as the base. Make enough to serve dinner for two days. Borscht tastes even better the second day.

4 cups (945 ml) beef broth or water
8 ounces (225 g) ground beef
2 medium beets, shredded or chopped
1 medium onion, chopped
1 medium carrot, chopped
2 cups (360 g) stewed tomatoes
2 cups (180 g) chopped cabbage or beet tops
2 cups (60 g) chopped spinach
½ teaspoon celery seed
1 teaspoon dill weed
Salt and pepper
Sour cream

Bring beef broth to a boil. Add ground beef, beets, onion, carrot, and stewed tomatoes; reduce heat and simmer for about 20 minutes. Add cabbage, spinach, celery seed, and dill weed; simmer for 10 minutes. Add salt and pepper to taste. Remove from heat and let cool slightly. Serve warm with a large scoop of sour cream. To increase the fat content, add butter or more sour cream.

Yield: Serves 4
Per serving: 10.5 g fat; 12 g net carbs; 23.5 g protein; 236 calories

Beef Stew

Most traditional beef stews are loaded with potatoes. In this low-carb version, the potatoes are replaced by more vegetables. The white-colored daikon radish, which tastes like a mild turnip, makes a reasonable substitute for potatoes both in taste and appearance.

5 cups (1180 ml) beef broth or water
10 ounces (280 g) chopped beef
¼ cup (56 g) butter, coconut oil, or red palm oil
1 large carrot, chopped
½ medium onion, chopped
2 cloves garlic, chopped
2 cups (200 g) chopped green beans

8 ounces (230 g) daikon radish or turnip, chopped
1 can (8 oz/125 g) tomato sauce
½ teaspoon oregano
Salt and pepper

Bring beef broth to a boil. Add chopped beef, butter, carrot, onion, garlic, green beans, daikon radish, and tomato sauce. Reduce heat and simmer for about 40 minutes. Add oregano and salt and pepper to taste. Simmer for 5 minutes. Remove from heat and serve.

Each serving supplies 6.3 grams of fat. You can easily increase the amount of fat by adding butter or coconut oil. One tablespoon of fat added to a serving will increase the total fat content to 20 grams.

Yield: Serves 4
Per serving: 20.5 g fat; 8 g net carbs; 30.5 g protein; 338 calories

Hearty Egg Drop Soup

Traditional Chinese egg drop soup consists of chicken broth, a little egg, and not much else. It tastes good, but it is not very filling. This is a heartier, more satisfying, version prepared with whole eggs, chicken, mushrooms, and onions.

7 cups (1650 ml) chicken broth
1½ cups (210 g) chopped chicken
1 medium stalk celery, thinly sliced
½ medium onion, chopped
8 mushrooms, sliced
¼ cup butter
4 eggs
Salt and pepper

Simmer chicken broth, chicken, celery, onion, mushrooms, and butter in a pot until the vegetables are tender. Crack the eggs open and pour into a bowl. Lightly beat the eggs and pour them into the hot soup. Simmer until the eggs are completely cooked. Add salt and pepper to taste. Top with chopped scallions as a garnish.

Yield: Serves 4
Per serving: 20 g fat; 4.5 g net carbs; 30.5 g protein; 320 calories

Chicken Chowder

2 tablespoons (28 g) butter
2 stalks celery, chopped
1 medium onion, chopped
4 cups (950 ml) chicken broth
2 ounces (56 g) mushrooms, chopped
1 teaspoon salt
¼ teaspoon black pepper
¼ cup (15 g) minced parsley
1 cup (240 ml) heavy cream
2 cups (280 g) chopped cooked chicken

Heat butter in a large skillet over medium heat. Sauté celery and onion until the onion begins to caramelize, about 10 minutes. Add chicken broth, mushrooms, salt, black pepper, and parsley, cover, and simmer for 30 minutes. Pour soup into a blender and blend until smooth. Pour back into the skillet, add cream and chicken and heat until hot, about 5 minutes.

Yield: Serves 4
Per serving: 31 g fat; 4.5 g net carbs; 27 g protein; 405 calories

Asparagus Cheese Soup

6 tablespoons (84 g) butter
½ medium onion, chopped
1 stalk celery, chopped
1 pound (450 g) asparagus, chopped
4 cups (950 ml) chicken broth
2 cloves garlic, chopped
1 teaspoon salt
¼ teaspoon black pepper
1 tablespoon (4 g) minced fresh parsley
1 cup (240 ml) heavy cream
2 teaspoons lemon juice
1 cup (115 g) shredded sharp cheddar cheese
4 strips sugar-free, nitrite-free bacon, cooked crisp and crumbled

Heat butter in a large skillet over medium heat. Sauté onion, celery, and asparagus until tender, about 10 to 15 minutes. Add broth, garlic, salt, and black pepper, cover, and simmer for 30 minutes. Remove from heat and let cool slightly. Add parsley and pour into a blender and puree. Pour puree back into skillet, add cream, lemon juice, and cheese and heat until hot. Serve with crumbled bacon sprinkled on top.

Yield: Serves 4
Per serving: 58 g fat; 6 g net carbs; 23 g protein; 638 calories

Cream of Tomato Soup

2 tablespoons (28 g) butter
½ medium yellow onion, chopped
2 large stalks celery, chopped
1 red bell pepper, chopped
1 clove garlic, chopped
3½ cups (830 ml) chicken or beef broth
16 ounces (470 ml) tomato sauce
¼ cup (15 g) minced fresh parsley
1 tablespoon (3 g) minced fresh basil or ½ teaspoon dried
½ teaspoon dried oregano
1¼ teaspoon salt
⅛ teaspoon freshly ground black pepper
1 tablespoon (15 ml) lemon juice
1 cup (240 ml) heavy cream
¼ cup (25 g) grated Parmesan cheese

Heat butter in a large saucepan over medium heat. Sauté onion, celery, and bell pepper until onion begins to caramelize, about 10 minutes. Add garlic and cook 1 to 2 minutes. Add broth, tomato sauce, parsley, basil, oregano, salt, and black pepper, cover, and simmer for 30 minutes. Pour into a blender and puree. Pour back into the pan, add lemon juice and cream, and reheat just until hot. Serve with Parmesan cheese sprinkled on top. Add a few pork rinds as croutons, if desired.

Yield: Serves 4
Per serving: 31 g fat; 9.5 g net carbs; 10.5 g protein; 359 calories

Fresh Tomato Soup

4 large tomatoes
¼ cup (56 g) butter
1 medium onion, chopped
2 stalks celery, chopped
1 medium carrot, chopped
2 cloves garlic, chopped
3 cups chicken broth
1 teaspoon salt
¼ teaspoon black pepper
½ teaspoon dried dill
1 teaspoon dried basil
½ teaspoon celery seed
¼ cup (15 g) minced parsley
½ cup (120 ml) heavy cream
½ cup (120 ml) sour cream
¼ cup (25 g) grated Parmesan cheese

Cut a small "X" on the bottom of each tomato and put them into a pot of boiling water for 1 minute. Using a slotted spoon, remove the tomatoes and peel off and discard the skin. Chop the tomatoes and set aside.

Heat the butter in a large skillet over medium heat. Sauté onion, celery, and carrot until tender, about 10 to 15 minutes. Add chopped tomatoes, garlic, broth, salt, pepper, dill, basil, and celery seed, cover, and simmer for 20 minutes. Remove from heat and let cool slightly. Add parsley, then pour into a blender and puree until smooth. Pour back into the skillet. Add cream and reheat until hot. Stir in sour cream. Serve topped with Parmesan cheese.

Yield: Serves 4
Per serving: 30 g fat; 11 g net carbs; 9 g protein; 350 calories

Cream of Mushroom Soup

¼ cup (56 g) butter
2 stalks celery, chopped
1 medium onion, chopped
10 ounces (280 g) mushrooms, chopped
5 cups beef or chicken broth
1 teaspoon salt

½ teaspoon black pepper
1 teaspoon tarragon
½ teaspoon thyme
½ cup (120 ml) heavy cream
½ cup (115 g) sour cream

Heat butter in a large skillet over medium heat. Sauté celery and onion until onion begins to caramelize, about 12 to 15 minutes. Add mushrooms, broth, salt, black pepper, tarragon, and thyme, cover, and simmer for 30 minutes. Remove from heat, add cream, and let cool slightly. Pour into a blender and puree. Return to the skillet and reheat. Stir in sour cream and serve.

Yield: Serves 4
Per serving: 30 g fat; 6.5 g net carbs; 10 g protein; 336 calories

Tomato Mushroom Bisque

4 large tomatoes, peeled and chopped
4 tablespoons (56 g) butter
1 small yellow onion, chopped
1 stalk celery, chopped
1 clove garlic, chopped
8 ounces (225 g) mushrooms
2 cups (480 ml) chicken broth
¼ teaspoon black pepper
4 teaspoons fish sauce
1 cup (240 ml) heavy cream or coconut milk

Fill a large pot with water and bring to a boil. Cut a small "X" on the bottom of each tomato and drop into the boiling water. Remove the tomatoes with a slotted spoon after about 1 minute and put them in a bath of cold water until cool enough to handle. Peel off the skins and discard. Chop the tomatoes.

Heat butter in a large saucepan or skillet over medium heat. Sauté onion and celery until the onion begins to caramelize, about 12 to 15 minutes. Add garlic and mushrooms, and cook 3 to 4 more minutes. Add broth, tomatoes, black pepper, and fish sauce, and simmer for 30 minutes. Put into a blender and puree. Pour puree back into the pan, add cream, and heat just until hot.

Yield: Serves 4
Per serving: 34.5 g fat; 10 g net carbs; 7.5 g protein; 380 calories

No-Bean Chili

This bean-free chili tastes just as good as the bean version. In this recipe, the beans are replaced by more vegetables, primarily daikon radish or turnip, either of which make a suitable substitute for beans when cut up into bean-size pieces.

¼ cup (56 g) coconut oil
1 pound (453 g) ground beef
1 medium onion, chopped
1 green bell pepper, chopped
6 cloves garlic, chopped
1 or 2 red chili peppers, chopped (optional)
1 pound (453 g) daikon radish or turnips, chopped
1⅓ cups (314 ml) tomato sauce
½ cup (118 ml) water
2 teaspoons chili powder
1½ teaspoons paprika
1 teaspoon oregano
1 teaspoon cumin
1½ teaspoons salt

Heat oil in a large skillet over medium heat. Add meat, onion, bell pepper, and garlic. Cook, stirring occasionally, until the meat is browned. Stir in chili peppers, daikon radish, tomato sauce, water, and spices, and simmer covered for about 30 minutes or until the chili thickens and vegetables are tender. Serve as is, or top with shredded cheese or sour cream.

Yield: 4 servings
Per serving: 21 g fat; 10 g net carbs; 38.5 g protein; 383 calories

Beef and Vegetable Chili

¼ cup (56 g) cooking oil
8 ounces (227 g) ground beef
½ onion, chopped
1 stalk celery, thinly sliced
1 green bell pepper, chopped
2 cloves garlic, finely chopped
6 ounces (170 g) turnip or daikon radish, chopped
2 teaspoons chili powder
1 teaspoon ground cumin
1 teaspoon dried oregano
½ teaspoon paprika
½ teaspoon salt
1 tablespoon (9 g) finely chopped jalapeño pepper
½ cup (125 g) tomato sauce
¾ cup (177 ml) water or beef broth
2 ounces (57 g) cheddar cheese, shredded

Heat oil in a large skillet over medium heat. Add beef, breaking it up, along with onion, celery, bell pepper, garlic, and turnip. Stirring occasionally, sauté for about 8 minutes or until meat is browned and vegetables are starting to soften. Stir in chili powder, cumin, oregano, paprika, salt, jalapeño pepper, tomato sauce, and water; cover and simmer for about 20 minutes or until vegetables are soft and flavors blended. Stir occasionally while cooking. Turn off the heat and sprinkle cheese evenly over the chili, cover and let sit for 1 to 2 minutes until cheese begins to melt. Serve in a bowl. Top with a dollop of sour cream or sliced avocado, if desired.

Yield: serves 2
Per serving: 45 g fat; 12 g net carbs; 44.5 g protein; 631 calories

Chicken Chili Stew

2 tablespoons (28 g) coconut oil
½ medium onion, chopped

1 stalk celery, chopped
1 red bell pepper, chopped
4 ounces (110 g) cooked chicken, chopped
4 ounces (110 g) mushrooms, sliced
¼ cup (35 g) finely chopped poblano or other chili pepper
1 teaspoon Tabasco sauce or other hot sauce
1 teaspoon cumin
½ teaspoon salt
1 cup (240 ml) chicken broth or water
½ cup (120 ml) heavy cream
1 cup (115 g) shredded Monterey Jack cheese
½ cup (115 g) sour cream

Heat oil in a large skillet over medium heat. Add onion, celery, and bell pepper, and sauté for 6 or 8 minutes or until the vegetables are tender. Add chicken, mushrooms, poblano pepper, Tabasco sauce, cumin, salt, broth, and cream, reduce heat, cover, and simmer for 10 minutes. Remove from heat and stir in cheese until it melts. Serve in a bowl topped with a dollop of sour cream.

Yield: serves 2
Per serving: 48 g fat; 10.5 g net carbs; 37.5 g protein; 624 calories

Chicken Gumbo

I love chicken gumbo. Traditional gumbo is made with rice, but this version leaves the rice out and adds more vegetables, three types of meat, and a burst of flavor. It's better tasting than the high-carb versions.

8 cups (1900 ml) Chicken Broth (page 77)
2 large tomatoes, cut in half
¼ cup (56 g) coconut or red palm oil
10 to 12 ounces (280 to 340 g) raw chicken, cut into bite-size pieces
14 ounces (400 g) shrimp
8 ounces (225 g) seasoned breakfast sausage, broken up
2 carrots, chopped
3 celery ribs, chopped
1 cup (100 g) chopped green beans
1 medium onion, chopped
4 cloves garlic, finely chopped
1 tablespoon (19 g) salt
1 teaspoon black pepper

8 ounces (225 g) okra
2 tablespoons (30 ml) fish sauce
2 tablespoons (30 ml) hot sauce

Put Chicken Broth into a 4-quart (4-liter) saucepan and bring it to a boil. Add tomatoes, reduce heat to a simmer, and cook for 10 minutes. Remove the tomatoes and set them aside to cool. Add coconut oil, chicken, shrimp, sausage, carrots, celery, green beans, onion, garlic, salt, and black pepper. Remove the skin from the stewed tomato halves and discard. Chop the tomatoes and add them to the soup. Simmer for 1 hour. Add okra, fish sauce, and hot sauce, and continue to simmer for 30 minutes.

Gumbo generally has a little kick to it, but not all people like spicy foods. This version is fairly mild. If you like your gumbo spicy hot, more hot sauce can be added to your individual serving. Store any leftover soup in an airtight container in the refrigerator or freezer.

You can easily increase the fat content of this soup by adding more fat. Red palm oil makes a good addition. It enhances the flavor and enriches the color. One tablespoon added to a cup of soup will add 14 grams of fat to the numbers below.

Yield: makes about 14 cups
Per cup: 11 g fat; 5 g net carbs; 20 g protein; 199 calories

New England Clam Chowder

¼ cup (56 g) butter
1 stalk medium celery, chopped
½ medium onion, chopped
8 ounces (170 g) daikon radish, chopped
2 cups (475 ml) chicken broth
2 cans (10 oz/280 g each) clams with juice, separated
½ teaspoon dried basil
½ teaspoon salt
¼ teaspoon freshly ground black pepper
4 teaspoons fish sauce
2½ cups (590 ml) heavy cream or coconut milk
10 pork rinds, broken into ½-inch (1.5-cm) size pieces (optional)

Heat butter in a large saucepan over medium heat. Sauté celery, onion, and daikon radish until tender, about 10 minutes. Add chicken broth, clam juice,

basil, salt, black pepper, and fish sauce, and simmer for about 5 minutes. Add clams and cream, and continue cooking until hot. Serve the chowder with pork rinds on top, as you would oyster crackers.

Yield: 4 servings
Per serving: 69 g fat; 5 g net carbs; 28 g protein; 753 calories

Seafood Chowder

2 tablespoons (28 g) coconut oil or bacon drippings
3 large shallots, chopped
3 garlic cloves, minced
½ teaspoon minced ginger
4 cups (950 ml) chicken broth
2 cups (470 ml) bottled clam juice
1 tablespoon (15 ml) fresh lime juice
2 teaspoons fish sauce
1 can (14 oz/396 g) coconut milk
2 teaspoons grated lime zest
½ teaspoon red pepper flakes
1 teaspoon salt

8 ounces (225 g) white fish fillets (such as halibut, cod, bass), cut into
   bite-size pieces
8 ounces (225 g) shellfish (such as carb, lobster, shrimp, scallops),
   peeled and cut into bite-size pieces
2 tablespoons (2 g) minced cilantro

Heat oil in a large pot. Sauté shallots, garlic, and ginger until fragrant, about
2 minutes. Add broth, clam juice, lime juice, fish sauce, coconut milk, lime zest,
red pepper flakes, and salt, and bring to a simmer. Add fish and shellfish, and
continue cooking until fish turns white and easily flakes. Serve garnished with
minced cilantro.

Yield: serves 6
Per cup: 22.5 g fat; 4.5 g net carbs; 22 g protein; 308 calories

Salmon Chowder

3 strips sugar-free, nitrite-free bacon, diced
1 medium onion, chopped
2 stalks celery, chopped
12 ounces (340 g) daikon radish or turnip, chopped
2½ cups (600 ml) chicken broth
1 teaspoon dried dill
1 bay leaf
½ teaspoon salt
⅛ teaspoon freshly ground black pepper
1 can (7.5 oz/212 g) salmon
2 tablespoons (28 g) butter
2 cups (470 ml) heavy cream or coconut milk

In a large pot over medium heat, sauté bacon, onion, celery, and daikon
until bacon is slightly crisp. Add chicken broth, dill, bay leaf, salt, and black
pepper, cover, and simmer for 20 minutes or until the vegetables are tender.
Add salmon, butter, and cream, and continue to simmer for about 5 minutes.
Remove the bay leaf and serve.

Yield: serves 4
Per cup: 22.5 g fat; 4.5 g net carbs; 22 g protein; 308 calories

Fish Bisque

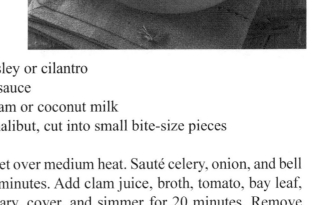

¼ cup (56 g) butter
2 stalks celery, chopped
1 medium onion, chopped
1 red bell pepper, chopped
8 oz (225 g) clam juice
2 cups (950 ml) fish or
  chicken broth
1 medium tomato,
  peeled and chopped
1 bay leaf
½ teaspoon salt
¼ teaspoon black pepper
¼ teaspoon rosemary
¼ cup (16 g) minced parsley or cilantro
8 ounces (225 g) tomato sauce
1 cup (240 ml) heavy cream or coconut milk
8 ounces (225 g) cod or halibut, cut into small bite-size pieces

Heat butter in a large skillet over medium heat. Sauté celery, onion, and bell pepper until tender, about 10 minutes. Add clam juice, broth, tomato, bay leaf, salt, black pepper, and rosemary, cover, and simmer for 20 minutes. Remove bay leaf, add parsley, remove from heat, and let cool slightly. Pour into a blender and puree. Pour puree back into the skillet, add tomato sauce and, cream, and reheat. Add fish and simmer for 5 minutes or until fish has turned white.

Yield: serves 4
Per cup: 35.5 g fat; 8 g net carbs; 20.5 g protein; 433 calories

Smoked Ham Hock Stew

1 to 1½ pounds (450 to 680 g) ham hock or ham shank
3 quarts (3 liters) water
1 medium onion, chopped
2 stalks celery, chopped
2 medium carrots, sliced
1 cup (120 g) chopped cauliflower
1 cup (120 g) chopped green beans
6 cloves garlic, chopped

1 teaspoon dried marjoram leaves
1 teaspoon dried basil
½ teaspoon dried dill
½ teaspoon salt
¼ teaspoon black pepper
6 tablespoons (84 g) butter

Fill a large pot with 3 quarts (3 liters) water, then add ham hock, bring to a boil, reduce heat, cover, and simmer for 6 to 8 hours. Remove ham hock and set aside to cool. Add to the water all of the remaining ingredients, cover, and simmer for 1 hour. When the ham hock is cool enough to handle, remove the bone and cut the meat into small, bite-size pieces. Discard the bone or save to make bone broth later. Add the meat back into the stew and heat thoroughly before serving.

Yield: serves 6
Per cup: 25.5 g fat; 5 g net carbs; 28 g protein; 361 calories

Chicken Almond Soup

2 tablespoons (28 g) coconut oil or butter
½ medium onion, chopped
6 ounces (170 g) broccoli, chopped
1 medium stalk celery, chopped
3 cloves garlic, minced
4 cups (950 ml) chicken broth
2 cups (280 g) chopped cooked chicken
1 teaspoon cumin
½ cup (70 g) whole almonds
1 tablespoon (14 g) roasted almond butter
Salt to taste

Heat the oil in a saucepan, add onion, and cook until it becomes translucent. Add broccoli, celery, and garlic. Cook until the vegetables soften and then add the broth. Stir in the chicken, cumin, almonds, and almond butter. The almond butter may form lumps, but these will dissolve as the soup cooks; stir occasionally. Simmer for 10 minutes. Add salt to taste and serve.

Yield: 4 servings
Per serving: 21.5 g fat; 6.5 g net carbs; 26 g protein; 323 calories

Beef Stroganoff Soup

This is a good recipe for tougher, less expensive cuts of meat like brisket, flank steak, and skirt steak. The slow cooking tenderizes the meat and brings out the flavor.

32 ounces (1 liter) water
1½ pounds (680 g) brisket or other cut of beef
¼ cup (56 g) butter
8 ounces (225 g) baby portobello mushrooms, cut in half
1 medium onion, chopped
4 cloves garlic, chopped
2 tablespoons (30 ml) Worcestershire sauce
1 tablespoon (4 g) dried thyme
8 ounces (225 g) cream cheese
½ teaspoon salt
½ teaspoon freshly ground black pepper
1 tablespoon (14 g) Dijon mustard
½ cup (120 ml) sour cream

Put water and beef into a slow cooker and cook at high setting for 4 hours. Remove the beef and set aside to cool. While the meat is cooling, put into the slow cooker butter, mushrooms, onion, garlic, Worcestershire sauce, thyme, cream cheese, salt, pepper, and Dijon mustard. Cut beef into bite-size pieces and add to the cooker. Cover and cook for 6 hours. Turn off heat. Just before serving add sour cream.

Yield: 8 servings
Per serving: 24 g fat; 4 g net carbs; 32 g protein; 360 calories

Chicken Bacon Chowder

This is a good dish for leftovers. Make it once and have enough for several days. Also tastes good in a thermos and taken to work.

12 strips sugar-free, nitrite-free bacon, cooked crisp and crumbled
3 large chicken breasts
2 cups (470 ml) chicken broth, separated
8 ounces (225 g) cream cheese
2 cups (470 g) heavy cream
2 tablespoons (30 g) butter
1 medium onion, chopped

1 bell pepper, chopped
2 medium stalks celery, chopped
8 ounces (225 g) mushrooms, sliced
6 cloves garlic, minced
1 teaspoon salt
½ teaspoon black pepper
1 tablespoon dried basil
1 tablespoon dried thyme

In a skillet, cook bacon and set aside. Pour off all but about 4 tablespoons (60 g) of bacon drippings. Save the excess drippings for another dish. Keep the remaining bacon drippings in the skillet, and cook chicken breasts at medium-high heat, searing each side. Remove the chicken and cut into small cubes. The chicken does not need to be fully cooked at this point.

Put 1 cup (235 ml) chicken broth into the skillet and bring it to a slow boil for about 2 minutes to absorb all the seared flavor from the pan. Pour the hot broth, including the bacon drippings, into a slow cooker. Add the remaining broth, cream cheese, cream, butter, onion, bell pepper, celery, mushrooms, garlic, salt, black pepper, basil, and thyme. Cover and cook at low heat for 6 hours.

Yield: 8 servings
Per serving: 55 g fat; 6.5 g net carbs; 26 g protein; 625 calories

Broccoli Cheddar Soup

¼ cup (56 g) butter
1 medium onion, finely chopped
2 stalks celery, finely chopped
4 cups (950 ml) chicken broth
4 cups (300 g) finely chopped broccoli
1 bay leaf
1 teaspoon salt
½ teaspoon black pepper
2 cups (470 ml) heavy cream
2 cups (225 g) sharp cheddar cheese, shredded
½ cup (50 g) grated Parmesan cheese

Heat butter in a large pot over medium heat. Add onion and celery, and cook, stirring until softened, about 8 to 10 minutes. Add chicken broth, broccoli,

bay leaf, salt, and black pepper, and bring to a boil. Reduce heat to medium-low and simmer for about 30 minutes, until broccoli is tender.

  Remove about half of the broccoli and set aside. Discard the bay leaf. Put the rest of the soup into a food processor and puree until smooth. Return the puree and cooked broccoli to the pot and set at medium-low heat. Add cream, cheddar cheese, and Parmesan cheese, and stir until well blended. Ladle the soup into bowls and top with a few pork rinds to serve as croutons.

Yield: 4 servings
Per serving: 39.5 g fat; 10 g net carbs; 26 g protein; 499 calories

Zucchini Soup

 ¼ cup (56 g) butter
 3 large zucchini (about 24 oz/680 g), sliced
 2 cups (470 ml) chicken broth
 ¼ teaspoon salt
 ⅛ teaspoon freshly ground black pepper
 1 tablespoon (15 ml) lemon juice
 2 tablespoons (6 g) chopped fresh chives or scallions

Heat butter in a large skillet over medium heat. Sauté zucchini until it starts to turn a light brown, stirring occasionally, about 8 to 10 minutes. Add broth, salt, black pepper, and lemon juice, and heat until hot. Pour into a blender and blend until smooth. Serve topped with fresh chives. It may also be served with a dollop of sour cream, if desired.

Yield: 4 servings
Per serving: 12.5 g fat; 4.5 g net carbs; 4.5 g protein; 148 calories

Minestrone

¼ cup (60 ml) extra virgin olive oil
1 medium yellow onion, chopped
1 carrot, chopped
1 stalk celery, chopped
6 ounces (170 g) cauliflower, chopped
5 cups beef, lamb, or pork broth
8 ounces (225 g) tomato sauce
3 cloves garlic, minced
½ teaspoon dried basil
½ teaspoon thyme
½ teaspoon salt
¼ teaspoon freshly ground black pepper
1 small zucchini, sliced in rounds and quartered
¾ cup (60 g) shredded Parmesan cheese

Heat oil in a large skillet over medium heat. Sauté onion, carrot, celery, and cauliflower until tender, about 12 to 15 minutes. Add broth, tomato sauce, garlic, basil, thyme, salt, black pepper, and zucchini, cover, and simmer for 20 to 30 minutes, until zucchini is tender. Remove from heat and add Parmesan cheese.

Yield: 4 servings
Per serving: 19.5 g fat; 9.5 g net carbs; 13.5 g protein; 267 calories

Vegetable Dishes

Vegetables are the heart and soul of a healthy ketogenic diet. That is why this is the largest and perhaps the most important chapter in this book. While many people think of vegetables as something they would rather avoid, when they are made the keto way, they transform into something delicious.

When you were growing up, did your mother serve green beans or other vegetables with nothing on them except maybe a little salt and pepper? Or perhaps your mother was into low-sodium diets as well, and you didn't even have salt to perk up your vegetables. Most vegetables, cooked by themselves with no seasonings or flavorings added, are dull and boring—that's why most children, and even adults, don't like to eat their vegetables. I don't like to eat bland, lifeless vegetables either, but I love vegetables when they are prepared properly with exciting ingredients. It doesn't take much to liven up vegetables. Otherwise ordinary green beans take on new life when combined with a few key ingredients, such as butter, onions, mushrooms, or bacon bits.

It is often difficult to incorporate enough fat into a low-carb diet to make it truly ketogenic. Vegetables provide a convenient and delicious way for you to increase the fat content of your diet. In addition, vegetables provide an excellent source of essential vitamins and minerals and add variety to your meals. Most vegetables are naturally low in fat, however, they can be prepared in ways that substantially increase their fat content, far more than even most meats and without the excess protein, making them a ketogenic dieter's best friend. Properly prepared vegetables are really the key to a successful and healthy ketogenic diet.

Many of the vegetable recipes and sauces used in the following dishes include butter and cream. If your preferences are vegan or Palo and you prefer not to use these ingredients, you can substitute the butter with coconut, red palm, or olive oils and replace the cream with coconut milk. Keep in mind that you are always free to alter the ingredients to your specific preferences. Be adventurous and experiment! The same is true for any of the recipes in this book.

Important note: The weight of the vegetables listed in the following recipes are calculated after they have been trimmed, peeled, cored, etc. For example, 8 ounces (225 g) of asparagus is the amount that is actually cooked and eaten; the weight does not include the woody stems that are routinely cut off and discarded. So be aware that when you purchase a 1 pound bunch of asparagus, after removing the stems, you may be left with just 8 ounces of asparagus.

Artichokes

I am surprised at how many people have not tried artichokes, simply boiled and served with butter or mayonnaise. Although artichokes themselves are low in fat, they provide an excellent way to boost fat intake when combined with butter or mayonnaise.

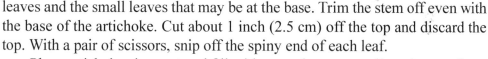

Each artichoke constitutes one serving. When preparing artichokes, first remove any discolored leaves and the small leaves that may be at the base. Trim the stem off even with the base of the artichoke. Cut about 1 inch (2.5 cm) off the top and discard the top. With a pair of scissors, snip off the spiny end of each leaf.

Place artichokes in a pot and fill with enough water to allow them to float. Add 1 teaspoon of salt. Heat water to boiling, then reduce heat, cover, and simmer for about 30 minutes or until the bottom of each artichoke is tender when pierced with a knife. Carefully remove artichokes from the water using tongs or a large slotted spoon. Place upside down to drain water.

Serve hot with butter, mayonnaise, or Hollandaise Sauce (page 30). To eat, pluck leaves one at a time and dip the base of the leaf into the sauce of your choice. Draw the base of the leaf between your teeth, scraping off the meaty portion. Discard the leaf.

After all the outer leaves have been removed, a center portion of light-colored tender leaves covering the fuzzy "choke" will be exposed. Using a spoon, scoop out these leaves and the choke and discard. What remains is the base or "heart" of the artichoke, generally considered the prized portion of the vegetable. Cut the heart into bite-size pieces and dip into the sauce.

A serving consists of 1 artichoke with 2 tablespoons (28 g) mayonnaise
Per serving: 21 g fat; 6.5 g net carbs; 4.5 g protein; 233 calories

Grilled Stuffed Avocados

2 tablespoons (28 g) coconut oil
1 medium yellow onion, finely chopped
2 garlic cloves, minced
8 ounces (225 g) ground beef
8 ounces (225 g) pork sausage
¼ teaspoon salt
1 tablespoon (7.5 g) chili powder
1 teaspoon paprika
1 teaspoon ground cumin
½ teaspoon cayenne pepper
1 can (15 oz/425 g) tomato sauce
6 avocados, halved and pitted, with skins on
2 cups (460 g) shredded Monterey Jack cheese
6 tablespoons (90 g) sour cream
½ cup (8 g) coarsely chopped cilantro

Heat oil in a medium saucepan over medium-high heat. Add the onion and garlic, and sauté for 5 minutes. Add ground beef, sausage, salt, chili powder, paprika, cumin, and cayenne, and sauté until the meat is browned and cooked through, about 8 minutes. Add tomato sauce and bring to a simmer. While the meat mixture is cooking, heat a grill to medium heat.

With the cut side of the avocados facing up, gently press down on them against the countertop to slightly flatten the bottom and allow them to sit without tilting.

Place the avocado halves on a baking sheet or large serving tray. Spoon a heaping mound of the meat mixture into the cavity of each avocado half. Sprinkle cheese over the top of each mound. Carefully set each avocado half on the cooking surface of the grill, close the grill lid, and cook for about 5 minutes, or until the cheese is melted and beginning to brown.

Arrange 2 avocado halves on each serving plate, and top each with a spoonful of sour cream and chopped cilantro.

Yield: 12 stuffed avocado halves
Per avocado half: 35 g fat; 4.5 g net carbs; 20 g protein; 413 calories

Creamed Asparagus

8 ounces (225 g) asparagus
Basic White Sauce (page 21)
Salt and black pepper, to taste

Steam, sauté, or parboil asparagus until tender. Make Basic White Sauce as directed. Serve covered with Basic White Sauce. The Mornay, Shrimp, Mushroom, and Mustard variations (pages 23-24) are especially good with asparagus. Add salt and black pepper to taste, if desired.

Yield: 2 servings
Per serving with ¼ cup (60 ml) Basic White Sauce: 28 g fat; 4 g net carbs; 3.5 g protein; 282 calories

Caramelized Onions and Asparagus

4 strips sugar-free, nitrite-free bacon, cooked crisp and crumbled
1 medium onion, coarsely chopped
1 pound (450 g) asparagus, trimmed
¼ teaspoon salt
¼ teaspoon lemon pepper

Cook bacon in a medium-size skillet and set aside. Heat bacon drippings over medium heat, add onion and asparagus, and cook uncovered until the onion begins to caramelize, about 10 to 14 minutes, stirring occasionally. Stir in salt and lemon pepper. Remove from heat. Serve topped with crumbled bacon.

Yield: 2 servings
Per serving: 23 g fat; 6 g net carbs; 18 g protein; 303 calories

Oven-Roasted Asparagus

1 pound (450 g) thin asparagus spears, trimmed
2 cloves garlic, minced
¼ cup (56 g) melted butter
1 tablespoon (15 ml) fresh lemon juice
1 teaspoon lemon zest
1 tablespoon (4 g) chopped fresh parsley
2 scallions, chopped
1 teaspoon chopped fresh rosemary
1 teaspoon chopped fresh thyme
⅛ teaspoon salt
⅛ teaspoon freshly ground black pepper

Preheat oven to 400° F (200° C). Arrange asparagus spears in a single layer in a baking pan. In a small bowl, stir together garlic, butter, lemon juice, and lemon zest. Stir in parsley, scallions, rosemary, thyme, salt, and pepper. Pour the mix over the asparagus, coating each stalk. Bake for 15 minutes or until asparagus is tender.

Yield: 2 servings
Per serving: 23 g fat; 4 g net carbs; 4 g protein; 239 calories

Asparagus with Hollandaise Sauce

Hollandaise Sauce (page 30)
8 ounces (220 g) asparagus

Steam asparagus in vegetable steamer until tender. Make Hollandaise Sauce as directed. Serve asparagus covered in Hollandaise Sauce.

Yield: 2 servings
Per serving with ¼ cup (60 ml) Hollandaise Sauce: 20 g fat; 3.5 g net carbs; 6.5 g protein; 220 calories

Broccoli with Cheese Sauce

This is a simple recipe that will transform ordinary broccoli into something even the kids will enjoy.

Cheese Sauce (page 24)
8 ounces (225 g) broccoli, cut into florets
Salt
Black pepper

Make Cheese Sauce according to directions. Cook broccoli in a vegetable steamer until tender. Serve broccoli covered in hot Cheese Sauce. Add salt and pepper to taste.

Yield: 2 servings
Per serving with ½ cup (120 ml) Cheese Sauce: 40.5 g fat; 7.5 g net carbs; 11 g protein; 438 calories

Variations:

Cheese Sauce makes a great topping for a variety of cooked vegetables. The following vegetables go well with Cheese Sauce, simply steam or cook in any manner you choose, and then cover with Cheese Sauce.

Artichoke hearts	Kale
Asparagus	Mushrooms
Brussels sprouts	Spinach
Cauliflower	Tomatoes
Chard	Turnips
Collard greens	Wax beans
Eggplant	Yellow crookneck squash
Green beans	Zucchini

Broccoli Au Gratin

20 ounces (560 g) broccoli, boiled and drained
1½ cups (360 ml) hot Cheese Sauce (page 24) or Mornay Sauce (page 23)
½ cup (75 g) diced sugar-free, nitrite-free ham or chicken
⅓ cup (38 g) shredded sharp cheddar cheese
1 tablespoon (14 g) butter, melted
2 strips sugar-free, nitrite-free bacon, cooked crisp and crumbled

Preheat broiler. Place precooked broccoli in an ungreased 1½-quart (1.5 -liter) casserole dish. Cover with hot Cheese Sauce, stir in ham, sprinkle with cheese, and drizzle butter on top. Broil 4 to 5 inches (10 to 12 cm) from the heat for 4 to 5 minutes or until lightly browned. Remove from the oven and sprinkle crumbled bacon on top before serving.

Yield: 6 servings
Per serving: 38 g fat; 8 g net carbs; 15 g protein; 434 calories

Variations:
Broccoli and Creamy Mushroom Sauce
Steam or parboil broccoli until tender. Cover with hot Creamy Mushroom Sauce (page 24), and cook as described above.

Creamy Broccoli with Shrimp
Steam or parboil broccoli until tender. Cover with hot Shrimp Sauce (page 23), and cook as described above.

Broccoli with Almonds

¼ cup (30 g) slivered almonds, toasted
¼ cup (56 g) butter
8 ounces (225 g) broccoli, cut into bite-size pieces
Salt
Black pepper
Juice from ½ fresh lemon

Heat oven or toaster oven to 350° F (180° C). Place almonds on baking sheet and cook until very lightly browned, about 6 minutes. Remove from oven and cool.

Heat butter in a skillet over medium heat. Add broccoli and sauté until tender, about 10 minutes. Remove from heat. Put on a serving plate and pour the butter over the broccoli. Add salt and pepper to taste. Top with toasted almonds and a squeeze of lemon juice.

Yield: 2 servings
Per serving: 30.5 g fat; 6 g net carbs; 6.5 g protein; 324 calories

Broccoli with Toasted Pecan Butter

2 cups (145 g) broccoli florets
2 tablespoons (28 g) butter
¼ cup (28 g) chopped pecans

Cook broccoli in a steamer until tender. Heat butter in a small saucepan over medium heat. Add pecans, stir gently. Remove the skillet from heat when the butter begins to turn brown. Pour over cooked broccoli and serve. Add salt and black pepper to taste.

Yield: 2 servings
Per serving: 21.5 g fat; 3.5 g net carbs; 3.5 g protein; 221 calories

Broccoli with Peanut Sauce

This dish combines broccoli with peanut butter. While this combination may sound unusual, it actually gives the broccoli a pleasant nutty flavor. If you prefer, you could make this recipe using almonds and almond butter.

¼ cup (60 g) butter
2 tablespoons (20 g) finely chopped, toasted peanuts
1 tablespoon (16 g) natural, sugar-free peanut butter
16 ounces (450 g) broccoli, cut into bite-size pieces

In a small saucepan over medium-low heat, melt butter. Stir in peanuts and peanut butter, and cook for about 2 minutes. Remove from heat and set aside, but keep warm. Steam or parboil broccoli until tender. Serve broccoli covered in peanut sauce.

Yield: 4 servings
Per serving: 17 g fat; 5.5 g net carbs; 5.5 g protein; 197 calories

Caramelized Onions and Broccoli

4 strips sugar-free, nitrite-free bacon, cooked crisp and crumbled
10 ounces (280 g) broccoli, cut into bite-size pieces
1 medium onion, coarsely chopped
2 tablespoons (28 g) butter
¼ teaspoon salt
¼ freshly ground black pepper
¼ cup (20 g) grated Parmesan cheese

Cook bacon in a medium-size skillet and set aside. Heat bacon drippings over medium heat, add broccoli and onion, and cook uncovered until the onion begins to turn golden brown, about 10 minutes, stirring occasionally. Stir in butter, salt, and black pepper, and cook until the onion is golden brown and broccoli is thoroughly cooked, about 4 to 5 minutes. Add crumbled bacon and remove from heat. Serve topped with Parmesan cheese.

Yield: 2 servings
Per serving: 35 g fat; 10 g net carbs; 22 g protein; 443 calories

Broccoli Casserole

16 ounces (450 g) broccoli, separated into florets
8 ounces (225 g) cream cheese, softened
¼ cup (60 g) mayonnaise (pages 37-40)
1 ounce (28 g) jalapeño pepper, diced
½ teaspoon salt
8 ounces (225 g) sharp cheddar cheese, shredded
6 strips sugar-free, nitrite-free bacon, cut into small pieces

Preheat oven to 375° F (190° C). Steam or boil broccoli until crisp tender, about 5 minutes. Remove from steamer or water, and let cool for a few minutes to allow moisture to evaporate. Arrange broccoli in a 2-quart (2-liter) casserole dish. Mix together cream cheese, mayonnaise, jalapeño pepper, and salt, and coat the broccoli. Sprinkle cheese evenly over the top, followed by the bacon pieces. Bake for 40 minutes, until hot and bubbly.

Yield: 4 servings
Per serving: 61 g fat; 7 g net carbs; 32.5 g protein; 707 calories

Brussels Sprouts Au Gratin

20 ounces (560 g) Brussels sprouts, boiled and drained
1½ cups (360 ml) hot Cheese Sauce (page 24) or Mornay Sauce (page 23)
⅓ cup (38 g) shredded sharp cheddar cheese
1 tablespoon (14 g) butter, melted
4 strips sugar-free, nitrite-free bacon, cooked crisp and crumbled

Preheat broiler. Place cooked Brussels sprouts in an ungreased 1½-quart (1.5 -liter) casserole dish. Cover with hot Cheese Sauce, sprinkle with cheese, and drizzle butter on top. Broil 4 to 5 inches (10 to 12 cm) from the heat for 4 to 5 minutes or until lightly browned. Remove from the oven and sprinkle crumbled bacon on top before serving.

Yield: 6 servings
Per serving: 29.5 g fat; 6.5 g net carbs; 13.5 g protein; 345 calories

Brussels Sprouts in Brown Butter

1½ pounds (680 g) Brussels sprouts
¼ cup (56 g) butter
½ cup (50 g) pecan halves
Salt
Black pepper
Lemon juice

Remove outer leaves of the Brussels sprouts and cut in half lengthwise. Place them in a large saucepan. Add water to a depth of ½ inch (1 cm), cover, and simmer for about 5 minutes, or until the sprouts are tender when pierced with a sharp knife. Remove from heat, drain, and set aside, but keep warm.

Melt butter in a large skillet over medium-low heat. Add pecans and cook until butter begins to turn brown and nuts become fragrant. Stir the Brussels sprouts into the hot butter and cook for about 5 minutes, stirring frequently. Remove from heat. Season with salt, black pepper, and lemon juice to taste.

Yield: 4 servings
Per serving: 21 g fat; 10.5 g net carbs; 7 g protein; 259 calories

Parmesan Roasted Brussels Sprouts

1 pound (450 g) Brussels sprouts
4 cloves garlic, minced
3 tablespoons (42 g) butter or bacon drippings, melted
6 tablespoons (30 g) Parmesan cheese, grated
Salt and black pepper

Preheat oven to 400° F (200° C). Cut the bottom of each sprout and remove the first layer of leaves. Cut each sprout in half, larger sprouts may be cut in fourths. Combine with garlic and melted butter and mix, coating each sprout evenly. Sprinkle with Parmesan cheese and salt and black pepper to taste. Place in a baking dish and bake for 40 to 50 minutes, until the center of the sprouts are tender. Stir once or twice while baking for even cooking and to prevent thinner pieces from burning.

Yield: 4 servings
Per serving: 10.5 g fat; 7 g net carbs; 6.5 g protein; 148 calories

Pennsylvania Dutch Cabbage

¼ cup (56 g) bacon drippings or butter
1 large yellow onion, chopped
1 medium green bell pepper, chopped
1 medium stalk celery, chopped
1 small head cabbage, shredded or chopped
2 cloves garlic, minced
1 large tomato, chopped
2 teaspoons dried tarragon
¼ teaspoon celery seed
1½ teaspoons salt
⅛ teaspoon freshly ground black pepper

Heat bacon drippings in a large skillet over medium heat. Sauté onion, bell pepper, and celery until tender, about 8 minutes. Add cabbage, garlic, tomato, tarragon, celery seed, salt, and black pepper, and cook for about 6 to 8 minutes, stirring frequently, until cabbage is tender.

Yield: 4 servings
Per serving: 14.5 g fat; 12 g net carbs; 3.5 g protein; 192 calories

Caraway Sauerkraut

¼ cup (56 g) butter
1 medium yellow onion, chopped
1 medium stalk celery, chopped
16 ounces (450 g) sauerkraut, drained
1 tablespoon (6 g) caraway seed

Heat butter in a large saucepan over medium heat. Sauté onion and celery until tender and onion begins to turn golden. Add sauerkraut and caraway seed, and cook for about 5 minutes, stirring frequently, until thoroughly heated.

Yield: 4 servings
Per serving: 12 g fat; 4 g net carbs; 1.5 g protein; 130 calories

Homemade Sauerkraut

You can buy sauerkraut in the store but the commercial bottling process generally uses heat pasteurization that kills all the beneficial bacteria that makes sauerkraut so helpful for digestive function. Homemade sauerkraut is easy to make and provides an excellent source of gut-friendly bacteria.

1 medium head green cabbage, shredded
2 tablespoons sea salt, not iodized

Wash cabbage and discard outer leaves. Cut out and discard the core. Shred or thinly slice the cabbage and put it in a bowl. Stir in salt, and let it sit for 30 to 60 minutes. Salt pulls out the juices so there will be a puddle of juice at the bottom of the cabbage. Pack cabbage with the juice tightly into a 2-quart (2-liter) glass jar. Wide mouth canning jars work really well. You should have enough cabbage juice to completely cover the shredded cabbage. If not, you can add a little water. Do not use chlorinated water. If you do not have non-chlorinated water, boil some water on the stove for 10 minutes and let it sit and cool to room temperature, this will allow the chlorine gas to evaporate.

The shredded cabbage should be completely submerged under the juices. If not, mold will tend to develop on the cabbage that is not submerged. If mold does grow, there is no need for alarm, it is not harmful. Just scoop it off and discard. The rest of the sauerkraut will be fine. The salty brine will prevent harmful bacteria and mold from growing, so don't skimp on the salt called for in the recipe.

Place a lid loosely over the mouth of the jar. It needs to be loose to allow gases to freely escape, yet still keep out dust and insects. Store the jar in a warm, dark place, such as in a kitchen cupboard, for 4 to 8 days, depending on the temperature of your home. Fermentation occurs faster when the temperature is on the warm side, and slower when it is cool. If you are making sauerkraut during the winter and your home is cool, you may need to allow extra time for the fermentation to occur.

The longer you let the cabbage ferment, the more sour it will become. When it reaches the level of sourness you prefer, tighten the lid and store it in the refrigerator. The cool temperature of the refrigerator will essentially stop any further fermentation.

Although sauerkraut is very low in fat, it is also very low in carbs and protein but rich in vitamins and healthy bacteria, making it very suitable for a ketogenic diet. It can be combined with other high-fat foods to enhance the flavor and improve the nutritional content of the meal.

Yield: make about 8 half cup (70g) servings
Per serving: 0 g fat; 1 g net carbs; 0.5 g protein; 6 calories

Cauliflower Rice

When cauliflower is finely chopped in a food processor it takes on the appearance of a bowl of cooked rice. Its mild taste and rice-like texture makes it a suitable replacement for ordinary rice in many traditional rice dishes. The only ingredient needed is cauliflower.

Chop the cauliflower into approximately 1-inch (2.5-cm) size pieces. Put the pieces into a food processor and pulse until the cauliflower is reduced to the size of rice grains. Be careful not to pulse too long or your cauliflower will be reduced to a grainy meal-like texture. If there are large chunks of cauliflower remaining after most of the rest is reduced to rice size, simply remove the larger pieces and pulse separately.

At this stage, the cauliflower rice is ready to be cooked or added to a "rice-free" rice dish.

Yield: varies
Per 1 cup (120 g) serving: 0 g fat; 3.5 g net carbs; 2.5 g protein; 24 calories

To make Cauliflower Rice, put chopped cauliflower into a food processor and pulse until it is reduced to rice size.

Mashed Cauliflower

This makes an excellent low-carb replacement for mashed potatoes—a popular low-carb/keto dish.

1 medium head cauliflower, cut into small pieces
4 ounces (110 g) cream cheese, softened
2 tablespoons (28 g) butter, melted
½ teaspoon salt
⅛ teaspoon freshly ground black pepper

Place cauliflower into a steamer and cook until very soft, about 30 minutes. Transfer the hot cauliflower to a food processor; do not let cool. Add cream cheese, butter, salt, and pepper. Process on high setting until the mixture is creamy. Serve topped with a pat of butter.

Yield: 4 servings
Per serving: 15.5 g fat; 5 g net carbs; 5 g protein; 179 calories

Variations:
Garlic Parmesan Mashed Cauliflower

In a small saucepan, sauté 1 clove finely chopped garlic in 1 tablespoon (14 g) butter; cook for about 2 minutes, just enough to soften and infuse the butter with the garlic flavor. Add the garlic butter and 2 tablespoons (10 g) Parmesan cheese to food processor and blend with the ingredients listed above.

Per serving: 19 g fat; 5 g net carbs; 6 g protein; 215 calories

Mashed cauliflower, chicken wings, and zucchini.

Sour Cream Mashed Cauliflower

Follow the recipe for Mashed Cauliflower above, but reduce the cream cheese to 2 ounces (55 g) and add 2 tablespoons (28 g) of sour cream and ¼ teaspoon of onion powder. Top with freshly cut chives.

Per serving: 12 g fat; 5 g net carbs; 6 g protein; 152 calories

Cheesy Mashed Cauliflower

Make Mashed Cauliflower as directed above, but top with shredded cheddar cheese and broil in the oven for 3 to 4 minutes, until cheese is hot and bubbly. Top with a dollop of sour cream and chopped chives.

Per serving: varies

Cauliflower Au Gratin

20 ounces (560 g) cauliflower, boiled and drained
1½ cups (360 ml) hot Cheese Sauce (page 24) or Mornay Sauce (page 23)
⅓ cup (38 g) shredded sharp cheddar cheese
1 tablespoon (14 g) butter, melted
4 strips sugar-free, nitrite-free bacon, cooked crisp and crumbled

Preheat broiler. Place cooked cauliflower in an ungreased 1½-quart (1.5 -liter) casserole dish. Cover with hot Cheese Sauce, sprinkle with cheese, and drizzle butter on top. Broil 4 to 5 inches (10 to 12 cm) from the heat for 4 to 5 minutes or until lightly browned. Remove from the oven and sprinkle crumbled bacon on top before serving.

Yield: 6 servings
Per serving: 44 g fat; 6.5 g net carbs; 18 g protein; 494 calories

Loaded Cauliflower

This is much like a loaded baked potato covered in your favorite toppings. Makes an excellent high-fat accompaniment to meat or fish.

8 ounces (225 g) cauliflower
4 tablespoons (56 g) butter
2 ounces (56 g) cheddar cheese, shredded
4 tablespoons (56 g) sour cream
2 strips sugar-free, nitrite-free bacon, cooked crisp and crumbled
2 teaspoons minced chives
Salt and black pepper

Steam or parboil cauliflower until tender. Put on a serving plate and top with butter, cheese, sour cream, bacon, and chives. Add salt and black pepper to taste.

Yield: 2 servings
Per serving: 46 g fat; 5 g net carbs; 17.5 g protein; 504 calories

Caramelized Onions and Cauliflower

4 strips sugar-free, nitrite-free bacon, cooked crisp and crumbled
1 medium onion, coarsely chopped
12 ounces (340 g) cauliflower, cut into bite-size pieces
¼ cup (56 g) butter
2 cloves garlic, finely chopped
¼ teaspoon salt
1½ teaspoons curry powder
Dash cayenne pepper (optional)

Cook bacon in a medium-size skillet and set aside. Heat bacon drippings over medium heat, add onion and cauliflower, and cook uncovered until the onion begins to turn golden brown, about 10 minutes, stirring occasionally. Stir in butter, garlic, salt, curry powder, and cayenne pepper, and cook until the onion is golden brown and cauliflower is thoroughly cooked, about 4 to 5 minutes. Remove from heat. Serve topped with crumbled bacon.

Yield: 2 servings
Per serving: 42 g fat; 10 g net carbs; 18 g protein; 530 calories

Cauliflower Espagnole

Espagnole Sauce (page 27)
2 tablespoons (30 g) coconut oil or bacon drippings
½ head cauliflower, cut into bite-size pieces
½ teaspoon coriander
⅛ teaspoon nutmeg

Make Espagnole Sauce according to directions. Make this sauce first as it takes the most time to prepare.

Heat oil in a skillet over medium heat. Cook cauliflower, stirring occasionally, until tender and lightly browned on all sides, about 10 to 15 minutes. Add Espagnole Sauce, coriander, and nutmeg. Bring to a simmer and cook for about 5 minutes. Remove from heat and serve.

Yield: 4 servings
Per serving: 15 g fat; 7 g net carbs; 12 g protein; 211 calories

Cauliflower in Curried Cream Sauce

2 tablespoons (28 g) coconut oil
1 tablespoon (15 g) butter
½ head medium cauliflower, cut into florets
½ medium onion, chopped
2 cloves garlic, minced
4 ounces (110 g) mushrooms, sliced
1 teaspoon yellow curry powder
¼ teaspoon turmeric

⅛ teaspoon cayenne pepper
¼ teaspoon salt
½ cup (120 ml) chicken broth
½ cup (120 ml) coconut milk
½ cup (120 g) sour cream

Heat coconut oil and butter in large skillet over medium heat. Add cauliflower and onion, and cook, stirring occasionally, until cauliflower begins to turn brown, about 10 to 15 minutes. Add garlic, mushrooms, curry powder, turmeric, cayenne pepper, and salt, and cook about 3 to 4 minutes or until the garlic becomes fragrant. Add chicken broth and coconut milk, and simmer for about 10 minutes, until flavors blend and vegetables are tender. Remove from heat and stir in sour cream.

Yield: 4 servings
Per serving: 24 g fat; 5.5 g net carbs; 4 g protein; 254 calories

Cauliflower de la Fontaine

1 medium head cauliflower, cut into florets and boiled
3 tablespoons (45 ml) extra virgin olive oil
1 small yellow onion, finely chopped
1 tablespoon (15 g) minced anchovies
¼ cup (30 ml) chicken broth
1 tablespoon (15 ml) lemon juice
1 teaspoon minced parsley
1 teaspoon minced cilantro
½ teaspoon minced fresh basil or ¼ teaspoon dried basil
Dash black pepper

Cook cauliflower in a steamer until tender and keep warm while preparing the other ingredients. Heat oil in a large skillet over medium heat. Sauté onion until lightly golden, about 6 to 8 minutes. Stir in anchovies and cook 1 minute. Stir in broth and lemon juice, cover, and simmer for 10 minutes. Add cauliflower, parsley, cilantro, basil, and black pepper, and simmer for 4 to 5 minutes, basting cauliflower occasionally until heated through.

Yield: 4 servings
Per serving: 11 g fat; 5 g net carbs; 4 g protein; 135 calories

Cauliflower Stuffed Peppers

2 green bell peppers
16 ounces (450 g) cauliflower, separated into florets
2 tablespoons (28 g) butter
¼ cup (56 g) cream cheese
1 egg
¼ teaspoon salt
⅛ teaspoon black pepper
¼ teaspoon garlic powder
¼ teaspoon onion powder
4 ounces (110 g) cooked pork, chicken, or sugar-free, nitrite-free ham
4 ounces (110 g) cheese, shredded

Preheat oven to 350° F (180° C). Cut each bell pepper in half lengthwise. Carefully remove the steam, seeds, and membranes. Fill a large pot with enough water to cover the peppers. Heat to boiling, add peppers, and cook for 6 minutes. Using a slotted spoon, remove the peppers from the water and set aside to cool and allow moisture to evaporate.

Steam or boil cauliflower until tender. Put cauliflower into a food processer along with butter, cream cheese, egg, salt, black pepper, garlic powder, and onion powder; blend until smooth. Stir in cooked meat and half of the cheese.

Place the bell peppers on a baking sheet or dish. Spoon an equal amount of filling into each bell pepper and sprinkle the rest of the cheese on the top. Bake for 30 minutes.

Yield: 4 stuffed peppers (halves)
Per serving: 22 g fat; 6 g net carbs; 19.5 g protein; 300 calories

Cauliflower Casserole

16 ounces (450 g) cauliflower, chopped
2 tablespoons (28 g) butter or bacon drippings
½ small onion, chopped
8 ounces (225 g) cream cheese, softened
½ teaspoon salt
¼ teaspoon black pepper
1 cup (230 g) sour cream
8 ounces (225 g) mushrooms, sliced

1 cup (150 g) chopped sugar-free, nitrite-free ham
6 ounces (170 g) cheddar cheese, shredded
¼ cup (15 g) chopped parsley

Preheat oven to 375° F (190° C). Steam cauliflower until tender. Heat butter in a small saucepan over medium heat, and sauté onion until tender. Remove from heat, add cream cheese, and stir until a creamy sauce forms. Stir in salt, black pepper, and sour cream. Combine cream sauce with cauliflower, mushrooms, and ham, then pour the mixture into an 11x7-inch (28x18-cm) casserole dish. Sprinkle cheddar cheese on top. Bake for 25 minutes. Serve garnished with chopped parsley.

Yield: 4 servings
Per serving: 55 g fat; 10.5 g net carbs; 27 g protein; 645 calories

Celery Au Gratin

1 bunch celery
¼ teaspoon salt
1½ cups (360 ml) Cheese Sauce (page 24) or Mornay Sauce (page 23)
⅓ cup (38 g) shredded sharp cheddar cheese
4 strips bacon, cooked crisp and crumbled

Cut celery into 1-inch (2.5-cm) lengths. Boil in water for 20 to 25 minutes until tender. Discard water and put celery into a 1-quart (1-liter) casserole dish. Mix celery with salt and hot Cheese Sauce and sprinkle with cheddar cheese. Broil 5 inches (12 cm) from heat for 3 to 4 minutes, until lightly browned. Remove from oven and sprinkle crumbled bacon on top before serving.

Yield: 4 servings
Per serving: 41 g fat; 5.5 g net carbs; 16.5 g protein; 457 calories

Daikon Radish

This is one of my favorite low-carb vegetables. Daikon is a large, mild-flavored white radish commonly used in Asian cuisine, but it is now available almost everywhere. There are a number of varieties of daikon; the most common is an elongated root that looks like a giant white carrot about a foot (30 cm) in length and 2 to 4 inches (5 to 10 cm) in diameter. Other varieties may be turnip-shaped or display various shades of green, pink, or purple. You will see it sold whole or cut into smaller lengths.

Although a root vegetable, daikon is relatively low in carbohydrate and in calories, making it suitable for low-carb and ketogenic diets. It is a versatile vegetable that tastes good raw, cooked, or pickled. When eaten raw, it tastes somewhat like a mild turnip. It makes a great addition to salads and relish trays, and when pickled, it imparts a nice tangy flavor to salads and other vegetables. When cooked, daikon softens, its taste mellows, and it absorbs the flavor of the cooking liquid, making it suitable for a variety of hot dishes. Daikon makes a suitable low-carb substitute for potatoes in cooked dishes such as soups, stews, and curries.

To prepare, peel the skin as you would a carrot and cut in whatever style your recipe calls for. The vegetable can be cut into strips, sliced, diced, shredded, or cubed.

Daikons are available at most good grocery, health food, and Asian markets.

Homemade Pickled Daikon

Pickled or fermented daikon radish makes a delicious vegetable complement to most any meal or can be used to liven up an otherwise ordinary salad. If you plan on making pickled daikon, allow at least three days for the fermentation process.

1½ pounds (680 g) daikon radish, shredded
1 tablespoon (18 g) sea salt, non-iodized

Mix the shredded daikon and salt and put into a large canning jar, then let it rest for 30 minutes. This allows the salt to pull out the liquid from the daikon.

Press down hard on the daikon with a wooden spoon to release more of the juice. Keep pressing until the juices rise to the surface and completely cover the daikon. If there is not enough juice to cover all of the daikon, you can add a little distilled or non-chlorinated water. Leave about ½ inch (2 cm) of air space at the top.

Cover loosely to keep out dust and insects and place in a warm, dark room or cupboard for at least 3 days. In cool weather you may need to extend the time another couple of days or even as much as a week or two. As the daikon ferments, it will develop a tangy flavor. The longer it ages, the stronger the flavor will become. Tighten the cover on the canning jar and store in the refrigerator. The cold temperature of the refrigerator will significantly slow down the fermentation process.

Use as a side to accompany a high-fat main dish.

Yield: 6 servings
Per serving: 0 g fat; 2 g net carbs; 2.5 g protein; 18 calories

Daikon Sauerkraut Slaw

This recipe is low in fat, but complements an otherwise high-fat meal.

1 cup (150 g) shredded daikon radish
1 carrot, shredded
1 cup (140 g) sauerkraut
¼ cup (60 ml) sauerkraut juice
¼ teaspoon celery salt

Combine daikon, carrot, sauerkraut, and juice, and mix. Put into a container with a tight fitting lid and place in the refrigerator for 6 to 24 hours, shake the container occasionally to distribute juices. Just before serving, drain the liquid and mix in celery salt. Serve as a condiment to meats or other vegetable dishes.

Yield: 2 servings
Per serving: 0 g fat; 4.5 g net carbs; 2.5 g protein; 28 calories

Izmir Eggplant

This is a traditional Turkish stew named after Izmir, a city on the Mediterranean coast of Turkey.

⅓ cup (80 ml) extra virgin olive oil
1 large yellow onion, chopped
1 medium eggplant, peeled and cubed
2 cloves garlic, minced
2 bay leaves
1 (8 ounce/225 g) can tomato sauce
½ tablespoon (8 ml) lemon juice
¼ teaspoon dried oregano
¼ teaspoon salt
⅛ teaspoon black pepper

Heat oil in a large skillet over medium heat. Sauté onion, eggplant, garlic, and bay leaves for 12 to 15 minutes or until the vegetables are tender. Add tomato sauce, lemon juice, oregano, salt, and black pepper, reduce heat to medium-low and simmer, uncovered, stirring occasionally, for 10 to 12 minutes. Discard bay leaves before serving.

Yield: 4 servings
Per serving: 19 g fat; 7 g net carbs; 2.5 g protein; 209 calories

Ratatouille

Ratatouille is a traditional French stew that is popular throughout the Mediterranean coast. It is typically prepared as a stew consisting of sautéed vegetables. Although made in a variety of ways, the main ingredients include eggplant, zucchini, onions, bell peppers, tomatoes, and garlic. This dish keeps well, so it makes an excellent meal for the following day. Can be eaten as a side or constitute the main dish.

¼ cup (60 ml) extra virgin olive oil
1½ cups (240 g) chopped onion
2 cloves garlic, minced
2 cups (160 g) peeled and chopped eggplant
½ teaspoon fresh thyme leaves or ¼ teaspoon dried
1 cup (150 g) chopped green bell pepper
1 cup (150 g) chopped red bell pepper
2 cups (240 g) chopped zucchini
1½ cups (270 g) chopped tomatoes

1 tablespoon (3 g) thinly sliced fresh basil or 1 teaspoon dried
1 tablespoon (4 g) minced fresh parsley
¼ teaspoon salt
⅛ teaspoon black pepper

Heat oil in a large saucepan over medium heat. Add onion and cook, stirring occasionally, until it is tender, about 6 to 7 minutes. Add garlic, eggplant, and thyme, and continue to cook, stirring occasionally, until the eggplant is partially cooked, about 5 minutes. Add green pepper, red pepper, and zucchini, and cook for an additional 5 minutes. Add tomatoes, basil, parsley, salt, and pepper, and cook a final 5 minutes. Stir well to blend.

Yield: 4 servings
Per serving: 15 g fat; 12 g net carbs; 3 g protein; 195 calories

Variation:
For a little extra kick, add ¼ to ½ teaspoon red pepper flakes with the bell peppers and zucchini.

Ratatouille

Eggplant Parmesan
This dish can also be made using zucchini, yellow crookneck, or pattypan squash.

Espagnole Sauce (page 27)
1 medium eggplant, peeled and sliced
½ cup (50 g) grated Parmesan cheese

Prepare Espagnole Sauce as directed. In a skillet, heat the sauce to a simmer, add eggplant, and cook for 5 to 6 minutes, stirring frequently, until eggplant is soft. Remove from heat and serve hot, topped with Parmesan cheese.

Yield: 6 servings (1 cup/240 g each)
Per serving: 12 g fat; 6.5 g net carbs; 10 g protein; 174 calories

Green Beans with Sausage Gravy

8 ounces (225 g) green beans, cut in bite-size pieces
Sausage Gravy (page 18) or Fiesta Gravy (page 19)

Boil, sauté, or parboil green beans until tender. Make Sausage Gravy as directed. Serve green beans covered with Sausage Gravy or Fiesta Gravy. Store leftover gravy, if there is any, in the refrigerator for use in another meal.

Yield: 2 servings
Per serving with ½ cup (120 ml) Sausage Gravy: 29 g fat; 8 g net carbs; 16 g protein; 357 calories

Variations:
Green Beans and Mushroom Sauce
Boil or parboil green beans until tender. Serve covered with Mushroom Sauce (page 24).

Green Beans under Sour Cream Sauce
This is a good way to liven up green beans. Boil or parboil green beans until tender. Serve covered with Sour Cream Sauce (page 23).

Green Bean Italiano

3 tablespoons (45 ml) olive oil
16 ounces (450 g) fresh green beans
½ cup (80 g) chopped onions
1 clove garlic, minced
1 large tomato, chopped
½ teaspoon salt
⅛ teaspoon freshly ground black pepper
¼ teaspoon dried dill weed

2 teaspoons minced parsley
¼ cup (25 g) grated Parmesan cheese

Heat oil in a large skillet over medium heat. Sauté green beans and onions until they are tender and start to turn light brown, about 6 to 8 minutes. Add garlic, tomato, salt, black pepper, and dill and cook for 4 to 5 minutes, stirring occasionally, until tomato is softened. Remove from heat and stir in parsley. Sprinkle with Parmesan cheese before serving.

Yield: 4 servings
Per serving: 12 g fat; 7.5 g net carbs; 5 g protein; 158 calories

Caramelized Onions and Green Beans

4 strips sugar-free, nitrite-free bacon, cooked crisp and crumbled
1 medium onion, coarsely chopped
8 ounces (225 g) fresh green beans, cut into bite-size pieces
¼ teaspoon salt
⅛ teaspoon freshly ground black pepper
½ teaspoon dill weed
¼ teaspoon celery seed

Cook bacon in a medium-size skillet and set aside. Heat bacon drippings over medium heat, add onions and green beans, and cook uncovered until the onions become caramelized, about 12 to 14 minutes, stirring occasionally. Stir in salt, black pepper, dill weed, and celery seed, and remove from heat. Serve topped with crumbled bacon.

Yield: 2 servings
Per serving: 23 g fat; 8.5 g net carbs; 16 g protein; 305 calories

Green Beans and Toasted Almonds

¼ cup (30 g) sliced or slivered almonds, toasted
¼ cup (56 g) butter
½ medium onion, chopped
8 ounces (225 g) fresh green beans, cut into bite-size pieces
¼ teaspoon salt
⅛ teaspoon freshly ground black pepper

Preheat oven or toaster oven to 350° F (180° C). Put almonds in a baking dish and bake until lightly toasted, about 6 to 8 minutes. Remove from oven and set aside.

Heat butter in a skillet over medium heat, add onion and green beans, and cook uncovered, stirring occasionally, until vegetables become tender, about 10 minutes. Stir in salt and black pepper, and remove from heat. Serve topped with toasted almonds.

Yield: 2 servings
Per serving: 30 g fat; 7.5 g net carbs; 6 g protein; 324 calories

Green Beans and Mushrooms

2 strips sugar-free, nitrite-free bacon, cooked crisp and crumbled
½ small onion, chopped
8 ounces (225 g) fresh green beans, cut into bite-size pieces
2 ounces (56 g) mushrooms, sliced
¼ teaspoon salt
⅛ teaspoon freshly ground black pepper
2 tablespoons (28 g) butter

Cook bacon in a medium-size skillet and set aside. Heat bacon drippings over medium heat, then add onion and green beans and cook uncovered until the onion becomes slightly tender, about 5 to 6 minutes, stirring occasionally. Add mushrooms, salt, and black pepper, and cook until tender, about 5 minutes. Serve topped with butter and crumbled bacon.

Yield: 2 servings
Per serving: 19.5 g fat; 6 g net carbs; 10 g protein; 239 calories

Green Beans with Bacon and Parmesan Cheese

Ketogenic recipes do not have to be complicated or time-consuming. This recipe is a good example of a tasty keto vegetable dish that is quick and simple.

4 strips sugar-free, nitrite-free bacon, cooked crisp and crumbled
8 ounces (225 g) fresh green beans, cut into bite-size pieces
2 tablespoons (28 g) butter
Salt
Black pepper
2 tablespoons (10 g) grated Parmesan cheese

In a medium-size skillet, cook bacon until crisp, then remove. Add green beans to the skillet and cook in the bacon drippings until tender. Add salt and black pepper to taste. Serve with crumbled bacon and Parmesan cheese.

Yield: 2 servings
Per serving: 17 g fat; 4.5 g net carbs; 17.5 g protein; 241 calories

Green Beans with Sofrito Sauce

1½ pounds (680 g) green beans, boiled and drained
3 strips sugar-free, nitrite-free bacon, diced
2 tablespoons (30 ml) lard or butter
1 medium yellow onion, finely chopped
1 clove garlic, minced
1 red bell pepper, finely chopped
1 large tomato, peeled, seeded, and coarsely chopped
Dash ground coriander
4 pitted green olives, finely chopped
¼ teaspoon capers, finely chopped
1 teaspoon dried oregano
⅓ cup (80 ml) water
½ teaspoon salt

Boil green beans until tender, about 25 minutes. While the beans are cooking, prepare the sauce. In a large skillet, fry bacon for 3 minutes over moderate heat. Add lard, onion, garlic, and red pepper, and sauté 7 to 8 minutes or until onions become lightly golden. Add tomato, coriander, olives, capers, oregano, water, and salt, and simmer for 8 to 10 minutes, stirring occasionally. Remove from heat and serve the sauce over the green beans.

Yield: 6 servings
Per serving: 9 g fat; 7.5 g net carbs; 6 g protein; 135 calories

Green Beans Espagnole
This is a great way to dress up, otherwise ordinary, green beans. Even your kids will enjoy eating green beans prepared this way.

Espagnole Sauce (page 27)
2 tablespoons (30 g) butter
8 ounces (225 g) fresh green beans

Prepare Espagnole Sauce as directed. Heat butter in a skillet over medium heat, add and cook green beans, stirring occasionally, until tender, about 8 to 10 minutes. Serve green beans covered in Espagnole Sauce.

Yield: 2 servings
Per serving with ½ cup (120 g) sauce: 22 g fat; 7.5 g net carbs; 2 g protein; 236 calories

Oriental-Style Green Beans

2 tablespoons (28 g) coconut oil
8 ounces (225 g) green beans, French cut if possible*
2 ounces (55 g) mushrooms, sliced
6 scallions, chopped
2 ounces (55 g) bamboo shoots, sliced lengthwise into matchstick strips
1 tablespoon (15 ml) soy sauce

Heat oil in a skillet over medium heat. Sauté green beans, stirring occasionally, until tender, about 5 to 7 minutes. Add mushrooms, scallions, and bamboo shoots, and cook until mushrooms are soft. Remove from heat and add soy sauce.

*If French-cut beans are not available and you use regular green beans, slice them lengthwise into matchstick strips.

Yield: 2 servings
Per serving: 14.5 g fat; 8 g net carbs; 5 g protein; 182 calories

Green Beans with Anchovies

2 tablespoons (28 g) butter
1 pound (450 g) green beans
2 cloves garlic, minced
4 anchovy fillets, minced or 1 tablespoon (14 g) anchovy paste
⅛ teaspoon freshly ground black pepper
⅛ teaspoon red pepper flakes
2 teaspoons red wine vinegar
¼ cup (28 g) pine nuts or slivered almonds, toasted
3 tablespoons (15 g) grated Parmesan cheese

Heat butter in a large skillet over medium heat. Add green beans and sauté until tender, about 7 to 8 minutes. Add garlic, anchovies, black pepper, and red pepper flakes, and cook until very fragrant, about 5 minutes. Stir in vinegar and toasted nuts, remove from heat, and transfer to a serving bowl. Top with Parmesan cheese.

Yield: 4 servings
Per serving: 16 g fat; 5.5 g net carbs; 5 g protein; 186 calories

Green Bean Casserole

½ cup (8 oz/225 g) cream cheese, softened
¼ cup (60 g) mayonnaise (pages 37-40)
1 teaspoon salt
¼ teaspoon black pepper
¼ teaspoon garlic powder
¼ cup (56 g) butter
3 cups (300 g) chopped green beans
2 medium stalks celery, chopped
1 medium onion, chopped

8 ounces (225 g) mushrooms, chopped
4 ounces (110 g) cheddar cheese, shredded

Preheat oven to 375° F (190° C). In a small bowl, blend together cream cheese, mayonnaise, salt, black pepper, and garlic powder, and set aside.

Heat butter in a large skillet over medium heat. Sauté green beans, celery, and onion until tender, about 6 to 8 minutes. Add mushrooms and cook 3 to 4 more minutes. In a bowl, combine cooked vegetables with cream cheese mixture, then place in a casserole dish. Top with shredded cheese. Bake for 20 minutes or until the cheese is hot and bubbly.

Yield: 4 servings
Per serving: 50.5 g fat; 9 g net carbs; 15.5 g protein; 552 calories

Green Beans Provencal

3 tablespoons (45 ml) extra virgin olive oil
16 ounces (450 g) fresh green beans
1 clove garlic, minced
2 teaspoons minced parsley
¾ teaspoon salt
⅛ teaspoon black pepper

Heat oil in a large skillet over medium heat. Sauté green beans until tender and slightly browned. Add garlic and cook 1 minute. Remove from heat, and add parsley, salt, and black pepper.

Yield: 4 servings
Per serving: 11 g fat; 5.5 g net carbs; 2 g protein; 129 calories

Sautéed Mushrooms

This is a simple and tasty side that can accompany meat, poultry, fish, or even a main vegetable dish.

3 tablespoons (42 g) butter
½ medium onion, sliced thin
8 ounces (225 g) mushrooms, sliced
Salt
Black pepper

Heat butter in a large skillet over medium heat. Sauté onion until it starts to turn golden, about 8 to 10 minutes. Add mushrooms, and cook until tender, about 5 minutes. Add salt and pepper to taste.

Yield: 4 servings
Per serving: 8.5 g fat; 2 g net carbs; 2 g protein; 92 calories

Stuffed Bell Peppers

    4 large bell peppers (any color)
    2 tablespoons (28 g) coconut oil
    12 ounces (340 g) ground beef or pork
    ½ medium yellow onion, chopped
    6 ounces (170 g) mushrooms, chopped
    1 clove garlic, finely chopped
    ½ teaspoon salt
    ¼ teaspoon freshly ground black pepper
    8 ounces (225 g) tomato sauce
    4 eggs, lightly beaten
    1 cup (115 g) shredded cheddar cheese
    4 tablespoons (56 g) butter

Preheat oven to 350° F (180° C). Cut the top stem portion off of each pepper. Carefully remove the seeds and membranes. Fill a large pot with enough water

to cover the peppers. Heat to boiling, add peppers, and cook for about 5 minutes. Set the peppers aside, and discard the water. This step is done to partially cook the peppers and ensure they will be tender after baking in the oven.

Heat coconut oil in a large skillet over medium heat. Add ground beef and onion, and cook, stirring occasionally, until the meat is browned and the onion is tender. Add mushrooms and garlic, and continue cooking until the mushrooms are soft. Remove from heat, and stir in salt, black pepper, tomato sauce, eggs, and cheese.

Stuff peppers with the beef mixture. Stand the peppers upright in a glass baking dish. Bake for 40 minutes. Remove from oven, place on serving plates, and top each with 1 tablespoon (14 g) butter.

Yield: 4 servings
Per serving: 41 g fat; 9.5 g net carbs; 42 g protein; 575 calories

Creamed Spinach

This recipe tastes great with spinach, but if you like, you may replace the spinach with another leafy green such as collard greens, beet greens, kale, or chard.

Basic White Sauce (page 21)
12 ounces (340 g) spinach

Make Basic White Sauce as directed. After the sauce thickens, add spinach and continue to cook and stir for 3 to 4 minutes, until leaves are wilted and immersed in the sauce.

This recipe can also be made using the Morney, Shrimp, Creamy Mushroom, Mustard, and Ham variations (pages 23-24) of the Basic White Sauce. Each sauce brings a little different flavor.

Yield: 4 servings
Per serving with Basic White Sauce: 35 g fat; 3.5 g net carbs; 3.5 g protein; 343 calories

Curried Spinach

20 ounces (560 g) spinach
2 tablespoons (28 g) butter
2 tablespoons (28 g) sour cream
2 teaspoons curry powder
⅛ teaspoon nutmeg
½ teaspoon salt
Dash black pepper

Cook spinach in a vegetable steamer until tender. Melt butter in a small saucepan over low heat. Blend in sour cream, curry powder, nutmeg, salt, and black pepper. Combine with cooked spinach and serve.

Yield: 4 servings
Per serving: 7.5 g fat; 2.5 g net carbs; 4.5 g protein; 95 calories

Fragrant Spinach in Coconut Milk

2 tablespoons (28 g) butter
½ large onion, finely chopped
½ teaspoon ground cumin
¼ teaspoon ground cardamom
¼ teaspoon ground turmeric
¼ teaspoon ground ginger
¼ teaspoon salt
16 ounces (450 g) spinach
½ cup (120 ml) coconut milk

Heat butter in large saucepan over medium heat. Sauté onion until soft, about 6 minutes. Add all seasonings and cook until fragrant, 1 to 2 minutes. Add spinach, cover, and cook until wilted, 2 to 3 minutes. Pour in coconut milk and continue to cook, uncovered, stirring occasionally, for 2 to 3 minutes.

Yield: 2 servings
Per serving: 26.5 g fat; 8 g net carbs; 8.5g protein; 304 calories

Spinach with Olive Oil and Vinegar
This is like a cooked spinach salad with oil and vinegar dressing.

¼ cup (60 ml) extra virgin olive oil
20 ounces (560 g) spinach
1 clove garlic, minced
3 tablespoons (45 ml) apple cider vinegar
½ teaspoon salt
Dash black pepper

Heat oil in a saucepan over medium-low heat. Add spinach and garlic, and cook uncovered, stirring occasionally, for about 8 minutes, until spinach is cooked. Remove from heat and add vinegar, salt, and black pepper. Toss to mix well and serve.

Yield: 4 servings
Per serving: 15 g fat; 2.5 g net carbs; 4 g protein; 161 calories

Fried Tomatoes
You can fry ripe or green tomatoes. It is best if they are ripe but still a little on the green side and firm.

3 tablespoons (42 g) butter or bacon drippings
4 large firm tomatoes, sliced ½-inch (1-cm) thick
½ teaspoon salt
⅛ teaspoon black pepper
¼ cup (60 g) sour cream

Heat oil in a skillet over medium heat. Add tomato slices, and fry 3 to 4 minutes on each side until lightly browned. Season with salt and black pepper, and top with a dollop of sour cream.

Yield: 4 servings
Per serving: 12 g fat; 5 g net carbs; 2 g protein; 136 calories

Variation:
Make the Fried Tomatoes as described above, but omit the sour cream and add grated Parmesan cheese to the top side of the tomato slice after it has been turned once. Allow the cheese to melt before removing it from the skillet.

Zucchini Au Gratin

2 pounds (900 g) zucchini, sliced
    into rounds
Salt
Black pepper
½ cup (50 g) freshly grated Parmesan cheese
2 tablespoons (28 g) butter, melted
2 strips sugar-free, nitrite-free bacon, cooked crisp and crumbled

Preheat oven to 400° F (190° C). Heat a pot of water to boiling, add zucchini, and cook for about 3 minutes. Drain water and let zucchini cool enough to handle. Arrange the zucchini in layers in a pie dish or casserole dish, sprinkling a little salt and black pepper over each layer. Top with Parmesan cheese and melted butter. Bake for 30 minutes. Set oven to broil, and place zucchini within 5 inches (12 cm) from heat for 3 to 5 minutes, until golden brown. Remove from oven, and sprinkle crumbled bacon on top before serving.

Yield: 4 servings
Per serving: 12.5 g fat; 5.5 g net carbs; 10 g protein; 174 calories

Broiled Tomatoes

4 large firm ripe tomatoes, cut in half crosswise
½ teaspoon salt
Dash black pepper
1 tablespoon (3 g) minced fresh chervil or 1 teaspoon dried chervil
1 tablespoon (3 g) minced fresh basil or 1 teaspoon dried basil
¼ cup (56 g) butter
Lemon juice (optional)

Preheat broiler. Arrange tomatoes cut side up in a shallow pan. Sprinkle each with salt, pepper, and herbs. Dot with butter. Broil 5 to 6 inches (12 to 15 cm) from heat for 10 to 12 minutes. Pour any melted butter from the pan on top of the tomatoes before serving. Sprinkle a few drops of lemon juice on each tomato half if desired.

Yield: 4 servings, 2 halves each
Per serving: 11.5 g fat; 5 g net carbs; 1.5 g protein; 129 calories

Sesame Zucchini

¼ cup (56 g) coconut oil
2 tablespoons (19 g) sesame seeds
½ onion, chopped
2 medium zucchini, sliced in rounds
¼ teaspoon minced ginger
2 cloves garlic, chopped
½ teaspoon salt
2 tablespoons (30 ml) soy sauce

Heat oil in a large skillet over medium-low heat. Add sesame seeds, and toast until lightly browned. Add onion, and cook at medium heat for about 5 minutes. Add zucchini, ginger, and garlic, and cook, stirring occasionally, until tender. Remove from heat, and add salt and soy sauce. Serve with pan drippings.

Yield: 2 servings
Per serving: 32 g fat; 9.5 g net carbs; 5.5 g protein; 348 calories

Caramelized Onions and Zucchini

4 strips sugar-free, nitrite-free bacon, cooked crisp and crumbled
1 medium onion, sliced
2 small or 1 medium zucchini, sliced
¼ teaspoon salt
⅛ teaspoon freshly ground black pepper
¼ teaspoon Italian herb mix (oregano, basil, marjoram, thyme)
8 cherry tomatoes, cut in half
2 tablespoons (10 g) grated Parmesan cheese

Cook bacon in a medium-size skillet and set aside. Heat bacon drippings to medium heat, then add onion and zucchini and cook, uncovered, until the onion becomes caramelized, about 10 to 14 minutes, stirring occasionally. Stir in salt, black pepper, Italian herb mix, tomatoes, and Parmesan cheese, and cook for 1 to 2 minutes to melt the cheese. Remove from heat. Serve topped with crumbled bacon.

Yield: 2 servings
Per serving: 24 g fat; 7.5 g net carbs; 17 g protein; 314 calories

Sausage and Summer Squash

This is a very simple, but delicious side dish that makes ordinary squash stand up and shout, "Yummm!" You can use any variety of summer squash—zucchini, yellow crookneck, pattypan, and so forth. Makes a great side dish, but could also serve as a main dish.

2 tablespoons (28 g) coconut oil
4 ounces (110 g) ground pork sausage
½ small onion, chopped
12 ounces (340 g) summer squash, sliced
½ teaspoon dill weed
Salt
Black pepper

Heat oil in a large skillet over medium heat. Cook ground pork, breaking it into small pieces, along with the onion until the meat is lightly browned. Add squash and dill weed, and cook, stirring occasionally, until the squash begins to brown and becomes tender. Add salt and black pepper to taste. Remove from heat and serve.

Yield 2 servings
Per serving: 16 g fat; 5 g net carbs; 16.5 g protein; 348 calories

Zucchini with Lemon Parmesan Sauce

This recipe works well with any type of summer squash. Try it with zucchini, yellow crookneck, pattypan (scallop), and others.

2 small or 1 large zucchini, sliced
¼ cup (56 g) butter
¼ cup (60 ml) heavy cream
¼ cup (20 g) grated Parmesan cheese
Dash of salt
⅛ teaspoon freshly ground black pepper
½ teaspoon fresh lemon juice

Put zucchini into a vegetable steamer and cook until tender. While the zucchini is cooking, prepare the sauce. Heat butter and cream in a small saucepan over medium-low heat. Stir in Parmesan cheese, salt, and black pepper. Stir constantly until the cheese dissolves and the sauce thickens, about 5 to 7 minutes. Stir in lemon juice, and remove from heat. Spoon sauce generously over hot steamed squash and serve.

Yield: 2 servings
Per serving: 35 g fat; 4 g net carbs; 4.5 g protein; 349 calories

Lasagna

This lasagna is made using summer squash in place of the pasta. Any type of summer squash can be used, zucchini, yellow, etc. The cooked squash produces a bit of excess moisture, but the lasagna tastes terrific.

1 tablespoon (14 g) coconut oil
8 ounces (225 g) ground beef
½ medium onion, chopped
2 cloves garlic, minced
1 teaspoon dried oregano
1 teaspoon dried basil
½ teaspoon salt
¼ teaspoon black pepper
4 ounces (110 g) tomato paste
2 medium summer squash (about 15 oz/425 g), thinly sliced
1½ cup (75 g) ricotta cheese
4 ounces (110 g) sharp cheddar cheese, shredded

Preheat oven to 350° F (180° C). Heat oil in a skillet over medium heat. Sauté ground beef and onion until meat is browned and onion is tender. Add garlic, oregano, basil, salt, black pepper, and tomato paste, and cook 3 to 4 minutes. Cut the squash into thin slices. Layer half of the squash on the bottom of an 11x7-inch (28x18-cm) casserole dish. Pour the meat mixture over the squash. Layer ricotta cheese over the meat mixture. Layer the rest of the squash over the ricotta. Top with cheddar cheese. Bake for 50 minutes.

Yield: 4 servings
Per serving: 18 g fat; 7.5 g net carbs; 28 g protein; 304 calories

Oven-Roasted Vegetables

This is one of my favorite vegetable recipes. Roasting vegetables in the oven gives them a unique flavor with a texture that is slightly crispy, yet tender. You can use a variety of both hard and soft vegetables, but you should not try to

cook them all at the same time. Harder vegetables like cauliflower and turnips need to be precooked before roasting.

Dense vegetables should be cut in approximately equal sizes, approximately 1½ to 2½ inches (4 to 6 cm) in length. This ensures that all the vegetables are evenly cooked. When you are through cutting, make sure the vegetables are thoroughly coated in oil. You can use most any type of oil—butter, coconut oil, red palm oil, or lard.

The cooking temperature must be hot (over 400° F/200° C) for proper roasting. The vegetables should be cooked in a large pan so they are not bunched together. Vegetables give off steam as they cook, and if they are overly crowded, they will steam rather than roast.

2 cups (80 g) cauliflower, cut into florets and sliced in half
2 cups (70 g) broccoli, cut into florets and sliced in half
1 turnip, peeled and quartered
2 carrots, cut into 2-inch (5-cm) lengths
1 cup (100 g) whole green beans
12 spears asparagus, cut in halves or thirds
2 red bell peppers, cut in half, with stem and seeds removed
8 mushrooms
1 small onion, quartered
6 tablespoons (84 g) butter, melted
½ teaspoon salt
¼ teaspoon freshly ground black pepper
½ to 1 teaspoon herbs or seasonings (optional)*

Preheat oven to 450° F (230° C). Steam the cauliflower, broccoli, turnip, and carrots, until just tender, about 6 minutes. Remove from the steamer and let cool slightly. Put the cooked vegetables into a large bowl. Add green beans, asparagus, bell peppers, mushrooms, and onion. Stir in melted butter, salt, and black pepper, tossing to evenly coat all the vegetables. Place the vegetables close together, but do not crowd, on a cooking sheet with a lip. Bake for 30 to 40 minutes, or until the vegetables begin to brown. For even roasting, you may want to toss the vegetables halfway through the cooking process. Herbs tend to lose their flavor and burn at high temperatures. If you want to add any herbs or seasonings, it is best to do so about 10 minutes before the vegetables are finished cooking.

*Generally salt and pepper are the only seasonings you need. However, you can add any combination of herbs and seasonings you desire, such as paprika, chili powder, cayenne pepper, rosemary, basil, thyme, sage, or garlic.

Yield: 4 servings
Per serving: 17.5 g fat; 11 g net carbs; 5 g protein; 221 calories

Wraps

Lettuce Wraps

Sandwiches are immensely popular. They are convenient, easy to make, travel well to school or work, and can taste delicious. The drawback with sandwiches, for a keto-conscious individual, is the high-carb content of the bread or bun that holds the sandwich together. A low-carb solution is to ditch the bread and instead wrap a large leaf of lettuce around the filling. The lettuce can hold the filling just as well as the bread, without all the carbs.

Bread is cheap, usually much cheaper than the filling. Consequently, many sandwiches have far too much bread and not enough of the good stuff—the tasty filling. Lettuce has a mild flavor and allows you to savor the flavorful filling.

Although most any type of lettuce can be used as the wrap, iceberg or head lettuce is the most suitable. Iceberg lettuce leaves are large, cup-shaped, and firm enough to hold the filling.

The easiest way to prepare lettuce leaves for wraps is to first remove the core from the head. To do this, locate the core of the head of lettuce. This is the white knob at the bottom of the head. With a sharp knife, cut all the way around the core. Pull the core out and discard. Without the core, the leaves are much easier to separate, with less tearing, providing many suitable leaves with which to make your wraps.

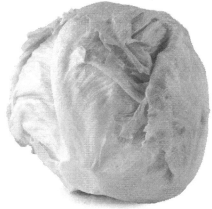

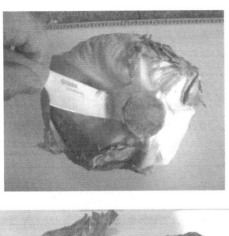
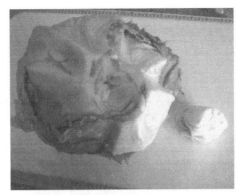

Cut and remove the core of the lettuce head, then peel off the leaves.

Wash the head of lettuce, and let all of the water drain out. You want to keep the head moist, but not soggy, so that the leaves don't dry out and become limp. While still slightly damp, place them in a plastic bag or other container and store in the coldest part of your refrigerator, usually on the lowest shelf.

Chicken Salad Wrap

This is the best chicken salad wrap I've ever eaten. It is important to use raw chicken and cook it until slightly crisp, as directed. I really like the chicken cooked in bacon drippings because it adds a little bacon flavor—and bacon makes anything taste better! The pork rinds give the wrap a nice crunch that complements the chicken and vegetables.

2 tablespoons (30 ml) bacon drippings or coconut oil
6 ounces (170 g) raw chicken, cut into bite-size pieces
¼ cup (60 g) diced celery
½ cup (55 g) shredded carrot
2 scallions, chopped
¼ cup (60 g) mayonnaise (pages 37-40)

½ teaspoon prepared mustard
⅛ teaspoon celery seed
⅛ teaspoon salt
Dash black pepper
½ teaspoon garlic powder
2 tablespoons (2 g) chopped cilantro
½ medium tomato, chopped
2 large lettuce leaves
Dash of paprika
10 pork rinds

Heat oil in a skillet over medium-high heat. Sauté chicken until it turns white and begins to develop a crisp, golden-brown skin, about 10 minutes. Remove from heat and set aside.

In a bowl, combine chicken, celery, carrot, scallions, mayonnaise, mustard, celery seed, salt, pepper, garlic powder, cilantro, and tomato. Spoon filling into lettuce leaves, add a dash of paprika, and top with pork rinds.

Yield: 2 servings
Per wrap: 41 g fat; 4 g net carbs; 35 g protein; 525 calories

Bacon Burger Wrap

This is a quick and tasty bun-less, or low-carb, hamburger. You can add or subtract the condiments to suit your preferences. Other condiments you might consider are mustard, barbecue sauce, jalapeño peppers, and sautéed mushrooms. I love a fried egg, with a runny yolk, on my burgers.

4 strips sugar-free, nitrite-free bacon, cooked crisp
6 ounces (170 g) ground beef
½ medium onion, sliced
Salt and black pepper to taste
2 ounces (57 g) cheese, shredded
2 large lettuce leaves
1 tablespoon (14 g) mayonnaise (pages 37-40)
½ small tomato, sliced
¼ cup (28 g) dill pickle, sliced

Cook bacon in a skillet until crisp. Remove bacon and set aside. Keep the bacon drippings in the skillet and add ground beef and onion. Break the beef into small chunks as it cooks and stir occasionally. Cook until the beef is browned and onion is tender. Add salt and pepper to taste. Push the meat and onion to the center of the pan and sprinkle with cheese. Cover, remove from heat, and set aside to allow the cheese to melt.

Open each lettuce leaf and spread an equal amount of mayonnaise on each. Add the tomato, pickle, and cooked bacon, followed by an equal portion of the cooked beef mixture. Wrap the lettuce around the filling and enjoy.

Yield: 2 servings
Per wrap: 35.5 g fat; 3.5 g net carbs; 47 g protein; 522 calories

Seafood Wrap

You can use any type of fish in this recipe. It is a great way to use leftover seafood. You can use fresh bass, catfish, perch, haddock, and others, or canned fish like tuna or salmon. Even crab and shrimp will work well.

6 ounces (170 g) fish or shellfish
1 hard-boiled egg, chopped
2 tablespoons (28 g) mayonnaise (pages 37-40)
¼ teaspoon curry powder
1 scallion, chopped
½ cup (60 g) shredded carrot
¼ teaspoon salt
⅛ teaspoon black pepper
2 large lettuce leaves
10 cherry tomatoes, sliced in half

Mix together fish, hard-boiled egg, mayonnaise, curry powder, scallion, carrot, salt, and pepper. Place the filling in 2 large lettuce leaves, and top with cherry tomatoes.

Yield: 2 servings
Per wrap: 19.5 g fat; 4.5 g net carbs; 25 g protein; 293.5 calories

Salmon Wrap

This wrap reminds me of the toasted tuna fish sandwiches I used to enjoy as a kid. One of the things I liked about the sandwiches I ate as I was growing up was the crunch of the toasted bread. The pork rinds used in this recipe give this otherwise soft lettuce wrap a nice crispy crunch. If you take this wrap to school or work, keep the pork rinds separate and add just before eating to keep them crunchy.

6 ounces (170 g) salmon
¼ cup (56 g) mayonnaise (pages 37-40)
2 tablespoons (25 g) chopped dill pickle
1 ounce (28 g) cheddar cheese, shredded
Salt and black pepper to taste
2 large lettuce leaves
10 pork rinds

Mix together salmon, mayonnaise, pickle, cheese, salt, and pepper. Divide the filling equally, and place in the lettuce leaves. Top with pork rinds just before serving.

Yield: 2 servings
Per wrap: 32 g fat; 0.5 g net carbs; 24.5 g protein; 388 calories

Avocado Bacon Wrap

This is one of my absolute favorite lettuce wraps. It's filled with bacon, avocado, and caramelized onions, so it's got to be good.

4 strips sugar-free, nitrite-free bacon
½ medium onion, sliced
1 avocado, peeled and pitted
2 tablespoons (28 g) mayonnaise (pages 37-40)
¼ teaspoon chili powder
⅛ teaspoon paprika powder
Salt to taste
2 large lettuce leaves
2 tablespoons (2 g) chopped cilantro

Cook bacon in a skillet until crisp, then remove from pan and set aside. Cook onion in bacon drippings until soft and beginning to caramelize, then remove from heat and set aside. In a small bowl, mash together the avocado, mayonnaise, chili powder, and paprika. Add salt to taste. Place an equal amount of the mashed avocado in the center of each lettuce leaf. Add two strips of bacon and half of the caramelized onions to each wrap. Garnish with cilantro. Wrap the lettuce around the filling and eat like a burrito.

Yield: 2 wraps
Per wrap: 46 g fat; 4.6 g net carbs; 16.5 g protein; 515 calories

Taco Wrap

If you like Mexican food but avoid it because of all the corn, beans, and rice, here is a keto-friendly version without the carbs but with all of the taste.

1 tablespoon (14 g) coconut oil
8 ounces (225 g) ground beef
½ small onion, chopped
1 tablespoon (9 g) jalapeño pepper, chopped
½ teaspoon chili powder or taco seasoning
¼ teaspoon salt
¼ cup (58 g) shredded cheddar cheese
2 large lettuce leaves
½ cup (90 g) chopped tomato
½ avocado, sliced
2 tablespoons (30 g) sour cream

Heat oil in a medium skillet over medium-high heat. Sauté ground beef and onion until the meat is browned and the onion is tender, about 8 to 9 minutes. Add jalapeño pepper, chili powder, and salt, and cook 2 to 3 minutes. Add cheese and remove from heat. Let cool for a few minutes. This will give time for the cheese to just start to melt. Scoop an equal amount of the filling into each of the lettuce leaves and add an equal amount of chopped tomato and avocado. Add a dollop of sour cream, roll up, and eat like a burrito or a taco.

Yield: 2 wraps
Per wrap: 34 g fat; 4.5 g net carbs; 43 g protein; 496 calories

Fajita Wrap

Fajitas are traditionally made using marinated and tenderized flank beef steak that is thinly sliced. You can use flank steak or any type of beef. Tough cuts of meat need to be tenderized first or precooked with moist heat. Fajitas provide a good way to use leftover meat. You can also make the fajita using chicken or a combination of chicken and beef.

    2 tablespoons (28 g) coconut oil
    ½ medium onion, sliced
    ½ green bell pepper, sliced
    ½ red bell pepper, sliced
    8 ounces (225 g) beef, thinly sliced
    ½ teaspoon chili powder
    ½ teaspoon paprika
    ¼ teaspoon onion powder
    ½ teaspoon ground cumin
    ¼ teaspoon cayenne pepper
    1 teaspoon salt
    2 large lettuce leaves
    ½ cup (120 g) salsa
    ½ avocado, sliced
    2 tablespoons (30 g) sour cream

Heat oil in a skillet over medium-high heat. Add onion and bell peppers, and sauté until the onion begins to caramelize, about 10 minutes. Add beef, chili powder, paprika, onion powder, cumin, cayenne pepper, and salt, and sauté until the meat is cooked to your liking. Obviously, if you use precooked meat it will take less time to cook than raw. Remove from heat, and let cool slightly.

Open lettuce leaves and scoop in meat filling. Add salsa, avocado, and sour cream. Wrap and eat.

Yield: 2 wraps
Per wrap: 32 g fat; 9 g net carbs; 37 g protein; 472 calories

Keto Burrito
This is the ketogenic version of a meat and bean burrito without the flour tortilla and beans.

    2 large lettuce leaves
    1½ cups (375 g) No-Bean Chili (page 88)
    2 ounces (57 g) cheddar cheese, shredded
    1 avocado, sliced
    2 tablespoons (30 g) sour cream

Place lettuce leaves on serving plates. Heat the No-Bean Chili until hot. Fill the leaves with an equal portion of No-Bean Chili, cheese, avocado, and sour cream. Wrap the lettuce around the filling and eat like a burrito.

Yield: 2 servings
Per serving: 27 g fat; 4 g net carbs; 19 g protein; 339 calories

Breakfast Keto Burrito

1 tablespoon (14 g) coconut oil
4 ounces (108 g) pork sausage
4 eggs, lightly beaten
¼ teaspoon salt
2 ounces (57 g) cheddar cheese, shredded
2 large lettuce leaves
2 tablespoons (30 g) sour cream
4 tablespoons (65 g) salsa

Heat oil in a skillet, then add sausage and cook until brown. Stir in eggs and salt, top with cheese, cover, and cook until the eggs set, about 5 minutes. Remove from heat. Put cooked egg mixture evenly into two lettuce leaves along with sour cream and salsa. Roll the lettuce leaves around the mixture to form a burrito.

Yield: 2 burritos
Per serving: 43.5 g fat; 3 g net carbs; 29.5 g protein; 521.5 calories

Philly Cheesesteak Wrap

For a great tasting cheesesteak you must start out with a good quality steak. The better the quality, the better the results. I recommend rib eye, New York strip, T-bone, and similar quality steaks. Select steaks that are well marbled in fat. Do not trim off the fat. Fat gives meat flavor.

Cut the meat into thin strips, about ⅛-inch (3-mm) thick. The butcher can do this for you when you purchase the meat. If you do it yourself, put the meat in the freezer for about 45 minutes to partially freeze and stiffen it first, to make it easier to cut.

2 tablespoons (28 g) coconut oil
½ medium onion, chopped

½ green pepper, chopped
8 ounces (227 g) beefsteak, thinly sliced
3 ounces (85 g) mushrooms, sliced
¼ teaspoon salt
¼ teaspoon black pepper
2 ounces (57 g) Monterey Jack, Munster, or provolone cheese
2 large lettuce leaves

Heat the oil in a skillet to medium-high. Sauté the onion for about 3 to 4 minutes, or until it starts to become translucent. Add green pepper, and continue to sauté for 5 to 8 minutes or until the peppers become tender. Add steak, mushrooms, salt, and black pepper, and sauté for another 4 to 5 minutes until the meat is lightly browned and onion begins to caramelize. Remove from heat and add cheese, cover, and wait for about 2 minutes or until the cheese just starts to melt. Uncover and spoon equal portions of the mixture into 2 large lettuce leaves.

Yield: 2 servings
Per serving: 30.5 g fat; 4 g net carbs; 43 g protein; 466 calories

Rueben Wrap

1 teaspoon coconut oil
6 ounces (170 g) corned beef or pastrami
2 ounces (56 g) Swiss cheese, sliced
2 large lettuce leaves

1 teaspoon prepared mustard
½ avocado, sliced
1 dill pickle, sliced in half lengthwise
¼ cup (60 g) sauerkraut

Heat oil in a skillet over medium heat. Cook meat until it is hot. Turn off the heat. Place cheese on top of the meat, cover the skillet, and let sit until the cheese begins to melt, about 2 minutes. Put meat and cheese into lettuce leaves, add mustard, avocado, pickle, and sauerkraut. Wrap and eat.

Yield: 2 servings
Per serving: 30.5 g fat; 3.5 g net carbs; 20.5 g protein; 370 calories

Asian Chicken Wrap

¼ cup (30 g) sliced or slivered almonds, toasted
2 tablespoons (28 g) coconut oil
½ cup (80 g) onion, chopped
1 teaspoon diced fresh ginger
2 ounces (55 g) bamboo shoots
4 ounces (110 g) cooked chicken, chopped
2 ounces (55 g) mushrooms, sliced
2 tablespoons (30 ml) rice vinegar

¼ teaspoon salt
⅛ teaspoon black pepper
2 large lettuce leaves
1 ounce (28 g) fresh alfalfa sprouts
1 tablespoon (15 ml) soy sauce or coconut aminos

Preheat oven or toaster oven to 350° F (180° C). Put almonds in an oven-safe baking dish and cook until golden brown, about 8 minutes. Remove from oven and set aside.

Heat oil in a skillet over medium-high heat. Sauté onion for about 5 minutes or until it starts to become translucent. Add ginger, bamboo shoots, chicken, and mushrooms, and cook 5 minutes, stirring occasionally. Add vinegar, salt, and black pepper, and cook another 3 to 4 minutes or until the vegetables are tender and chicken is cooked. Remove from heat. Put filling into lettuce leaves. Top with toasted almonds, sprouts, and soy sauce.

Yield: 2 servings
Per serving: 23 g fat; 6.5 g net carbs; 22 g protein; 321 calories

Asian Beef Wrap

2 tablespoons (28 g) coconut oil
½ cup (80 g) onion, chopped
8 ounces (220 g) beefsteak, cut in bite-size pieces
3 ounces (85 g) bok choy, chopped
2 ounces (55 g) mushrooms, chopped
2 cloves garlic, minced
¼ teaspoon salt
⅛ teaspoon black pepper
2 large lettuce leaves
Soy sauce or coconut aminos to taste

Heat oil in a skillet over medium-high heat. Sauté onion and beef for about 6 minutes, or until the beef is lightly browned. Add bok choy, mushrooms, garlic, salt, and pepper, and continue cooking until the vegetables are tender, about 6 to 8 minutes. Remove from heat. Spoon filling into lettuce leaves. Add soy sauce to taste.

Yield: 2 servings
Per serving: 21 g fat; 6 g net carbs; 36 g protein; 357 calories

Deli Wrap

You can enjoy your favorite deli sandwiches without the carbs by replacing the bread with lettuce. Any type of deli meat will do: turkey, chicken, ham, pastrami, beef, etc. Check ingredient labels and make sure they are sugar-free, nitrite-free, and contain no unwanted additives. These sandwiches are eaten cold, so they can be taken to school, to work, or on family outings. You can modify the following recipe to suit your tastes by deleting ingredients or adding others like green bell peppers, banana peppers, jalapeño peppers, cilantro, onions, avocado, etc.

4 ounces (110 g) deli meat
2 ounces (55 g) Monterey Jack, Munster, or provolone cheese
2 large lettuce leaves
1 tablespoon (14 g) mayonnaise (pages 37-40)
½ teaspoon yellow mustard (optional)
2 ounces (55 g) pickles, sliced
½ medium tomato, sliced
1 ounce (28 g) fresh alfalfa sprouts

Layer the meat and cheese inside the lettuce leaves. Spread on the mayonnaise and mustard. Follow with pickles and tomatoes, and top with sprouts. Fold the lettuce around the filling and eat like a burrito.

Yield: 2 servings
Per serving: 12 g fat; 4.5 g net carbs; 17 g protein; 194 calories

Chicken Bacon Wrap

4 strips sugar-free, nitrite-free bacon, cooked crisp
4 ounces (120 g) chicken (cooked or raw)
½ avocado, sliced
½ medium tomato, sliced
2 large lettuce leaves
1 tablespoon (14 g) mayonnaise (pages 37-40)
1 scallion, chopped
Salt and black pepper to taste

Cook bacon in a skillet until crisp, remove from pan, and set aside. Cut chicken into bite-size pieces, and cook in the skillet with the bacon grease. You can use either raw chicken or precooked chicken, cooking in the bacon grease gives additional flavor to the chicken. If you are using raw chicken, cook until the meat turns white and starts to brown, about 10 minutes. If you are using precooked chicken, cook until it begins to brown around the edges, about 5 to 8 minutes. Put the chicken in a small bowl and set aside to cool.

Layer an equal amount of sliced avocado, tomato, and bacon in each lettuce leaf. Combine the chicken with mayonnaise, chopped scallion, salt, and pepper, and put an equal amount into each lettuce leaf.

Yield: 2 servings
Per serving: 33 g fat; 3 g net carbs; 33 g protein; 441 calories

Turkey and Ham Wrap

2 large lettuce leaves
4 ounces (110 g) sliced turkey
2 ounces (60 g) sliced sugar-free, nitrite-free ham
1 small tomato, cut into wedges
½ avocado, sliced
2 ounces (50 g) fresh alfalfa sprouts
2 teaspoons fresh lime juice
¼ cup (60 ml) Ranch Dressing (page 43)

Layer in each lettuce leaf an equal portion of turkey, ham, tomato, avocado, and sprouts. Mix lime juice into the Ranch Dressing and pour over the filling. Wrap and eat.

Yield: 2 servings
Per serving: 15 g fat; 3 g net carbs; 23.5 g protein; 241 calories

Chinese Spring Rolls

2 tablespoons (28 g) coconut oil
½ cup (55 g) carrots, shredded
½ cup (80 g) onion, chopped
1 clove garlic, minced
1 cup (70 g) cooked chicken, chopped
½ cup (45 g) cabbage, chopped
1 teaspoon minced fresh ginger

1 tablespoon (15 ml) soy sauce or coconut aminos
2 large lettuce leaves

Heat oil in a skillet over medium-high heat. Sauté carrots, onion, and garlic for about 5 minutes or until slightly limp. Add chicken, cabbage, and ginger, and cook until cabbage is soft, about 5 minutes. Remove from heat and stir in soy sauce. Divide filling evenly between the lettuce leaves.

Yield: 2 servings
Per serving: 15 g fat; 7 g net carbs; 11.5 g protein; 209 calories

Ham Salad Wrap

1½ cups (225 g) cooked sugar-free, nitrite-free ham, chopped
1 hard-boiled egg, peeled and chopped
1 tablespoon (8 g) finely chopped celery
2 teaspoons chopped dill pickle or pickle relish
1 scallion, chopped
½ cup (115 g) mayonnaise (pages 37-40)
½ tablespoon (5 g) prepared mustard
2 large lettuce leaves

Mix ham, egg, celery, pickle, and scallion together in a bowl. In a separate bowl, stir together mayonnaise and mustard. Combine the two mixtures together. Scoop the mixture into lettuce leaves and serve.

Yield: 2 servings
Per serving: 31 g fat; 1.5 g net carbs; 22 g protein; 373 calories

Egg Salad Sandwich

2 tablespoons (14 g) slivered or sliced almonds, toasted
2 hard-boiled eggs, peeled and chopped
1½ tablespoons (21 g) mayonnaise (pages 37-40)
1 teaspoon prepared mustard
⅛ teaspoon salt
2 tablespoons (25 g) chopped dill pickle or pickle relish
1 tablespoon (2 g) diced cilantro
1 large lettuce leaf
1 teaspoon diced chives

Heat oven or toaster oven to 350° F (180° C). Put almonds in an oven-safe baking dish and toast almonds until they are a golden brown, about 7 minutes. The almonds can burn easily so you need to check them frequently. Remove the almonds from the oven and set aside.

Mix together chopped eggs, mayonnaise, mustard, salt, pickle, and cilantro. Spoon the filling into the lettuce leaf. Top with chives and toasted almonds.

Yield: 1 serving
Per serving: 15.5 g fat; 1.5 g net carbs; 7.5 g protein; 175.5 calories

Bacon and Egg Salad Wrap

2 strips sugar-free, nitrite-free bacon, cooked crisp and crumbled
2 hard-boiled eggs, peeled and chopped
2 tablespoons (28 g) mayonnaise (pages 37-40)
2 tablespoons (7 g) finely chopped celery
1 scallion, chopped
Dash of curry powder (optional)
Salt and black pepper to taste
1 large lettuce leaf

Mix together crumbled bacon, hard-boiled eggs, mayonnaise, celery, and scallion. Sprinkle with curry powder, salt, and black pepper to taste. Fill lettuce leaf and enjoy.

Yield: 1 serving
Per serving: 35 g fat; 2 g net carbs; 25 g protein; 423 calories

Shrimp Salad Wrap

6 ounces (170 g) precooked shrimp
½ cup (65 g) Cocktail Sauce (page 33)
1 tablespoon (15 ml) fresh lemon juice
2 teaspoons lemon zest
1 cup (120 g) chopped cucumber
½ cup (50 g) chopped celery
2 tablespoons (6 g) chopped chives or scallions
2 tablespoons (2 g) chopped cilantro
Salt and black pepper to taste
2 large lettuce leaves

In a medium bowl, mix together shrimp, Cocktail Sauce, lemon juice, lemon zest, cucumber, celery, chives, cilantro, salt, and pepper. Spoon mixture into lettuce leaves. Wrap filling in the lettuce and enjoy.

Yield: 2 servings
Per serving: 1.5 g fat; 7 g net carbs; 20 g protein; 121.5 calories

Shrimp Avocado Wrap

6 ounces (170 g) precooked shrimp
¼ cup (60 g) mayonnaise (pages 37-40)
1 tablespoon (9 g) chopped jalapeño pepper

½ medium tomato, chopped
1 avocado, chopped
2 tablespoons (2 g) chopped cilantro
2 scallions, chopped
⅛ teaspoon salt
2 large lettuce leaves

In a medium bowl, combine cooked shrimp, mayonnaise, jalapeño pepper, tomato, avocado, cilantro, scallions, and salt. Toss the ingredients together until well mixed. Scoop mixture into lettuce leaves, wrap, and enjoy.

Yield: 2 servings
Per serving: 37 g fat; 5 g net carbs; 22 g protein; 441 calories

Shrimp Scallop Wrap

3 stalks celery (1 cut in quarters, 2 thinly sliced)
2 cloves garlic (2 smashed, 1 chopped)
Juice of 1 lemon, divided
8 ounces (227 g) baby carrots, quartered lengthwise
12 ounces (340 g) small raw shrimp, peeled and deveined
8 ounces (227 g) sea scallops, halved horizontally
1 avocado, peeled, pitted, and cut in half
3 teaspoons capers, plus 1 tablespoon (15 ml) of brine from the jar
1 tablespoon (14 g) mayonnaise (pages 37-40)
½ teaspoon salt
¼ teaspoon black pepper
½ cup (55 g) chopped almonds, toasted
4 large lettuce leaves

In a large saucepan, combine 10 cups of water with the quartered celery, smashed garlic, and half of the lemon juice. Cover and bring to a boil. Uncover, add carrots, and cook 2 minutes. Add the shrimp and cook for about 4 minutes, until the shrimp becomes white. Transfer the carrots and shrimp to a colander and rinse under cold water.

Bring the water back to a boil, add the scallops, and cook until white, about 2 minutes. With a slotted spoon, remove the scallops and add them to the colander. Rinse under cold water.

Ladle out ⅓ cup (80 ml) of the broth and set aside to cool. Refrigerate or freeze the remaining broth and use it as the base for soup in another recipe. Using a food processor or blender, puree half of the avocado, the reserved broth, the remaining lemon juice, the caper brine, chopped garlic, mayonnaise, salt, and black pepper. Set the puree aside.

Chop whole almonds or use slivered almonds and put them in an oven-safe dish. With the oven or toaster oven at 350° F (180° C) cook the almonds until they are a light golden brown, about 7 minutes. Check often because they burn easily. Remove from the oven and set aside.

Chop the remaining half of avocado and put it in a bowl along with the cooked carrots, shrimp, and scallops, and the sliced celery, capers, and toasted almonds. Add the puree and mix well. Scoop equal portions of the filling into each lettuce leaf. Wrap and eat.

Yield: 4 servings
Per serving: 22 g fat; 11 g net carbs; 34 g protein; 378 calories

Fried Chicken Finger Wrap

2 tablespoons (30 ml) bacon drippings or coconut oil
2 (3 oz/85 g each) boneless chicken breasts, cut in finger-size strips
½ cup (55 g) shredded carrot
½ cup (65 g) chopped cucumber
2 scallions, chopped
½ cup (75 g) chopped green bell pepper
½ medium tomato, chopped
¼ cup (60 ml) Asian Almond Dressing (page 41)
2 large lettuce leaves
10 pork rinds

Heat oil in a skillet over medium-high heat. Fry chicken strips, turning occasionally, until they start to turn golden brown, about 10 to 15 minutes. Remove chicken from the pan and set aside to cool.

In a bowl, combine carrot, cucumber, scallions, green pepper, and tomato. Toss vegetables with the Asian

Almond Dressing. Spoon vegetables into lettuce leaves, add an equal portion of chicken strips, and top with pork rinds. Wrap and enjoy.

Yield: 2 servings
Per serving: 41 g fat; 7 g net carbs; 31 g protein; 521 calories

Ham and Cheese Salad Sandwich

Wraps are almost like eating a salad by hand—a salad sandwich. All of the salad ingredients are wrapped up in the lettuce and topped with a favorite salad dressing.

2 large lettuce leaves
4 ounces (110 g) sugar-free, nitrite-free ham, sliced
2 ounces (55 g) cheddar cheese, sliced
1 medium tomato, chopped
½ avocado, sliced
1 ounce (28 g) alfalfa sprouts
2 tablespoons (30 ml) Vinaigrette Salad Dressing (page 42)

Open lettuce leaves and layer on ham, cheese, tomato, avocado, and sprouts. Sprinkle salad dressing on top, wrap, and eat.

Yield: 2 servings
Per serving: 21 g fat; 3.5 g net carbs; 17 g protein; 432 calories

Garden Salad Sandwich

This is a tossed salad sandwich wrapped in lettuce. The recipe calls for Ranch Dressing but you can use any salad dressing of your choice.

2 large lettuce leaves
½ medium tomato, chopped
¼ cup (35 g) chopped bell pepper
¼ cup (30 g) shredded carrot
½ cup (35 g) shredded cabbage
½ cup (55 g) sliced cucumber
2 scallions, chopped
4 strips sugar-free, nitrite-free bacon, cooked crisp and crumbled
2 ounces (55 g) feta cheese
¼ cup (56 g) Ranch Dressing (page 43)

Open lettuce leaves and fill with equal amounts of tomato, bell pepper, carrots, cabbage, cucumber, scallions, bacon, and feta cheese. Top with salad dressing, wrap, and eat.

Yield: 2 servings
Per serving: 28 g fat; 7.5 g net carbs; 20 g protein; 362 calories

Almond Chicken Wrap

¼ cup (30 g) chopped almonds, toasted
2 tablespoons (28 g) coconut oil
6 ounces (170 g) raw chicken, cut into bite-size pieces
1 medium carrot, cut into julienne strips
2 teaspoons minced fresh ginger
2 ounces (55 g) bamboo shoots
½ cup (40 g) shredded cabbage
¼ teaspoon salt
2 tablespoons (30 ml) rice vinegar
2 scallions, chopped
2 tablespoons (30 ml) soy sauce or coconut aminos
2 large lettuce leaves

Preheat oven or toaster oven to 350° F (180° C). Put chopped almonds on an oven-safe baking dish and cook until light golden brown, about 7 minutes. Remove from oven and set aside.

Heat oil in skillet over medium-high heat Sauté chicken and carrot until the chicken turns white, about 8 minutes. Add ginger, bamboo shoots, and cabbage, and cook for 5 minutes or until the cabbage is cooked. Stir in salt, vinegar, and scallions, and cook about 1 minute. Remove from heat and add toasted almonds and soy sauce. Let cool slightly then spoon into lettuce leaves.

Yield: 2 servings
Per serving: 24 g fat; 7 g net carbs; 30 g protein; 364 calories

Chicken Mango Wrap

2 tablespoons (30 ml) bacon drippings or coconut oil
6 ounces (170 g) raw chicken, cut in strips

½ cup (90 g) fresh mango, diced
2 scallions, chopped
¼ cup (75 g) red bell pepper, chopped
½ cup (60 g) chopped cucumber
¼ cup (25 g) chopped almonds, toasted
¼ cup (60 ml) Cilantro Lime Salad Dressing (page 46)
2 large lettuce leaves

Heat oil in a skillet over medium-high heat. Sauté chicken strips until the meat becomes white and begins to brown, about 10 minutes. Remove from heat and let cool. In a bowl, toss together mango, scallions, bell pepper, cucumber, almonds, and dressing. Spoon filling into lettuce leaves and top with chicken strips. Wrap and enjoy.

Yield: 2 servings
Per serving: 23 g fat; 11 g net carbs; 28 g protein; 363 calories

Beef

Beef is the meat from full-grown cattle about two years old. A live steer weighs about 1,200 pounds (544 kg) and yields about 490 pounds (222 kg) of edible meat. There are at least 50 breeds of beef cattle, but fewer than 10 make up most cattle produced.

All cattle start out eating pasture grass, however, three-fourths of them are "finished" (reach full maturity) in feedlots where they are fed specially formulated feed based on corn or other grains to bulk them up for market. Beef that is labeled "grassfed" is raised and finished on organically grown grass, without exposure to hormones or antibiotics, making it preferable to feedlot beef.

There are four basic major (primal) cuts into which beef is separated: chuck, loin, rib, and round. Often, packages of fresh beef purchased in the supermarket are labeled with the primal cut as well as the product, such as "chuck roast" or "round steak." This helps consumers know how to cook the product for best results. Generally, chuck and round are less tender and require moist heat, such as braising; loin and rib can be cooked by dry heat methods, such as broiling or grilling.

Unfortunately, names for various cuts can vary regionally in stores, and the primal may not be identified, causing confusion over the choice of cooking method. For example, a boneless top loin steak is variously called strip steak, Kansas City Steak, New York strip steak, hotel cut strip steak, ambassador steak, or club sirloin steak. If in doubt, ask the butcher to identify the primal or offer cooking suggestions.

If the product has a "use by" date, follow that date. If it has a "sell by" date or no date, cook or freeze the product by the times on the following chart.

Storage Times for Beef Products

Product	Refrigerator 40° F (4° C)	Freezer 0° F (-18° C)
Fresh beef roast, steaks, chops, or ribs	3 to 5 days	6 to 12 months
Fresh beef liver or variety meats	1 or 2 days	3 to 4 months
Home cooked beef, soups, stews, or casseroles	3 to 4 days	2 to 3 months
Store-cooked convenience meals	1 to 2 days	2 to 3 months
Cooked beef gravy or beef broth	1 or 2 days	2 to 3 months
Beef hot dogs or lunch meats, sealed in package	2 weeks (or 1 week after a "Use By" date)	1 to 2 months
Beef hot dogs, opened package	7 days	1 to 2 months
Lunch meats, opened package	3 to 5 days	1 to 2 months
TV dinners, frozen casseroles	Keep frozen	3 to 4 months
Canned beef products in pantry	2 to 5 years in pantry; 3 to 4 days after opening	After opening, 2 to 3 months
Jerky, commercially vacuum packaged	1 year in pantry, refrigerate 2 to 3 months	Do not freeze

CUTS OF MEAT

What is the difference between a skirt steak, a round steak, and a blade steak? Most people don't know. Many people judge the tenderness and flavor of a cut of meat based on its cost. This isn't a good way to judge. Although tough cuts of meat generally are cheaper than other cuts, they are not necessarily cheap. Each cut of meat will produce good results if you know how to properly prepare and cook it. If you tried to cook a flank steak like you would a sirloin, you would be greatly disappointed. For this reason, if you want to have great tasting steaks, roasts, and chops, it is advisable that you understand a little about the different cuts of meats and how best to prepare them.

A half carcass ready for cutting is divided into large sections known as primals. Beef is generally divided into eight primals, while pork and lamb are cut into four and five respectively. Each primal is sliced into the individual cuts you see in the store. The meat in each primal is of similar quality. For example, meat from the rib, short loin, and sirloin primals of a steer are the prime cuts and are the most costly. Cuts from the brisket and shank, short plate, flank, and round are generally the toughest and cheapest.

Although the names for the various cuts of meat can vary somewhat, commercial cuts of meat are fairly consistent. Whether you are buying an entire side of beef or individual cuts at the market, the type of cuts you have to choose from are basically the same. Cuts from the shoulder, called the chuck, are all similar in texture and quality. Likewise, the various cuts from the ribs, rump (round), shank (leg), breast (short plate), and belly (flank) are all similar in quality. When you order a sirloin steak (tender and fatty) or a flank steak (lean and tough), you know exactly what you are getting. Some cuts may be thicker or larger, some may include the bone and some not, and some may include more or less fat, but the quality of the cuts are similar for each primal.

Muscle meats tend to become tougher if they are exercised more and if they contain more sinew and connective tissue. Cuts from the legs (shank) or rump (round) get a lot of exercise and tend to be tougher. Prime cuts of meat from the loins (back) and ribs get far less use and are more tender and generally are marbled in fat. Fatty, marbled meats are more tender and flavorful than lean cuts. Bones also tend to give the surrounding meat more flavor. This is why rib eye roast (prime rib), which has very little connective tissue and is richly marbled in fat and attached to multiple rib bones, is among the most tender and delicious cuts of meat.

Generally, ground meat is made from the less tender and less popular cuts of beef. Trimmings from more tender cuts may also be used. Grinding tenderizes the meat and the fat reduces its dryness and improves flavor.

Chuck

The chuck is the steer's shoulder and comprises about 26 percent of the carcass weight. This primal contains the upper portion of the backbone, five rib bones, and portions of the shoulder (blade) and arm bones. Because these muscles are heavily used, the chuck contains a high percentage of connective tissue. Much of the ground beef comes from the chuck, the rest comes from meat and fat trimmed from the other primals. The most characteristic cut is the 7-bone steak or pot roast, which gets its name from the shape of the bone in this cut.

Common cuts are: arm roast, blade steak, 7-bone pot roast, stew meat, and short ribs.

Brisket and Shank

The brisket comes from the animal's breast and the shank from the front legs, and makes up approximately 10 percent of the carcass weight. The boneless brisket is one of the toughest cuts of meat, but when cooked properly, it makes fantastic barbecue, corned beef, and pastrami. The brisket and shank make excellent soup stock.

Common cuts are: brisket and shank (foreshank).

Rib

The rib cuts contribute about 10 percent to the carcass weight and are among the most tender and valued. It yields prime rib (rib eye) roast, rib eye (Delmonico) steak, and ribs. The roast is often sold with the ribs attached, but it can be divided and sold separately.

Common cuts are: prime rib, rib eye steak, and ribs.

Short Plate and Flank

The short plate and flank are located in the chest and abdominal region of the steer. Combined, they account for about 10 percent of the overall weight of the carcass. The muscles in this area get a lot of use, so the cuts contain a lot of connective tissue and are very tough, therefore, these cuts must be braised or marinated to make them chewable. Steaks are usually cut very thin and across the grain and are often used in fajitas and Asian stir-fries. Much of it is turned into ground beef.

Common cuts are: flank steak, skirt steak, and ground beef.

Short Loin

The loin consists of the muscles along the back on both sides of the spine between the shortest ribs and hip bone. It makes up about 8 percent of the carcass. Short loin yields many of the most tender, marbled, and expensive cuts of beef, including the most prized tenderloin (filet mignon). Porterhouse and T-bone steaks include a portion of the tenderloin. When a carcass is butchered, it can yield either filet mignon or Porterhouse and T-bone steaks, but not both. A T-bone steak, however, can be cut along the central bone, yielding a filet mignon and a New York strip steak. When you eat a T-bone steak, you can notice the difference in tenderness between the filet mignon and the New York strip sides. A Porterhouse steak is similar to a T-bone, except it is cut further down the back and contains a larger portion of the tenderloin.

Common cuts are: T-bone steak, Porterhouse steak, tenderloin roast, tenderloin steaks, top loin steak, and New York strip steak.

Sirloin

The sirloin is located between the short loin and the round (rump) and contains part of the backbone and part of the hip bone. It makes up about 9 percent of the carcass weight. Sirloin yields the second most tender meat, next to the short loin. Sirloin steaks and roasts are called by several names, including sirloin tip, round tip, or just tip steak or tip roast. Sirloin cuts are excellent for dry-heat cooking, such as roasting, broiling, and grilling.

Common cuts are: sirloin steak, sirloin tip roast, and tri-tip roast.

Round

Round cuts come from the rump and back legs of the steer and account for about 27 percent of the carcass. The meat is lean and well exercised, and therefore, much tougher than sirloin. Steaks can be marinated and should not be overcooked; medium rare is best. These cuts are often used to make chicken-fried steak and jerky.

Common cuts are: round steak, top round steak, bottom round steaks, round rump roast, tip roast or steak, and eye round roast.

TENDERIZING TOUGH CUTS OF MEAT

At some time in your life, you have probably tried to eat a piece of meat that was so tough and chewy it seemed like you were eating shoe leather. Improper cooking can make tough cuts of meat even tougher. Yet no meat, regardless of the cut, should be unpleasantly tough. If prepared properly, even the toughest cuts can be made tender and delicious.

Age tends to make meat tougher; the older the animal, the tougher the meat. Heavily used muscles tend to become stronger and are filled with tough sinew and connective tissues. The most frequently used muscles—the legs, neck, shoulder, rump, and flank—will be tougher than the less-used muscles in the ribs and loin.

It is to your advantage to become familiar with the various cuts of meat so that you can cook them properly and achieve the best results. For instance, you don't need to buy expensive top round for stew, when less expensive neck, shank, and chuck will produce a richer, heartier flavor and overall better results. Save the more tender cuts for frying, roasting, and grilling.

Tough cuts can be tenderized, improving their palatability and usefulness. Meat can be tenderized mechanically or chemically. Mechanical tenderizing involves breaking up tough meat fibers by pounding, cubing, scoring, or grinding. Chemical tenderizing softens the fibers by using enzymes, acid marinades, or moist heat cooking. Using enzymes isn't a modern development, but has been used for generations. Certain fruits contain protein digestive enzymes that are useful in tenderizing meats. Papaya juice contains the enzyme papain, and pineapple has one called bromelain, which are both very effective in breaking down tough meat fibers. Many commercial tenderizers are simply crystalline forms of these enzymes. Vinegar, lemon juice, and wine are acidic. The acids break down the fibers.

Marinating, by itself, isn't an effective method of tenderizing because the juices of the marinade barely penetrate the surface of the meat. Combining the marinade with mechanical tenderizing, such as scoring, greatly improves the results, allowing the marinade to penetrate deeper into the meat.

Meat should be marinated for at least 4 hours and as long as overnight. Marinating longer than 24 hours is not recommended because it causes the meat fibers on the surface to break down too much, resulting in a mushy texture.

A heavy-duty plastic bag is convenient for marinating; a glass utility dish may also be used. Select dishes in which the meat will fit snugly but lie flat. Turn meat occasionally during marinating so that all sides are equally exposed to the marinade.

Quick, dry cooking (frying, broiling, grilling) dries out and toughens meat. The less you cook the meat, the more tender it will be. For best results, cheaper, tougher cuts of meat should be marinated/tenderized and cooked no more than medium rare. Very tough meat, like brisket and pot roast, can be made deliciously tender with slow moist cooking by boiling. Slow moist cooking breaks down the tough connective tissue so that the meat melts in your mouth. It is the most effective way to soften tough cuts of meat.

STEAKS
How to Broil Beef Steaks

Prime cuts of beef, such as tenderloin, T-bone, Porterhouse, sirloin, top loin, and rib eye, all produce great results when broiled. If the steak has fat along the outer edge, cut the fat diagonally at 1-inch (2-cm) intervals, without cutting into the meat. This will prevent the steak from curling while it is cooking.

Set the temperature of the oven to broil or 550° F (280° C). Place the steaks on the rack in the broiler pan. When placed into the oven, the medium-thick steaks (¾ to 1 inch/1.5 to 2 cm) should be 2 to 3 inches (5 to 7 cm) from the heating element. Thick steaks (1 to 2 inches/2 to 5 cm) should be 3 to 5 inches (7 to 12 cm) from the heat.

Broil until the surface of the steaks are brown, then turn and broil the other side until brown. See the chart on the following page for total cooking times.

The internal temperature for rare steaks is 140° F (60° C), medium rare 145° F (63° C), and medium 160° F (70° C). It is generally not recommended to cook more than medium.

Beef Cooking Chart

Type of Beef	Size	Cooking Method	Cooking Time	Internal Temperature
Rib Roast, bone in	4 to 6 lbs 1.8 to 2.7 kg	Roast 325° F 170° C	23-25 min/lb 25-27 min/0.5 kg	
Rib Roast, boneless rolled	3 to 4 lbs 1.3 to 1.8 kg	Roast 325° F 170° C	28-30 min/lb 31-33 min/0.5 kg	
Chuck Roast, Brisket	2.5 to 4 lbs. 1.1 to 1.8 kg	Braise* 325° F 170° C	2-3 hours	Medium rare 145° F 63° C
Round or Rump Roast	4 to 6 lbs 1.8 to 2.7 kg	Roast 325° F 170° C	30-35 min/lb 33-39 min/0.5 kg	Medium 160° F 70° C
Tenderloin, whole	¾ in. thick 1.9 cm	Roast 425° F 220° C	45-60 min total	
Steaks	1 to 1.5 in. thick 2.5 to 3.8 cm	Broil/Grill	4-5 min per side	Well Done 170° F 76° C
Stew or Shank Cross Cuts	4 in. long 2 in thick	Cover with liquid, simmer	2-3 hours	
Short Ribs	10 cm long, 5 cm thick	Braise* 325° F 170° C	1.5 to 2.5 hours	
Hamburger patties, fresh	4 oz/110 g	Grill, broil, or fry	3-5 min per side	160° F 70° C

*Braising is roasting or simmering less-tender meats with a small amount of liquid in a tightly covered pan.

How to Pan-Fry the Perfect Steak

Pan-frying is a great way to cook prime cuts of steak, especially those that are marbled in fat. Fat improves the flavor of the meat, and pan-frying allows the steak to cook in its own juices as opposed to losing them through the grates of a grill or rack of a broiling pan. Although cooking a steak in a frying pan is easy, unless you follow a few simple steps, you can ruin a choice cut of meat.

The secret to great tasting pan-fried steaks is to sear the outside surfaces of the steak while leaving the inside slightly red. Searing gives a nice flavor to the outer surfaces of the steak, sealing in the juices for a deliciously juicy steak. You don't want to cook it too long, medium rare to medium is ideal. The less you cook the steak, the more tender and juicy it will be.

Start with a prime cut of steak from the rib, short loin, or sirloin section of beef (see pages 165-166). The best cuts are richly marbled in fat and are a nice pink color. A dark red color indicates the meat may be old.

Allow the steak to come to room temperature. You don't want to cook a piece of meat that has a cold or frozen center. If it is frozen, make sure it is thoroughly thawed and at room temperature before cooking. To warm a refrigerated steak, let it sit, covered, at room temperature for 20 to 30 minutes. Do not rinse the meat in water. If it becomes wet, dry it off with a paper towel before cooking. If the steak is wet, it will steam rather than sear.

Heat a skillet to medium-high. It is important that you use fairly high heat to sear the outside of the steak. Add 1 tablespoon (14 g) of coconut oil or lard to the pan followed by 1 tablespoon (14 g) of butter. The oil or lard is used to prevent the meat from sticking to the pan, the butter is use solely for flavor. Sprinkle salt and black pepper on both sides of the steak and place it into the hot pan. The salt is helpful at this stage because it will help draw out moisture from the surface of the steak, allowing the surface to sear and lock the moisture inside.

Let the meat cook undisturbed for about 5 to 7 minutes or until the meat is nicely seared. Do not move the steak around or flip it from side to side. Let it sit and cook. Do not cover. When the first side is finished cooking, flip and cook the other side for 5 to 7 minutes. One of the tricks of pan-frying a great steak is to turn it only once.

Do not cook other foods in the same pan alongside the steak. Cook the steak separately. Cook vegetables in another pan or, preferably, in the same pan with the meat juices after removing the steak.

Remove the meat from the pan and allow it to sit for a few minutes before eating. When meat is put into a hot pan, it tends to tense up. Resting for a few minutes allows the meat to relax and soften and brings out the flavor. Top with a dollop of butter, if desired, and serve.

Cooking time will vary due to the thickness of the meat and how much you want it cooked. Obviously, a 1-inch (2.5-cm) steak will take less time to cook

Broiling Times for Steaks (minutes)			
Cut	**Rare**	**Medium Rare**	**Medium**
T-bone			
1-inch (2.5 cm)	20	22	25
1½ inches (3.8 cm)	30	32	35
Porterhouse			
1 inch (2.5 cm)	20	22	25
1½ inch (3.8 cm)	30	32	35
Tenderloin (filet mignon)			
4 ounces (113 g)	10	12	15
8 ounces (226 g)	15	17	20
Top Loin			
1 inch (2.5 cm)	15	17	20
1½ inches (2.8 cm)	25	27	30
2 inches (5 cm)	35	40	45
Sirloin			
1 inch (1.5 cm)	20	22	25
1½ inches (2.8 cm)	30	32	35
Ribeye			
1 inch (1.5 cm)	15	17	20
1½ inches (2.8 cm)	25	27	30
2 inches (5 cm)	35	40	45

than a 2-inch (5-cm) steak and a rare steak less time than a medium cooked one. With experience you will be able to judge very accurately how long to cook a steak. A helpful aid in determining the doneness of a steak is the finger test, see following page.

How to Tell When Your Steak Is Done (The Finger Test)

There are various methods cooks use to tell if a steak has reached the desired level of doneness during the cooking process. Most inexperienced cooks will simply take a knife and cut into the center of the steak and look inside. This is not recommended. Once you cut into the steak, the juices escape, juices that you want kept inside the steak. Another approach is to measure the temperature at the center of the steak. This requires inserting a meat thermometer into the steak, but again, this releases the juices.

Most experienced cooks rely on the finger test. This test relies on touch, and allows you to compare the firmness of your thumb muscle to that of a steak at various stages of cooking. It takes a little practice, but once you get the feel for it, it is a good way to determine doneness.

Raw

With your hand open and relaxed, press the muscle at the base of your thumb. It feels soft and fleshy. The firmness of this muscle is about the same as if you pressed on a raw steak.

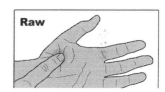

Rare

Bring the tip of your first (index) finger to the tip of your thumb, making a circle. Press the muscle at the base of your thumb. This position requires the muscle at the base of the thumb to tighten slightly. The firmness of this muscle is about the same as a rare steak.

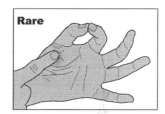

Medium Rare

Press the tip of your second (middle) finger to the tip of your thumb. The muscle at the base of your thumb tightens up more. It will still feel soft, but not squishy. In this position the muscle feels like a medium rare steak.

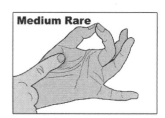

Medium

Without straining, press the tip of your third (ring) finger to the tip of your thumb. Pressing the muscle at the base of your thumb gives you an indication of the firmness of a medium cooked steak.

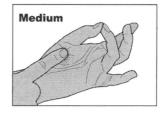

Well Done

Press the tip of your fourth (pinkie) finger to the tip of your thumb. It will feel firm. The amount of pressure required to make an indentation in the muscle at the base of your thumb is about the same as if you pressed on a well done steak.

How to Grill the Perfect Steak

If you want a great steak, you need to start with a prime cut of beef. An economy cut will produce substandard results. The best steaks for the grill are the prime cuts—rib eye, T-bone, Porterhouse, tenderloin, New York strip, top loin, and sirloin. These cuts produce the tastiest and most tender steaks. It can be bone-in or boneless, although the bone tends to add flavor.

It's best to get a thick steak, 1½ to 2 inches (4 to 5 cm). The thickness is not just about quantity, but about flavor. If the steak is too thin, it is very difficult to get the contrast between a perfectly seared exterior and a soft, tender, juicy interior. Once you get the right amount of searing on the outside, the inside of a skinny steak will be cooked too much, unless you like your steak well done—a tragedy for a high-end steak. A 1½- to 2-inch steak may weigh 12 ounces (340 g) or more. This is a lot of meat. It is better to cook one large steak and share it between two people than it is to grill two smaller steaks.

Before cooking, remove the steak from the refrigerator, cover, and let sit for 20 to 30 minutes to bring it to room temperature. A cold center delays cooking, increasing the chance of a raw center when the outside is done.

Heat your grill to high. Brush the steak on both sides with oil and season liberally with salt and black pepper. The oil will prevent the steak from sticking to the grill, and the salt will help pull out moisture from the surface of the meat to seal in the juices. Place the steak on the grill and cook until seared, 5 to 6 minutes. Searing makes steaks delicious because it seals in juices and enriches the flavor. The perfect steak should have a crusty, lightly charred exterior surrounding a core of lightly pink, juicy, tender meat that extends from edge to edge.

Use tongs to place your steak on the grill, turn it, and remove it (wash the tongs after they have touched raw meat). Do not use a fork. A fork will puncture the steak, releasing the juices and drying out the meat. In addition, if the steak is richly marbled, the juices will be full of grease that will fall into the coals or burner, causing flare-ups that can leave your expensive steak seriously charred in a matter of seconds.

Although some people like their steaks medium well or even well done, the longer a steak is cooked, the less tender it becomes, and frankly, less tasteful. Medium rare to medium is enough to safely cook the meat but still keeps it tender and delicious. Since it is difficult to judge the temperature on a grill, cooking time may vary. Use the finger test to check for doneness.

Remove the meat from the pan and allow it to sit for at least 5 minutes before eating. When meat is exposed to high temperatures it tends to tense up. Resting for a few minutes allows the meat to relax and soften and brings out the flavor.

STEAK SAUCES

Generally, all a good quality steak needs for seasoning is salt and black pepper. High quality steaks, when properly cooked, taste terrific all by themselves, however, sometimes you may want something a little different. Here are a few steak sauces you can try. You don't need to restrict them to just prime cuts, they can enhance the more economical cuts as well.

Barbecue Sauce

1 tablespoon (15 ml) extra virgin olive oil
1 small onion, finely chopped
2 tablespoons (32 g) tomato paste
1 teaspoon chili powder
1 teaspoon ground cumin
¾ teaspoon garlic powder
¾ teaspoon dry mustard
¼ teaspoon nutmeg
⅛ teaspoon cayenne pepper
1½ cups (350 ml) tomato sauce
1½ tablespoons (23 ml) apple cider vinegar
2 teaspoons Worcestershire sauce

Heat oil in a small saucepan over medium heat. Sauté onion until it begins to turn golden brown, about 8 minutes. Stir in all the remaining ingredients and simmer, stirring occasionally for about 8 minutes. Use immediately or store in an airtight container in the refrigerator.

Yield: about 2 cups (448 g)
Per serving (2 tablespoons/28 g): 1 g fat; 1.5 g net carbs; 0.5 g protein; 17 calories

Horseradish Mustard Sauce

1 tablespoon (14 g) prepared horseradish
1 tablespoon (11 g) Dijon mustard
¼ cup (60 ml) buttermilk
2 tablespoons (28 g) sour cream
1 teaspoon freshly ground black pepper
½ teaspoon salt

Thoroughly mix all ingredients in a small bowl. Recipe makes enough for 2 to 4 steaks.

Yield: about 8 tablespoons (112 g)
Per serving (2 tablespoons/28 g): 1.5 g fat; 1.5 g net carbs; 1 g protein; 23 calories

Mustard Shallot Sauce

¼ cup (60 ml) extra virgin olive oil
¼ cup (44 g) Dijon mustard
¼ cup (60 ml) red wine vinegar
2 medium shallots, chopped
¾ teaspoon salt

Combine all ingredients into a blender and blend until smooth. Pour over steak and hot cooked vegetables.

Yield: about 1 cup (224 g)
Per serving (2 tablespoons/28 g): 7 g fat; 1 g net carbs; 0.5 g protein; 69 calories

Chimichurri Sauce

This is a traditional steak sauce in Argentina. It a tangy, brightly colored sauce with herbs, garlic, and vinegar. In Argentina, grilled meats are always served with a side of chimichurri sauce.

1 cup (60 g) packed fresh Italian parsley leaves
2 medium garlic cloves, crushed or minced
¼ cup (4 g) packed fresh cilantro
2 tablespoons (8 g) fresh chopped oregano leaves
   (or 2 teaspoons dried oregano)

¼ cup (60 ml) red wine vinegar
¼ teaspoon red pepper flakes
¼ teaspoon salt
½ cup (120 ml) extra virgin olive oil

Combine parsley, garlic, cilantro, oregano, vinegar, red pepper flakes, and salt in a food processor. Process until finely chopped, stopping and scraping down the sides of the bowl with a rubber spatula as needed. With the processor running, add oil in a steady stream. Scrape down the sides of the bowl and pulse a few times to combine. Transfer sauce to an airtight container and refrigerate for at least 2 hours and up to 24 hours to allow the flavors to blend. Stir before serving. Will last refrigerated for up to 1 week.

Yield: about 1 cup (224 g)
Per serving (2 tablespoons/28 g): 14.5 g fat; 1 g net carbs; 0.5 g protein; 136 calories

Provolone Sauce

2 tablespoons (28 g) butter
½ cup (120 ml) heavy cream
2 cups (225 g) shredded provolone cheese
¼ cup (20 g) grated Parmesan cheese
½ teaspoon salt
¼ teaspoon fresh ground black pepper

In a small saucepan, melt butter over medium heat. Stir in cream. Turn the heat to low and add the cheeses, salt, and black pepper. Stir constantly for 4 to 5 minutes, until cheese is melted and sauce is thickened.

Yield: about 4 servings
Per serving: 15.5 g fat; 1.5 g net carbs; 11 g protein; 189 calories

Shallot Steak Sauce

This is a thin sauce made in the juices of a pan-fried steak.

3 tablespoons (30 g) minced shallots
2 tablespoons (30 ml) drippings from a broiled or pan-fried steak
½ cup (60 ml) beef broth
2 tablespoons (30 ml) red wine vinegar
1 tablespoon (4 g) minced fresh parsley (optional)

Sauté shallots in steak drippings over moderate heat for 3 to 5 minutes, or until limp. If you don't have enough drippings to make 2 tablespoons (30 ml) worth, add butter. Add beef broth, vinegar, and parsley and bring to a gentle boil for about 5 minutes.

Yield: 3 servings, ¼ cup (60 ml) each
Per serving: 8 g fat; 2 g net carbs; 0.5 g protein; 82 calories

STEAK RUBS

Rubs can be used in place of steak sauces. Rubs are applied to the exterior surface of the meat just before cooking; they need no standing time. However, for convenience, rubs may be applied several hours in advance; the coated meat should be refrigerated until cooking time. Flavors become more pronounced the longer the rub is on the meat. You can create your own blend of seasonings for rubs or use one of the recipes here.

Emeril's Steak Rub

Celebrity chef Emeril Lagasse says this is his favorite steak rub.

2 teaspoons salt
½ teaspoon fresh ground black pepper
1 teaspoon paprika
1 teaspoon cumin
1 teaspoon chili powder

Lemon-Rosemary Rub

1½ teaspoons grated lemon peel
1 teaspoon ground dried rosemary leaves
¼ teaspoon dried thyme
¼ teaspoon salt
¼ teaspoon fresh ground black pepper
2 large cloves garlic, minced

Southwestern Rub

1½ teaspoons chili powder
1 teaspoon garlic powder
½ teaspoon dried oregano
¼ teaspoon ground cumin

Combine all ingredients and evenly coat meat before cooking. Makes enough rub to season 2 pounds (900 g) of meat.

Yield: makes enough for 2 steaks
Per serving: 0 g fat; 0.5 (or less) g net carbs; 0 g protein; 0 calories

BEEF RECIPES

Steak and Caramelized Onions with Provolone Sauce

Steak rub (below)
2 tablespoons (28 g) butter
1 large Spanish onion, thinly sliced
8 ounces (225 g) mushrooms, sliced
1 teaspoon salt
1 tablespoon (14 g) coconut oil or red palm oil
12 ounces (340 g) beef steak
Provolone Sauce (page 175)

Steak Rub:
½ tablespoons paprika
½ teaspoon chili powder
¼ teaspoon ground cumin
¼ teaspoon ground coriander
¼ teaspoon dry mustard
¼ teaspoon dried oregano
¼ teaspoon salt
¼ teaspoon black pepper

To make the rub, mix all the steak rub ingredients together and set aside.

To cook the vegetables, heat butter in a large skillet over medium heat. Sauté onion until it begins to turn light brown, about 10 to 12 minutes. Add mushrooms and continue to cook until soft, about 5 minutes. Add salt and place on warm plate. The onions and mushrooms can be added back into the skillet to warm up just before removing the steaks (as shown above).

To cook the steak, add coconut oil to the skillet. Increase heat to medium-high. Spread the steak rub evenly over the meat. Place steak in the hot skillet and cook both sides until browned, about 5 minutes per side. Serve the steak topped with the caramelized onions and Provolone Sauce.

Yield: serves 2
Per serving (with Provolone Sauce): 45 g fat; 9.5 g net carbs; 67 g protein;
711 calories

Sliced Beef with Mushroom Sauce

This recipe uses beef tenderloin or rib eye, cut into thin slices.

½ cup (35 g) thinly sliced mushrooms
2 tablespoons (20 g) chopped onion
1 teaspoon lemon juice
1 teaspoon Worcestershire sauce
⅛ teaspoon salt
1 clove garlic, crushed
¼ cup (56 g) butter
2 tablespoons (2 g) chopped fresh parsley or cilantro
2 tablespoons (28 g) butter
1 pound (454 g) beef tenderloin or rib eye steak, cut into 8 thin slices

In a small saucepan over medium heat, cook and stir mushrooms, onion, lemon juice, Worcestershire sauce, salt, and garlic in ¼ cup (56 g) butter until mushrooms are tender. Remove from heat and stir in parsley; keep sauce warm as you cook the meat.

Heat 2 tablespoons (28 g) of butter in a skillet over medium-high heat. Cook the beef, turning once, until desired doneness, about 5 to 7 minutes per side (see page 171). Serve topped with mushroom sauce along with a vegetable side dish.

Yield: 4 servings (2 slices each)
Per serving: 27 g fat; 0.5 g net carbs; 33 g protein; 377 calories

Broiled Steak with Mushrooms, Onions, and Green Peppers

8 ounces (225 g) steak
3 tablespoons (42 g) coconut oil or butter
½ medium yellow onion, chopped
1 green bell pepper, chopped
8 ounces (225 g) mushrooms, sliced
2 teaspoons soy sauce or coconut aminos
Salt
Black pepper

Broil steak as described on page 167. To cook vegetables, heat oil in a large skillet to medium heat. Sauté onion and bell pepper until the onion begins to turn golden, about 8 to 10 minutes. Add mushrooms and cook until tender. Add soy sauce and salt and pepper to taste. Serve over broiled steak.

Yield: 2 servings
Per serving: 27 g fat; 7 g net carbs; 45 g protein; 451 calories

New England Pot Roast
This pot roast can be cooked in a Dutch oven or a slow cooker. The juices and vegetables are pureed together to make a delicious gravy.

2 tablespoons (28 g) coconut oil or lard
1½ pounds (680 g) beef arm, blade, or 7-bone pot roast
1½ cups (350 ml) water
2 teaspoons salt
1 teaspoon freshly ground black pepper
1 bay leaf
¼ cup (60 g) tomato paste or 1 large tomato, chopped
4 medium carrots, cut into 1-inch (2.5-cm) pieces
4 medium stalks celery, cut into 1-inch (2.5-cm) pieces
2 medium red peppers, coarsely chopped
1 large onion, cut into fourths
4 cloves garlic
2 teaspoons dried marjoram

2 teaspoons dried basil
16 ounces (450 g) button mushrooms, whole
¼ cup (56 g) butter, softened

Heat oil in a Dutch oven over medium-high heat. Add pot roast and brown both sides. Add water, salt, black pepper, bay leaf, tomato paste, carrots, celery, red peppers, onion, garlic, marjoram, and basil. Reduce heat, cover, and simmer for 2 hours (if you are using a slow cooker, add mushrooms and cook on high for 4 hours). Check water level and add more if necessary, but don't use too much or it will make the gravy runny. Add whole mushrooms and simmer about 20 minutes or until the mushrooms are tender.

Separate the meat and mushrooms from the broth and vegetables. Remove and discard the bay leaf. Combine the broth, vegetables, and butter into a food processor or blender and puree until smooth to make the gravy. Taste and add more salt and black pepper if desired. Serve meat and mushrooms covered in gravy.

Yield: serves 4
Per serving: 59.5 g fat; 13 g net carbs; 52 g protein; 795 calories

Corned Beef and Cabbage

The corned beef you get at the store always contains sugar and sodium nitrite, which are used in the curing process. In this recipe, you make your own sugar-free, chemical-free corned beef—a much healthier option. Corned beef is normally prepared using brisket, the toughest cut of meat. In this recipe, we use a pot roast, but you can use brisket or any of the tougher cuts of meat.

Marinade (below)
1 pot roast or brisket (about 2 pounds/900 g)
1 onion, quartered
1 large carrot, coarsely chopped
1 stalk celery, coarsely chopped
4 turnips, quartered
½ teaspoon celery seed
1 teaspoon coriander seed
½ teaspoon dry mustard
½ teaspoon dill weed
1 small head cabbage, chopped into thick wedges
½ cup (120 g) butter

Marinade:
1 to 2 quarts/liters water
½ cup (150 g) kosher salt
1 cinnamon stick, broken into several pieces
1 teaspoon mustard seeds
1 teaspoon black peppercorns
8 whole cloves
8 whole allspice berries
12 whole juniper berries
2 bay leaves, crumbled
½ teaspoon ground ginger
Ice

To make the marinade: Place the water into a large 6 to 8 quart/liter stockpot along with salt, cinnamon stick, mustard seeds, peppercorns, cloves, allspice, juniper berries, bay leaves, and ginger. Cook over high heat until the salt dissolves. Remove from the heat and add the ice. Stir until the ice has melted and marinade is cool.

Once it has cooled, place the meat in a large 2 gallon zip-close bag and add the marinade. Seal the bag and lay it flat inside a casserole dish or other container, and place it in the refrigerator for 7 to 10 days. Check daily and turn the bag over to make sure both sides of the meat are equally soaked in the marinade.

To cook the meat and vegetables: After 7 to 10 days, remove the meat from the marinade and rinse well under cool water. Discard the marinade. Place the meat into a pot just large enough to hold it, add the onion, carrot, celery, turnips, cloves, celery seed, and coriander seed, and cover with water by 1 inch (2.5 cm). Set over high heat and bring to a boil. Reduce the heat to low, cover, and gently simmer for to 2 hours. Stir into the broth the mustard and dill weed. Put the cabbage on top of the meat and continue to simmer for 30 to 60 minutes or until the meat is tender. Remove from the pot and slice across the grain. Serve the corned beef with vegetables topped with butter. Save the broth and use it in another dish or drink it as a beverage or soup.

Yield: 8 servings
Per serving: 39 g fat; 10.5 g net carbs; 33.5 g protein; 527 calories

Rolled Flank Steak

A tenderized flank steak piled with vegetables and bacon and rolled up into a "roast" is delicious and amazingly tender. You will need butcher's string to tie the roll together. You can get the string from your butcher or online. Butcher's string is made from cotton and is safe to use in cooking. When you buy the steak, get the string at the same time.

1 pound (450 g) beef flank steak, butterflied
½ cup (120 ml) soy sauce or coconut aminos
2 tablespoons (30 ml) apple cider or rice vinegar
6 strips sugar-free, nitrite-free bacon
1 red bell pepper, cut into thin strips
½ cup (80 g) chopped onion
1 cup (70 g) sliced mushrooms
1 tablespoon (14 g) butter
2 teaspoon salt
¼ teaspoon black pepper
4 ounces (110 g) thinly sliced provolone cheese (optional)
1 cup (30 g) fresh spinach leaves

Butterfly the steak to make it thinner and larger. Start at one edge of the steak and cut it horizontally to within ½ inch (1.5 cm) of the opposite edge. When you open up the steak it will lie flat like a butterfly spreading its wings. The butcher can also do this for you and save you the time and trouble (highly recommended).

Tenderize the steak by placing it on a cutting board and pound it with a meat tenderizing hammer. Beat one side, slightly stretching the steak to increase its size, then flip and do the same on the other side. The steak will be thinner with a slightly larger surface area. Place the steak in a large dish or container. Mix soy sauce and vinegar, and pour the mixture over the steak, covering the

surface of the meat with the marinade. Place in the refrigerator for 4 to 12 hours, or overnight.

When you are ready to cook the steak, preheat oven to 350° F (180° C). Cook bacon in a large skillet over medium until almost crisp. Remove from the skillet and set aside. Sauté bell pepper and onion in the bacon drippings until slightly tender, about 6 minutes. Add mushrooms, butter, salt, and black pepper, and cook an additional 2 minutes. You don't need to thoroughly cook the vegetables at this point; they will finish cooking in the oven.

Remove the steak from the marinade, and hold it up for a half minute or so to let the excess marinade drip off, but do not wash it off. Lay the steak out flat on a cutting board. Layer the provolone cheese across the steak, leaving a 1-inch (2.5-cm) border around the edge. Arrange the bacon and cooked vegetables evenly over the steak. Pour any remaining bacon drippings over the vegetables. Top with a layer of raw spinach leaves.

Roll the steak firmly into a log and tie it in place with butcher's string, tying a piece of string every 3 to 5 inches (7 to 12 cm). This is the most difficult step in the process. If you have a helper, it makes the job a little easier.

Place the log in a baking dish and bake for 1 hour. Remove from the oven and let rest for 5 to 10 minutes before cutting. Serve with the meat drippings from the baking dish spooned on top. Goes well with a side salad.

Yield: 4 servings
Per serving: 31.5 g fat; 6 g net carbs; 52 g protein; 515 calories

Marinated Flank Steak with Spinach

3 cloves garlic, minced, divided
2 tablespoons (30 ml) extra virgin olive oil
1 tablespoon (15 ml) red wine vinegar
Salt
Black pepper
⅛ teaspoon red pepper flakes
1 tablespoon (14 g) coconut oil
1 pound (450 g) flank steak
¼ cup (56 g) butter
2 pounds (900 g) fresh baby spinach
Lemon juice
Grated Romano cheese

In a bowl, combine half of the garlic with the olive oil, vinegar, 1 teaspoon salt, ½ teaspoon black pepper, and the red pepper flakes. Coat both sides of the steak with the marinade, place on a plate, cover, and refrigerate at least 4 hours and as long as overnight.

When ready to cook, heat coconut oil in a large skillet over medium-high heat. Take the steak and pat dry with paper towels. Place the steak in the hot skillet and cook for about 5 minutes per side for medium rare, longer if desired. Remove the steak from the pan and set aside.

Heat the butter in the skillet over medium heat. Add the remaining garlic and cook for 1 minute. Add the spinach and cook until wilted, about 3 to 4 minutes. Remove from heat and season with salt, black pepper, and lemon juice to taste. Slice the steak thinly across the grain and serve with spinach topped with Romano cheese.

Yield: 4 servings
Per serving: 25 g fat; 4 g net carbs; 38 g protein; 393 calories

Steak and Broccoli with Vegetable Sauce

This recipe is made using one of the more economical cuts of meat, such as top round, tip, or chuck steak. A rich, chunky vegetable sauce is produced that is poured over the steak and broccoli.

1 pound (450 g) boneless beef steak
¼ cup (56 g) coconut oil, lard, or red palm oil
1 cup (230 g) crushed or stewed tomatoes
1 large onion, coarsely chopped
2 cloves garlic, whole
1 green pepper, coarsely chopped
1 red pepper, coarsely chopped
2 stalks celery, coarsely chopped
1 teaspoon dried oregano
1 teaspoon thyme
½ teaspoon celery seed
1 teaspoon salt
½ teaspoon black pepper
16 ounces (450 g) broccoli, cut into florets and steamed

Tenderize both sides of the meat with a hand held meat tenderizer or mallet, or cut crisscross patterns ⅛-inch (0.5-cm) deep on both sides. Heat the oil in a large skillet over medium-high heat. Brown both sides of the beef in the hot oil, about 5 minutes per side. Add tomatoes, onion, garlic, green and red peppers, celery, oregano, thyme, celery seed, salt, and black pepper. Reduce heat, cover, and simmer for 45 minutes or until beef is tender. Serve steaks with steamed broccoli covered with the chunky vegetable sauce. Add salt and butter to taste.

Yield: serves 4
Per serving: 21.5 g fat; 12.5 g net carbs; 39.5 g protein; 401 calories

Barbecue Beef Short Ribs

Barbecue sauce is normally high in sugar, and therefore, not suitable for a ketogenic diet. This recipe uses a homemade reduced-carb barbecue sauce that works with low-carb and keto diets. Beef ribs are generally tough and require tenderizing or a long period of moist cooking before putting them on the barbecue or in the oven to finish off.

2 pounds (900 g) beef short ribs
2 tablespoons (28 g) coconut or red palm oil

2 tablespoons (30 ml) apple cider vinegar
1 teaspoon salt
¼ teaspoon black pepper
1 teaspoon dry mustard
1 tablespoon (6 g) granulated onion
2 cloves garlic, minced
4 ounces (110 g) tomato sauce
8 ounces (220 g) crushed pineapple, with juice
1 tablespoon (15 ml) Worcestershire sauce

Put the ribs in a large pot and cover with water by about 1 inch (2.5 cm). Bring to a boil, reduce heat, cover, and simmer for 1 hour or until the meat is fork tender. Reserve the broth for another dish or use as a base for soup.

In a medium saucepan, combine oil, vinegar, salt, black pepper, mustard, onion, garlic, tomato sauce, crushed pineapple, and Worcestershire sauce. Cook over medium heat, stirring occasionally, for approximately 15 minutes until sauce has thickened. Coat the ribs in the sauce.

Transfer the ribs to a hot outdoor grill, meat side down first, and cook 8 to 10 minutes on each side. Or you can put the ribs in a casserole dish, meat side up, and cook them in the oven at 400° F (200° C) for 20 to 30 minutes. Serve with remaining sauce along with a keto vegetable side dish.

Yield: serves 6
Per serving: 18.5 g fat; 6 g net carbs; 43.5 g protein; 364 calories

Sirloin Tip Roast with Roasted Vegetables

This recipe makes plenty to share with guests or to keep for leftovers.

6 medium carrots, cut in 1-inch (2.5-cm) pieces
1 bulb fennel, chopped
12 ounces (340 g) cauliflower, chopped in 1-inch (2.5-cm) pieces
2 medium onions, cut in wedges
½ teaspoon rosemary
½ teaspoon salt
¼ teaspoon freshly ground black pepper
2 pounds (900 g) sirloin tip roast
½ cup (112 g) butter, softened

Preheat oven to 450° F (230° C). Put carrots, fennel, cauliflower, and onion in a baking dish. Sprinkle with rosemary, salt, and pepper. Place the roast on top of the vegetables. Rub the butter over the top of the roast. Insert meat thermometer, place the roast in the oven, and cook for 15 minutes. Reduce heat to 350° F (180° C) and cook until thermometer reads 145° F (63° C) for a medium rare roast, about 60 minutes. Serve slices of roast with the vegetables and meat drippings.

Yield: 10 servings
Per serving: 20 g fat; 6 g net carbs; 26 g protein; 308 calories

Zucchini-Beef Casserole

¼ cup (56 g) butter
6 ounces (170 g) ground beef
½ teaspoon salt
¼ teaspoon freshly ground black pepper
½ teaspoon oregano
½ teaspoon garlic powder
¼ cup (20 g) grated Parmesan cheese
2 medium zucchini (about 12 oz/340g), sliced
¼ cup (110 g) tomato sauce
3 ounces (85 g) Monterey Jack cheese, shredded
12 pork rinds, broken into small bite-size pieces (optional)

Preheat oven to 350° F (180° C). Heat butter in a skillet to medium heat. Sauté ground beef, onion, and bell pepper until meat is browned and vegetables slightly tender, about 5 minutes. Stir in salt, black pepper, oregano, and garlic powder, and remove from heat. Mix in Parmesan cheese and sliced zucchini. Pour zucchini mixture evenly into an 11x7x1½-inch (28x18x4-cm) baking dish. Drizzle tomato sauce over the top, followed by the Monterey Jack cheese. Bake in the oven for 45 minutes. Sprinkle pork rinds on top before serving.

Yield: 2 servings
Per serving: 43 g fat; 10 g net carbs; 43 g protein; 599 calories

Beef Espagnole

This is an excellent recipe for leftover beef roast or steak. The recipe below specifies sirloin, however, you can use a less expensive cut of meat like brisket, flank steak, and round roast or steak. If you use these cuts, they need to be cooked slowly over several hours to make them tender before they are used in this recipe.

Espagnole Sauce (page 27)
1 tablespoon (14 g) coconut oil or red palm oil
12 ounces (340 g) sirloin, cut into bite-size pieces
1 green bell pepper, cut into strips
4 ounces (110 g) mushrooms, sliced
2 tablespoons (30 ml) Worcestershire sauce
¾ cup (175 g) sour cream

Make Espagnole Sauce as directed. The sauce requires the greatest amount of time, so make it first.

Heat oil in a large skillet over medium heat. Sauté sirloin and bell pepper until meat is browned. Add mushrooms and cook until tender, about 5 minutes. Add Espagnole Sauce and Worcestershire sauce to the meat. Bring to a simmer and cook for about 5 minutes. Remove from heat and stir in sour cream.

Yield: 4 servings
Per serving: 33.5 g fat; 10 g net carbs; 38.5 g protein; 495 calories

Beef Patties Smothered in Cheese Sauce

Cheese Sauce (page 24)
2 tablespoons (28 g) coconut oil
8 ounces (215 g) ground beef

¼ teaspoon salt
⅛ teaspoon black pepper
1 medium yellow onion, cut in thin slices
4 ounces (110 g) mushrooms, sliced

Make Cheese Sauce according to directions. Heat oil in skillet over medium heat. Mix ground beef, salt, and black pepper, and shape into 2 patties. Place the patties in the skillet. Add onion slices along the sides of the patties. Cook beef patties until brown, turn, and brown the other sides. Cook onion slices, stirring occasionally, until they become tender. Add mushrooms and cook until soft.

Remove patties and place on plates, top with mushrooms and onions, and cover with Cheese Sauce. Goes well with steamed broccoli also topped with Cheese Sauce.

Yield: 2 servings
Per serving with ½ cup (120 ml) Cheese Sauce: 62 g fat; 8 g net carbs; 43 g protein; 762 calories

Beef-Cauliflower Goulash

12 ounces (340 g) boneless chuck steak
2 tablespoons (28 g) coconut or red palm oil
1 medium onion, chopped
2 medium carrots, chopped
2 cloves garlic, finely chopped
4 cups (400 g) chopped cauliflower
2 tablespoons (14 g) paprika
4 cups (950 ml) beef broth or water
1 green bell pepper, chopped
½ teaspoon caraway seeds
Salt and black pepper

Cut the meat into bite-size pieces. Heat the oil in a large saucepan or skillet over medium heat. Add the meat and brown on all sides. Remove the meat and set aside. Add onion, carrots, and garlic, and cook until onion is tender, about 5 minutes. Return the beef to the pan and add cauliflower, paprika, broth, bell pepper, and caraway seeds. Bring to a simmer, cover, and cook over low heat for 1 hour. Season with salt and pepper to taste and serve.

Yield: 4 servings
Per serving: 21.5 g fat; 10.5 g net carbs; 25.5 g protein; 337 calories

Fajita Flank Steak

There is no tortilla in this fajita, it is eaten as a steak with cooked vegetables.

12 ounces (340 g) flank or skirt steak
Marinade (below)
2 tablespoons (28 g) coconut oil
1 small onion, sliced
1 green bell pepper, thinly sliced
1 red bell pepper, thinly sliced
Salt
Black pepper

Marinade:
¼ cup (45 ml) red wine vinegar
Juice of 2 limes
2 tablespoons (30 ml) extra virgin olive oil
2 teaspoons coriander
1 teaspoon chili powder
2 cloves garlic, minced
1 teaspoon oregano
½ teaspoon ground cumin
½ teaspoon black pepper

Lay the steak out on a cutting board and beat it with a tenderizing hammer. Beat both sides. Place the steak in a glass casserole dish that will allow the steak to lie flat. Mix all of the marinade ingredients, then pour the mixture over the steak, making sure to coat both sides. Cover the dish with plastic wrap and place in the refrigerator for at least 4 hours and as long as overnight. While marinating, flip the steak over a couple of times to make sure it is evenly coated.

When you are ready to cook the steak, heat oil in a large skillet over medium heat. Remove the steak from the marinade and let excess drip off. Place the steak into the hot skillet and cook until browned, then flip and cook the other side, about 4 to 5 minutes per side. Remove the steak and keep warm. Add onion and bell peppers and sauté until tender. Add salt and black pepper to taste. Serve the steak with cooked vegetables. Goes well with a little cilantro, sour cream, and guacamole.

Yield: 2 servings
Per serving: 30 g fat; 8.5 g net carbs; 49 g protein; 500 calories

Beef and Sweet Potato Hash

"Hash" simply means a combination of chopped food. Traditional hash mixes chopped beef and potatoes. In this recipe, we use ground beef with chopped sweet potato, plus other vegetables. Sweet potatoes are moderately high in carbohydrate, so this recipe uses only a small amount—just enough to give the dish a potato taste but keeping it ketogenic.

2 tablespoons (28 g) cooking oil
3 ounces (85 g) sweet potato, chopped
3 ounces (85 g) onion, coarsely chopped
4 ounces (113 g) green beans, cut into 1-inch (2.5-cm) long pieces
4 ounces (113 g) bell pepper, chopped
6 ounces (170 g) ground beef
2 ounces (57 g) mushrooms, chopped
Salt and black pepper to taste
Soy sauce or coconut aminos to taste (optional)

Heat the oil in a skillet over medium heat. Chop sweet potato into ½-inch (1-cm) cubes. Put the sweet potato, onion, green beans, and bell pepper into the skillet, cover, and cook, stirring once or twice, for about 12 minutes, or until the vegetables are crisp tender. Stir in the ground beef, mushrooms, salt, and pepper, and cook uncovered for 4 to 5 minutes, until the meat is cooked and the vegetables are soft, but not mushy. Stir occasionally. Remove from heat, add soy sauce to taste, and serve.

Yield: 2 servings.
Per serving: 19.5 g fat; 15 g net carbs; 40 g protein; 396 calories

Hamburger Hash

Hash is commonly a pan-fried dish made using meat (often corned beef) and potatoes. In this version, we use ground beef for the meat and replace the potatoes with a chopped daikon radish. When cooked, daikon radishes have a mild taste, making them suitable low-carb substitutes for potatoes. If you don't have daikon radishes available you can also use turnips, but daikon radishes have a slightly lower carb content.

2 tablespoons (28 g) coconut oil or bacon drippings
8 ounces (226 g) ground beef
9 ounces (250 g) daikon radish, chopped in ¼-inch (0.5-cm) cubes
½ medium onion, chopped
1 green bell pepper, chopped
5 ounces (142 g) mushrooms
1 teaspoon thyme
¼ teaspoon black pepper
½ teaspoon salt
2 tablespoons Worcestershire sauce (optional)

Heat oil in a large skillet. Add ground beef, daikon radish, onion, and bell pepper, cover and cook for about 12 to 14 minutes, stirring occasionally. Add mushrooms, thyme, black pepper, and salt, and cook uncovered for another 5 to 7 minutes or until the mushrooms are cooked and vegetables are soft. Stir in Worcestershire sauce and remove from heat.

Yield: Serves 2
Per serving: 21 g fat; 11.5 g net carbs; 39.8 g protein; 413 calories

Pork

Pork is the most commonly consumed meat in the world. However, beginning in the 1970s consumption in some countries has declined somewhat because of pork's high fat content. Many consumers are opting for leaner meats. The food industry has responded to customers' preferences for leaner meats and today hogs have much less fat due to modern breeding and feeding practices.

The domestication of pigs (immature hogs) for food dates back to at least 7,000 B.C. in the Middle East. However, evidence shows that Stone Age man hunted and ate wild boar, the hog's ancestor. The earliest known pork recipe comes from a 2,000 year-old Chinese text. For generations pork has served as a food staple throughout the world.

Pork is generally produced from young animals (6 to 7 months old) that weigh from 175 to 240 pounds (79 to 108 kg). Much of a hog is cured and made into ham, bacon, and sausage. Uncured meat is called "fresh pork."

It isn't necessary to wash raw pork before cooking it. Any bacteria that might be present on the surface will be destroyed by cooking.

Never brown or partially cook pork, then refrigerate and finish cooking later, because any bacteria present wouldn't have been destroyed. It is safe to partially precook pork immediately before transferring it to the hot grill to finish cooking.

You have probably heard that pork should be well cooked to ensure its safety. Most of us learned to fear undercooked pork from our mothers, as well as from public health officials and cookbook authors who have insisted for years that pork should always be cooked well done. As a consequence, pork has been habitually served dry and overly cooked.

Storage Times for Pork Products

Product	Refrigerator 40° F/4° C	Freezer 0° F/-18° C
Fresh pork roast, steaks, chops or ribs	3 to 5 days	4 to 6 months
Fresh pork liver or variety meats	1 to 2 days	3 to 4 months
Home cooked pork; soups, stews, or casseroles	3 to 4 days	2 to 3 months
Store-cooked convenience meals	1 to 2 days	2 to 3 months
Frozen dinners & entrees	Keep frozen before cooking	3 to 4 months
Canned pork products in pantry	2 to 5 years in pantry, 3 to 4 days after opening	After opening, 2 to 3 months

These short, but safe, storage time limits will help keep refrigerated pork from spoiling. Because freezing keeps food safe indefinitely, recommended storage times are for quality only.

New guidelines for cooking pork now eliminate the special attention it has received in the past. Pork is exposed to the same types of bacteria that contaminate other meats, and the same rules of cooking apply.

So why has pork been singled out for special treatment in the past? The reason given is the potential danger of contamination from a certain parasite, the roundworm *Trichinella spiralis.* Trichinella is widely dreaded for its ability to burrow into the muscles of pigs and other livestock, infecting people who eat undercooked, contaminated meat. This was a legitimate fear at one time. In days gone by, this parasite was a much greater threat than it is today. However, improvements in pork farming and processing have virtually eliminated parasite contamination in commercially produced pork in developed countries.

It is much less likely nowadays for commercially produced pork to be contaminated with Trichinella. Even if the meat was contaminated, excessive heat is not needed to kill the parasite, ordinary cooking temperatures will adequately do the job. Exposure to a temperature of 130 degrees F (54 C) for 30 minutes, or 140 degrees F (50 C) for just 1 minute, is all that is needed. Any temperature above 140 degrees F (50 C) kills the parasite in seconds. An internal temperature of 145 degrees F (63 C), which is medium rare, is ample enough to guarantee the safety of the meat. Cooked muscle meats may be pink even after the meat has reached a safe internal temperature. If fresh pork has reached 145 °F (63 C) throughout, even though it may still be pink in the center, it should be safe. The pink color can be due to the cooking method or added ingredients.

In addition, freezing kills any parasites that may be in the pork—an advantage our ancestors didn't have. For this reason, virtually all pork and pork products sold in the US have been frozen even if they are labeled "fresh." If in doubt, when you get home from the store put your pork in the freezer for a day or two before thawing and cooking.

The US Food and Drug Administration (FDA) 2009 Food Code makes no special provisions for cooking pork. Instead, it recommends using the same times and temperatures used for all meats. For approximate cooking times, see the chart on page 196. Times are based on pork at refrigerator temperature (40° F/4° C). Remember that appliances and outdoor grills can vary in heat. Use a meat thermometer to check for safe cooking and doneness.

PORK CUTS
Shoulder

The shoulder cuts are taken from the shoulders and front legs and make up about 25 percent of the carcass weight. These cuts yield mostly roasts and steaks along with the hocks (shank or legs). The hocks usually contain the bone and make excellent stews and soups. These cuts contain the highest percentage of connective tissue in the whole animal because of the hog's extensive use of its front legs and shoulders. This is the source of most of the ground pork and sausage.

Common cuts are: arm roast, shoulder steak, shoulder roast, sausage, and hocks.

Loin

The loin provides the most prized cuts, with the tenderloin being the most tender. It consists of the back muscles and part of the ribs, making up about 22 percent of the carcass. Baby back ribs are cut from the center sections of the loin when making boneless chops and deboned whole loin. Pork chops can be cut with or without the attached rib bone.

Common cuts are: whole loin, baby back ribs, tenderloin, and pork chops.

Side

The side or belly of the hog provides spare ribs and bacon and accounts for about 23 percent of the carcass. Pork belly is streaked in fat and makes up about half of the side cuts. The belly can be eaten fresh (fresh side) or cured to make bacon.

Common cuts are: spare ribs and bacon.

Fresh Pork Cooking Chart

Cut	Thickness or Weight	Cooking Time	Minimum Internal Temp
ROASTING: Set oven at 350° F (180° C). Roast in a shallow pan, uncovered.			
Loin Roast, bone-in or boneless	2 -5 lb (0.9-2.3 kg)	20 min/ lb (0.45 kg)	145° F (63° C)
Crown Roast	10 lb (4.5 kg)	12 min/ lb (0.45 kg)	145° F (63° C)
Leg, (fresh ham) whole, bone-in	18-20 lb (8-9 kg)	15 min/lb (0.45 kg)	145° F (63° C)
Leg, (fresh ham) Half, bone-in	5-8 lb (2.3-3.6 kg)	22-25 min/lb (0.45 kg)	145° F (63° C)
Boston Butt	3-6 lb (1.3-2.7 kg)	45 min/lb (0.45 kg)	145° F (63° C)
Tenderloin, roast at 425° F (220° C)	½-1½ lb (0.23-0.68 kg)	20-27 min	145° F (63° C)
Ribs (back, country-style or spareribs)	2-4 lb (0.9-1.8 kg)	1½-2 hours	145° F (63° C)
BROILING: (4 in/10 cm from heat; turn once) or GRILLING (over direct, medium heat; turn once halfway through grilling).			
Loin Chops, bone-in or boneless	¾ -1½ in (0.6-3.8 cm)	8-9 or 12-16 min	145° F (63° C)
Loin Kabobs	1 inch (2.5 cm) cubes	10-15 min	145° F (63° C)
Tenderloin	½-1½ lb (0.23-0.68 kg)	20 min	145° F (63° C)
Ribs (indirect heat)	2-4 lb (0.9-1.8 kg)	1½-2 hours	145° F (63° C)
Ground Pork Patties	½ inch (1.3 cm)	8-10 min	160° F (70° C)
IN A SKILLET ON STOVE			
Loin Chops or Cutlets	¼-¾ inch (0.6-1.9 cm)	3-4 or 7-8 min	145° F (63° C)
Tenderloin Medallions	¼-½ inch (0.6-1.3 cm)	4-8 min	145° F (63° C)
Ground Pork Patties	½ inch (1.3 cm)	8 to 10 min	160° F (70° C)
BRAISING: Cover and simmer with a liquid.			
Loin Chops, bone-in or boneless	¼ -¾ inch (0.6-1.9 cm)	6-8 min	145° F (63° C)
Loin Cubes and Tenderloin Medallions	½-1 inch (1.3-2.5 cm)	8-10 min	145° F (63° C)
Shoulder Butt, boneless	3-6 lb (1.3-2.7 kg)	2-2½ hours	145° F (63° C)
Ribs, all types	2-4 lb (0.9-1.8 kg)	1½-2 hours	145° F (63° C)
STEWING: Cover pan; simmer, covered with liquid.			
Loin or Shoulder Cubes	1 inch (2.5 cm)	45-60 min	145° F (63° C)

Leg

This primal consists of the hind legs and makes up about 30 percent of the carcass weight. When cured and smoked, the legs produce hams, and when fresh and uncured, they produce ham roasts and steaks. Ham can be boneless or bone-in and typically are fully cooked. The lower portions of the legs are cut into hocks.

Common cuts are: ham and ham roast.

PORK RECIPES

Roast Pork

Allow about ½ pound (225 g) per person. Place the roast in a shallow roasting pan fat side up. Some recipes suggest placing roasts on a rack to keep it separated from the drippings, but you need not do that. The drippings actually keep the meat moist and add flavor. Insert a meat thermometer into the center or the thickest part of the roast, but avoid touching bone. Position the thermometer so that you can easily read it while it is in the oven. Do not add water and do not cover.

Roast the meat at 350° F (180° C) according to the chart above. You do not need to preheat the oven when cooking a roast, since doneness is determined by the temperature of the meat and not by time cooked.

Roasts are easier to carve if allowed to rest for about 10 to 15 minutes after being removed from the oven. Meat retains heat for several minutes after removal from the oven, continuing the cooking process as it rests. Therefore, the roast can be removed from the oven when the thermometer registers 5° F (2° C) lower than the desired temperature.

Lemon-Pepper Roasted Pork Tenderloin

This is a keto friendly recipe. It does not contain enough fat to be ketogenic itself, but it can be combined with ketogenic side dishes to make it such.

2 lemons, zested
1½ teaspoons salt
1 teaspoon dried thyme
1 teaspoon garlic powder
½ teaspoon black pepper
1 tablespoon (14 g) coconut oil, melted
1 pound (450 g) pork tenderloin

Preheat the oven to 425° F (220° C). In a small bowl, mix together lemon zest, salt, thyme, garlic powder, and black pepper. Drizzle the melted coconut oil over the pork tenderloin, then spread it over the meat to evenly coat. Sprinkle the lemon zest mixture evenly over all sides of the tenderloin. Put the pork in a greased baking dish, then roast it for 15 minutes, or until the center reads 145° F (63° C) on a meat thermometer. Remove from the oven and let it rest for at least 5 minutes before carving. Cut into ¼-inch (0.5-cm) slices. Serve with a squeeze of lemon along with a keto side dish.

Yield: 4 servings
Per serving: 7.5 g fat; 0 g net carbs; 29.5 g protein; 185 calories

Roasted Rolled Pork Belly with Mushroom Stuffing

Roasted Pork Belly is the next best thing to a succulent whole roasted pig. While cooking, the fatty outside layer develops a deliciously crisp coat encasing the entire roast. When you slice the roast, you reveal the tasty mushroom stuffing in the center. Since pork belly contains a lot of fat, much of it will be rendered into the baking dish, as much as a pint (470 ml). Store the drippings in the refrigerator and use whenever bacon drippings or another oil are called for in a recipe.

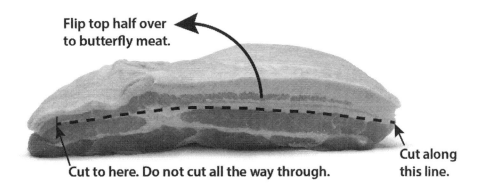

Flip top half over to butterfly meat.

Cut to here. Do not cut all the way through.

Cut along this line.

3 to 4 pounds (1360 to 1800 g) whole pork belly
4 cloves garlic, chopped
½ medium red onion
4 ounces (110 g) mushrooms, chopped
1 small carrot, finely chopped
1 tablespoon (2 g) fresh chopped rosemary leaves
½ teaspoon salt
¼ teaspoon freshly ground black pepper

Preheat the oven to 375° F (190° C). Lay the pork belly out flat on the countertop, fatty side down. It should be at least 16 inches (40 cm) long in order to roll up completely. If the pork belly is not that long (and they usually aren't), take a sharp knife and slice it lengthwise to butterfly it and open it up. Layer on top of the meaty side the garlic, onion, mushrooms, carrot, rosemary, salt, and black pepper. Leave a 2-inch (5-cm) border around the edges of the meat. Starting at the least fatty edge, tightly roll the pork belly into a log. You want the outside of the log to have the thickest layer of fat. Secure the log in place using 3 lengths of butcher's string; one near each end and one in the middle.

Put the roast in a casserole or roasting pan that has at least a 2-inch (5-cm) lip, to contain the rendered fat. Insert a meat thermometer into the center of the roast. Bake until the thermometer reads at least 160° F (70° C) and the outside layer of fat is a dark golden brown and crispy. Remove from the oven and let rest for 10 minutes. Slice and serve with a keto side dish.

Yield: about 6 servings
Per serving: 48 g fat; 2 g net carbs; 40 g protein; 600 calories

Pork Provencale

 1 clove garlic, minced
 ½ teaspoon dried basil
 ¼ teaspoon black pepper
 2 pork chops
 2 tablespoons (28 g) coconut oil
 1 tablespoon (15 ml) extra virgin olive oil
 ¼ cup (40 g) diced yellow onion
 2 zucchini, thinly sliced
 6 cherry tomatoes, halved
 ¼ teaspoon dill weed
 2 tablespoons (10 g) Parmesan cheese
 ¼ teaspoon salt

Combine garlic, basil, and black pepper, and then divide mixture in half. Press half of the seasoning mixture evenly onto both sides of the pork chops. Heat coconut oil in a large skillet over medium heat. Add pork chops and cook each side until browned, 4 to 5 minutes per side. Remove from heat and place on a warm plate to keep warm.

Put olive oil and remaining seasoning mixture into the skillet. Add onion and zucchini and cook 3 to 4 minutes, stirring occasionally. Add tomatoes and dill, and cook 1 to 2 minutes or until the zucchini is tender. Remove vegetables, sprinkle with cheese, and serve with the pork chops. Add salt to taste.

Yield: serves 2
Per serving: 42.5 g fat; 7 g net carbs; 22.5 g protein; 500 calories

Spinach-Stuffed Ham with Horseradish Sauce

 ½ cup (80 ml) chilled heavy cream
 3 tablespoons (45 g) prepared horseradish
 ½ teaspoon salt
 2 tablespoons (28 g) coconut oil
 1 medium stalk celery, chopped
 ¼ cup (120 g) chopped onion
 4 ounces (110 g) mushrooms, sliced
 8 ounces (220 g) fresh spinach
 4 teaspoon salt
 ⅛ teaspoon black pepper

2 fully cooked slices of smoked ham, ½ inch (5 cm) thick
1 tablespoon (14 g) butter, melted

Preheat oven to 325° F (170° C). While the oven is warming up, prepare the horseradish sauce. To make the sauce, beat cream until stiff peaks form. Fold in well-drained horseradish, and salt. Set aside.

To make the filling, heat oil in skillet over medium heat and sauté celery and onion until vegetables are tender. Stir in mushrooms, spinach, salt, and black pepper, and cook until mushrooms are tender.

Place 1 slice of ham in an ungreased shallow baking dish. Spread with the vegetable filling. Cover with the second slice of ham and brush with butter. Cover and bake in the oven for 15 minutes. Uncover and cook an additional 15 minutes. Serve with horseradish sauce.

Yield: 4 servings
Per serving: 26 g fat; 8 g net carbs; 22 g protein; 354 calories

Pork Chops and Green Beans

2 tablespoons (28 g) coconut oil
2 pork chops
½ medium onion, chopped
3 cups (300 g) green beans
4 ounces (110 g) mushrooms, sliced
Salt
Black pepper

Heat oil in a large skillet over medium heat. Add pork chops and cook until browned on one side. Turn pork chops over and add onion and green beans. Cook, stirring the vegetables occasionally, until chops are browned on second side and vegetables are tender. Stir in mushrooms and cook until tender, about 2 to 3 minutes. Remove from heat. Add salt and black pepper to taste. Pour meat drippings over the vegetables and serve with the chops.

Yield: 2 servings
Per serving: 34 g fat; 9 g net carbs; 22.5 g protein; 337 calories

Roasted Pork Chops and Veggies

5 ounces (150 g) cauliflower, separated into florets
5 ounces (150 g) broccoli, separated into florets
2 tablespoons (30 ml) extra virgin olive oil
3 tablespoons (42 g) butter, melted
5 cloves garlic, minced
½ teaspoon dried thyme
¼ teaspoon black pepper
½ teaspoon salt
2 pork chops
⅔ cup (50 g) shredded Parmesan cheese
2 tablespoons (8 g) chopped fresh parsley

Preheat oven to 400° F (200° C). Steam cauliflower and broccoli for about 10 minutes or until tender, but not overcooked, and set aside. In a large, self-sealing plastic bag, combine olive oil, melted butter, garlic, thyme, black pepper, and salt. Add cooked cauliflower and broccoli florets, seal bag, and thoroughly coat the vegetables with the oil mixture. Place the vegetables in a casserole dish.

Put the pork chops into the plastic bag and coat with the remaining oil mixture. Place the chops into the casserole dish, side by side with the vegetables. Pour any remaining oil mixture over the meat and vegetables and sprinkle Parmesan cheese evenly over the top. Bake for 35 to 40 minutes, until the meat is cooked and vegetables start to turn brown. Serve the chops and roasted vegetables with the pan drippings poured on top, garnished with parsley.

Yield: 2 servings
Per serving: 55.5 g fat; 8 g net carbs; 30 g protein; 651 calories

Rosemary-Lemon Pork Chops

¼ cup (60 ml) extra virgin olive oil
Juice from ½ lemon
½ teaspoons dried rosemary
4 garlic cloves, chopped
1½ teaspoon dried sage
¼ teaspoon salt
¼ teaspoon black pepper
2 pork chops
1 tablespoon (14 g) coconut oil

½ medium onion, chopped
2 zucchini, thinly sliced

In a small bowl, combine olive oil, lemon juice, rosemary, garlic, sage, salt, and black pepper. Place the chops into a shallow pan or plate and pour olive oil mixture over them, coating them on both sides. Set aside for 30 to 60 minutes.

Heat coconut oil in a large skillet over medium heat. Lift each pork chop out of the marinade and place in the hot skillet. Reserve the marinade. Cook chops until well browned, about 6 minutes per side. Remove from the skillet and place on a warm plate. Pour the remaining marinade into the skillet and sauté the onion and zucchini, stirring occasionally, until the vegetables are tender. Serve the chops with the vegetables.

Yield: 2 servings
Per serving: 49 g fat; 8.5 g net carbs; 21 g protein; 559 calories

Creamed Pork and Mushrooms

2 tablespoons (28 g) coconut oil
2 pork chops or pork steaks
½ medium onion, sliced
1 red bell pepper, sliced
1 green bell pepper, sliced
2 cloves garlic, chopped
8 ounces (225 g) mushrooms, sliced
½ cup (120 ml) heavy cream
1 teaspoon poultry seasoning
½ teaspoon salt
¼ teaspoon black pepper
¼ cup (60 g) sour cream

Heat oil in a large skillet over medium heat. Fry the pork until browned on both sides, about 5 minutes per side. Remove from the skillet and set aside. Sauté onion and bell peppers until tender, about 6 to 8 minutes. Add garlic and mushrooms, and cook until the mushrooms are soft. Return the pork to the skillet, and add cream, poultry seasoning, salt, and black pepper. Cook, stirring frequently, for about 4 minutes. Remove from heat and stir in sour cream. Serve pork covered with the vegetables and sauce.

Yield: 2 servings
Per serving: 51.5 g fat; 12 g net carbs; 24.5 g protein; 609 calories

Asparagus Divan

   1 pound (450 g) cooked asparagus
   4 slices (about 3 ounces/85 g each) sugar-free and nitrite-free ham
   1 cup hot Cheese Sauce (page 24)
   ¼ cup (20 g) grated Parmesan cheese

Preheat broiler. Arrange hot asparagus on ham slices in a shallow roasting pan. Pour Cheese Sauce over asparagus and sprinkle Parmesan cheese on top. Broil 4 inches (10 cm) from heat for 3 to 4 minutes, until sauce is speckled with brown and bubbly.

   Yield: 4 servings
   Per serving: 28.5 g fat; 5 g net carbs; 22 g protein; 364 calories

Variation:
Asparagus and Egg Divan
   Prepare Asparagus Divan, but add a very soft poached egg on top of each of the four slices of ham and asparagus, then cover with sauce and broil as directed.

   Yield: 4 servings
   Per serving: 33 g fat; 6 g net carbs; 27.5 g protein; 330 calories

Pork Parmesan

   2 tablespoons (28 g) coconut or red palm oil
   2 pork chops or pork steaks
   ½ medium onion, sliced
   1 green bell pepper, sliced
   1 medium carrot, sliced
   2 cloves garlic, minced
   2 cups (170 g) chopped and peeled eggplant
   ½ cup (120 g) crushed tomatoes
   ½ teaspoon dried oregano
   ½ teaspoon dried basil
   ½ teaspoon salt
   ¼ teaspoon black pepper
   2 tablespoons (10 g) grated Parmesan cheese

Heat oil in a large skillet over medium heat. Fry the pork until browned on both sides, about 5 minutes per side. Remove the pork from the pan and set aside. Put onion, bell pepper, and carrot into the skillet, and sauté in the pork drippings until tender. Add garlic and eggplant and cook 4 minutes, stirring occasionally. Add crushed tomatoes, oregano, basil, salt, and black pepper, and cook and stir for another 4 minutes until hot. Return the pork to the skillet to reheat. Serve pork covered with the vegetables and sauce topped with Parmesan cheese.

Yield: serves 2
Per serving: 35 g fat; 12.5 g net carbs; 23 g protein; 457 calories

Roasted pork belly.

Roasted Pork Belly with Vegetables

Roasted pork belly is delicious, and the drippings with seasonings make the vegetables stand out. As with all the recipes in this book, the nutritional values are based on the foods after they have been cooked. Pork belly, being mostly fat, reduces in size by more than half as it cooks, so a 10 ounce slice of pork belly ends up weighing less than 5 ounces.

10 ounces (280 g) uncooked pork belly
4 ounces (110 g) cauliflower, separated into florets
4 ounces (110 g) broccoli, separated into florets

4 ounces (110 g) asparagus spears
½ medium yellow onion, cut in quarters
4 ounces (110 g) whole mushrooms
½ teaspoon ground rosemary
¼ teaspoon salt
⅛ teaspoon freshly ground black pepper

Preheat oven to 425° F (220° C). Place pork belly into in a 2-quart (2-liter) casserole dish and roast for about 20 minutes. Remove the meat from the oven. Add the cauliflower, broccoli, asparagus, and onion to the casserole dish and spoon meat drippings over the vegetables until they are completely coated.

Return the meat with the vegetables to the oven and cook another 20 minutes. Add the mushrooms and continue cooking for about 10 minutes, or until the mushrooms are cooked and the fat on pork belly becomes golden and begins to turn crisp. Add salt and black pepper to taste and serve.

Yield: 2 servings
Per serving: 38 g fat; 8 g net carbs; 41 g protein; 538 calories

Spring Roll in a Bowl

This dish is like a wrapper-free spring roll served in a bowl. It can be made with pork, ham, sausage, or chicken.

¼ cup (56 g) bacon drippings or red palm oil
6 ounces (170 g) pork, ham, sausage, or chicken
1 medium onion, chopped
1 medium carrot, cut in julienne slices
1 stalk celery, cut in 2-inch (5-cm) long julienne slices
3 cups (210 g) shredded cabbage
1½ tablespoons (22 ml) soy sauce or coconut aminos
1 teaspoon rice vinegar
Salt and pepper

Heat oil in large skillet over medium heat. Sauté meat, onion, carrot, and celery for 5 minutes, or until tender. Add cabbage and continue cooking for 5 minutes until cabbage is tender. Remove from heat and add soy sauce and rice vinegar, and salt and black pepper to taste.

Yield: 2 servings
Per serving: 31 g fat; 10.5 g net carbs; 25 g protein; 421 calories

Bratwurst and cooked cabbage.

Bratwurst and Cabbage

This delicious single-skillet meal can be enjoyed for breakfast or dinner.

2 tablespoons (28 g) coconut oil
2 bratwursts or Polish sausages
1 small onion, chopped
1 green bell pepper, chopped
4 cups (360 g) chopped cabbage
Salt
Black pepper

Heat oil in a skillet over medium heat. Add sausage, onion, and bell pepper. Sauté until the vegetables are tender and sausage is browned. Stir in cabbage, cover, and cook, stirring occasionally, until tender. Add salt and black pepper to taste.

Yield: 2 servings
Per serving: 39 g fat; 11 g net carbs; 15 g protein; 455 calories

Hot Ham and Cabbage Slaw

This recipe combines freshly cooked cabbage with sauerkraut, ham, and other vegetables for a very tasty one-dish dinner.

2 tablespoons (28 g) cooking oil
½ cup (50 g) chopped fennel or sliced celery
½ medium onion, sliced
¼ green bell pepper, chopped
1 cup (116 g) chopped cooked ham
3 cups (270 g) chopped cabbage
½ teaspoon dry mustard
¼ teaspoon salt
1 cup (142 g) sauerkraut

Heat oil in a skillet over medium heat. Sauté fennel, onion, and bell pepper for about 6 to 8 minutes or until the vegetables are slightly soft. Stir in ham, cabbage, dry mustard, and salt, then cover and cook, stirring occasionally for about 5 to 6 minutes or until the cabbage is soft. Turn off the heat, layer sauerkraut on top, cover, and let sit for 1 to 2 minutes. You are not cooking the sauerkraut, just warming it up. Stir the sauerkraut into the rest of the vegetables and serve.

Yield: Serves 2
Per serving: 19.5 g fat; 10 g net carbs; 13 g protein; 267 calories

Lamb

Sheep are classified as lamb, yearling mutton, or mutton, depending on their age. The flavor of lamb is milder and the meat more tender than mutton. Lamb comes from animals that are typically less than a year old, while mutton is produced from older animals. Most lambs are brought to market at about 6 to 8 months old. A lamb weighs about 140 pounds (63 kg) and yields approximately 46 to 49 pounds (20 to 22 kg) of edible lean retail lamb cuts.

If the phrase "Spring Lamb" is on a meat label, it means the lamb was produced between March and October. The term comes from times past when lambs born in harsh winter weather would have little chance to survive until the next year. Today, with more protected animal husbandry conditions, lamb is available all the time.

Lambs are generally raised on pasture grass and coarsely ground grain. They are fed hay and feed consisting of corn, barley, milo (a type of sorghum), and/or wheat supplemented with vitamins and minerals. Lambs are usually "finished" in feedlots where they are fed specially formulated feed. While most lambs are finished on grains, some lambs are raised on pasture and are finished on grass instead of grains. Grass-finished lamb is usually distinguished on the label.

There are five basic primal cuts into which the lamb carcass is separated: shoulder, rack, shank/breast, loin, and leg. Preferably, packages of fresh lamb purchased in the supermarket should be labeled with the primal cut as well as the product, such as "shoulder roast" or "loin chop."

You often hear the term "rack of lamb." The "rack" is the primal cut more commonly known as the rib. The rack contains nine full ribs and can be split (along the backbone) into two lamb rib roasts. A "lamb crown roast" is made by sewing two rib roasts together to form a circle or crown.

Chops can come from various primal cuts. "Loin" chops come from the loin and "rib" chops come from the rack (or rib); these are the most tender and most expensive chops. "Blade" and "arm" chops (from the shoulder) and "sirloin" chops (from the leg) are less expensive, but they may be just as tender.

Lamb is aged to develop additional tenderness and flavor. Usually only the higher-quality, more expensive primals, such as racks, ribs, and loins, are aged, and these are mainly sold to restaurants. Aging is done commercially under controlled temperatures and humidity.

Lamb patties and ground lamb mixtures, such as meat loaf, should be cooked to a safe minimum internal temperature of 160° F (70° C) as measured by a food thermometer. Cook all organ and variety meats (such as heart, kidney, liver, and tongue) to 160° F (70° C). Cook all raw lamb steaks, chops, and roasts to a minimum internal temperature of 145° F (63° C) as measured with a food thermometer before removing meat from the heat source. For safety and quality, allow meat to rest for at least 5 minutes before carving or consuming. For reasons of personal preference, you may choose to cook meat to higher temperatures. For approximate cooking times for use in meal planning, see the chart on page 213.

Times are based on lamb held at refrigerator temperature (40° F/4° C). Remember that appliances and outdoor grills can vary in heat. Use a food thermometer to check for safe cooking and doneness of lamb.

After cooking bone-in lamb leg or roast, 1 pound (½ kg) of raw weight will yield 8 to 9 ounces (225 to 255 g) of edible meat. Ground lamb or boneless cuts will yield about 10.5 ounces (298 g) of edible meat.

LAMB CUTS
Shoulder
The shoulder includes the front legs, shoulders, and upper portion of the neck. These muscles get a lot of use and are full of connective tissue, making the meat tougher than most other cuts.

Common cuts are: shoulder on the bone, blade roast, blade chop, arm chop, stew meat, ground lamb, and sausage.

Breast and Foreleg
The breast is one of the most inexpensive cuts of lamb. It contains a high amount of fat and a lot of flavor. Lamb breast is cut into thin strips and is usually stuffed, rolled, and braised slowly. The foreleg or shank is the leanest cut of lamb. It is a strong muscle with a lot of connective tissues, which requires slow braising.

Common cuts are: rolled roast, riblets, and lamb shank.

Rib

The ribs produce very tender, mild-flavored meat. A rack of lamb has seven to eight ribs and can either be cut and cooked as individual chops or as a rib roast. It is one of the most prized cuts. The crown roast is composed of two or three racks tied together to form a crown.

Common cuts are: rack of lamb, crown roast, and rib chops.

Loin

The loin consists of the muscles along the lamb's back and extends from the lower ribs to the hip bone. The loin is the most highly prized and expensive of the cuts. As with beef and pork, the tenderloin is the most tender cut.

Common cuts are: loin roast, loin chops, tenderloin, and medallion.

Leg

The lamb's hind legs are sold as the traditional leg of lamb. It is sold whole, weighing 5 to 9 pounds (2 to 4 kg) or cut into sirloin and shank. The meat is lean and tender and can be cooked in a variety of ways.

Common cuts are: leg of lamb, sirloin, leg roast or steak, and cubes for kebabs.

LAMB RECIPES

Roast Leg of Lamb

5 to 7 pounds lamb leg, bone-in
3 tablespoons (42g) coconut or red palm oil, melted
Salt and freshly ground black pepper
6 cloves garlic
3 stems fresh rosemary

Take the lamb out of the refrigerator an hour before cooking and let it come to room temperature. This promotes faster and more even cooking.

Rub the entire surface of the lamb with coconut or red palm oil. Set the lamb on a roasting pan. Season liberally with salt and black pepper. Set the oven to broil. Position roast so that the top of the meat is only 3 or 4 inches (7 to 10 cm) from the heating element. Broil for 5 minutes or until the top of the lamb leg looks seared and browned. Flip the lamb over and broil the other side until browned.

Roast leg of lamb.

Remove the roast from the oven. Turn the oven to 325° F (170° C) and reposition the oven rack to the middle of the oven. Mince the garlic and rosemary leaves. Flip the lamb leg over again and rub the top with the chopped garlic and rosemary. Insert a meat thermometer into the center of the lamb. Cover the lamb loosely with foil. Put the lamb back in the oven and cook for one hour.

Remove the foil and check the temperature. If it is not yet done, return the lamb to the oven without the foil, and continue cooking. For a medium rare to medium roast, remove the lamb when the temperature reaches 140° to 145° F (60° to 63° C). Refer to the cooking chart above for general roasting times. Let it rest a few minutes before carving. Even though it is not in the oven, the internal heat will continue to cook the meat for several minutes.

To carve, turn the lamb so the bone is parallel to the cutting board. Make perpendicular slices to the bone, angling straight down until your knife hits the bone. Cut the lamb off the bone by slicing through the bottom of the slices with your knife parallel to the bone.

Serve with your choice of keto side dishes.

Yield: varies depending on the size of the roast
Per 3 ounce (85 g) serving: 18 g fat; 0 g net carbs; 14 g protein; 218 calories

Lamb Cooking Chart

Cut	Size	Cooking Method	Cooking Time
Leg, bone-in	5-7 lb (2.3-3.2 kg) 7-9 lb (3.2-4 kg)	Roast 325° F (170° C)	20-25 min/lb (0.45 kg)
Leg, boneless, rolled	4-7 lb (1.8-3.2 kg)	Roast 325° F (170° C)	15-20 min/lb (0.45 kg)
Shoulder Roast or Shank Leg Half	3-4 lb (1.4-1.8 kg)	Roast 325° F (170° C)	25-30 min/lb (0.45 kg)
Cubes, for kabobs	1-1½ in (2.5-3.8 cm)	Roast 325° F (170° C)	30-35 min/lb (0.45 kg)
Ground Lamb Patties	2 in (5 cm)	Broil/Grill	8-12 min/lb (0.45 kg)
Chops, Ribs, or Loin	1-1½ in (2.5-3.8 cm)	Broil/Grill	5-8 min/lb (0.45 kg)
Leg Steaks	¾ in (2 cm)	Broil/Grill	7-11 min/lb (0.45 kg)
Stew Meat, pieces	1-1½ in (2.5-3.8 cm)	Broil/Grill	14-18 min/lb (0.45 kg)
Breast, Rolled	1½-2 in (3.8-5 cm)	Braise* 325° F (170° C)	1½-2 hours
Shanks	¾-1 in (2-2.5 cm)	Cover with liquid; simmer	1½-2 hours

The minimum internal temperature for all cuts of meat should be 145° F (63° C) except ground lamb patties which should be 160° F (70° C).

*Braising is roasting or simmering less-tender meats with a small amount of liquid in a tightly covered pan.

Roast Leg of Lamb in a Garlic Nest

Rosemary sprigs
4 pound (1800 g) boneless leg of lamb
40 to 50 cloves garlic, unpeeled
¼ cup (60 ml) butter or coconut oil, melted
1 teaspoon salt
¼ teaspoon freshly ground black pepper

Preheat oven to 425° F (220° C). Arrange rosemary sprigs on the bottom of a roasting pan. Place the lamb on top of the sprigs and tuck the garlic around the edge. Drizzle butter over the roast, then sprinkle with salt and pepper. Insert a meat thermometer into the center of the roast.

Cook the lamb for 10 minutes, then reduce the heat to 325° F (170° C) and cover loosely with foil. Roast until the meat thermometer reads 130° F (54° C), about 1½ to 2 hours. Remove the foil and continue cooking until the thermometer reads 145° F (63° C), about 15 minutes. Let the roast rest for about 10 to 15 minutes before carving. Squeeze the roasted garlic out of their skins and serve with the pan drippings drizzled over the sliced lamb. Add a keto side dish.

Yield: 8 servings
Per serving: 48 g fat; 0.5 g net carbs; 38 g protein; 586 calories

Slow-Roasted Rolled Leg of Lamb

2 tablespoons (28 g) coconut oil
3 medium cloves garlic, minced
3 medium shallots, minced
2 tablespoons (4 g) finely chopped fresh rosemary leaves
1 tablespoon (6 g) lemon zest
½ teaspoon red pepper flakes
1 tablespoon (18 g) salt
½ teaspoon freshly ground black pepper
1 whole butterflied boneless leg of lamb (about 4 lb/1800 g)

Adjust oven rack to lower-middle position and preheat oven to 275° F (140° C). Heat oil in a small saucepan over medium heat. Add garlic, shallots, rosemary, lemon zest, and red pepper flakes. Cook, stirring occasionally, until shallots and garlic are softened, about 5 minutes. Transfer to a small bowl. Add salt and black pepper, and mix with a fork to combine.

Rub half of mixture into inside of the butterflied lamb leg. Roll leg and tie securely at 1- to 2-inch (2.5- to 5-cm) intervals with butcher's string. Rub remaining mixture over exterior of lamb.

Place lamb in a baking dish. Transfer to oven and roast until a thermometer inserted into the middle of lamb registers 125° to 130° F (51° to 54° C) if you want it medium-rare, or 130° to 135° F (54° to 57° C) for medium. Remove from oven and let rest for 30 minutes; as it rests it will continue to cook from the internal heat. The following step finishes off the cooking.

While lamb is resting, increase oven temperature to 500° F (260° C). Return lamb to oven and roast until exterior is deep brown and crisp, about 15 minutes.

Remove from oven and let rest 5 minutes. Remove string with kitchen shears, transfer lamb to cutting board, and slice into ¼-inch (0.6-cm) slices. Serve with pan drippings and a keto side dish.

Yield: 8 servings
Per serving: 52 g fat; 1 g net carbs; 38 g protein; 606 calories

Roast Lamb with Anchovies

Anchovies and lamb many sound like a strange combination, but they really work well together in this recipe. The mustard/mayonnaise coating develops a nice crust over the roast to make the meat succulent and tasty.

4 pound (1.8 kg) boneless leg of lamb
1 jar (3.35 oz/94 g) anchovies packed in olive oil
3 cloves garlic, crushed
1 teaspoon powdered rosemary
¼ cup (44 g) Dijon mustard
¼ cup (60 g) mayonnaise (pages 37-40)

Preheat oven to 425° F (220° C). Remove netting on the lamb, if present. Make cuts over the surface of the lamb ½ inch (1 cm) deep. Chop anchovy fillets into quarters, and insert the pieces into the cuts in the lamb. Place the lamb on a rack in a roasting pan. In a small bowl, mix garlic, rosemary, mustard, and mayonnaise, then spread over the surface of the roast. Cook the lamb for 30 minutes, then reduce the temperature to 350° F (180° C) and roast for about 90 minutes or until the internal temperature reaches 145° F (63° C). Serve with keto vegetables or salad to make a full meal.

Yield: 10 servings
Per serving: 18.5 g fat; 0.5 g net carbs; 53 g protein; 380 calories

Lamb Patties with Mushroom Gravy

1 tablespoon (15 ml) coconut oil or bacon drippings
6 ounces (170 g) ground lamb
2 teaspoons dried granulated onion
½ teaspoon salt
Mushroom Gravy (below)

Mushroom Gravy:
2 tablespoons (28 g) butter
1 ounce (28 g) finely chopped onion
4 ounces (110 g) mushrooms, chopped
⅓ teaspoon ground rosemary
⅓ teaspoon salt
⅓ teaspoon freshly ground black pepper
¼ cup (60 ml) heavy cream

Heat the oil in a skillet to medium heat. Combine lamb, granulated onion, and salt into 2 patties and cook, uncovered, until browned and cooked through, about 5 minutes per side. Remove the patties and set aside.

Make the gravy using the same pan. Add butter, onion, mushrooms, rosemary, salt, and pepper, and cook for 5 minutes or until the mushrooms soften. Add cream and continue to cook, stirring occasionally, until slightly thickened, about 3 to 4 minutes. Serve poured over the lamb patties along with a side of keto vegetables.

Yield: 2 patties
Per serving: 26 g fat; 3 g net carbs; 26 g protein; 350 calories

Lamb and Egg Hash

2 tablespoons (28 g) coconut oil or red palm oil
1 medium carrot, chopped
4 ounces (110 g) daikon radish, chopped
½ red onion, chopped
½ red bell pepper, chopped
2 cloves garlic, finely chopped
6 ounces (170 g) ground lamb
4 ounces (110 g) mushrooms, chopped
½ teaspoon salt
¼ teaspoon black pepper
¼ teaspoon chili powder
¼ cup (4 g) chopped cilantro
2 eggs, poached or fried

Heat oil in a skillet to medium-high heat. Sauté carrot and daikon for 5 minutes. Add onion, bell pepper, garlic, and lamb, and cook until vegetables are crisp tender, about 8 minutes. Add mushrooms, salt, black pepper, and chili powder, and cook until all the vegetables are tender, about 4 to 5 minutes. Remove from heat. Put on serving plate, and top with cilantro and a poached or fried egg.

Yield: 2 servings
Per serving: 24.5 g fat; 9 g net carbs; 33 g protein; 338 calories

Lamb Chops and Asparagus

3 tablespoons (42 g) coconut oil
2 lamb chops (3 oz/85 g each)
1 pound (450 g) asparagus, cut into bite-size pieces
Salt
Black pepper

Heat oil in a large skillet over medium heat. Add lamb chops, cover, and cook until one side is browned. Turn chops over and add asparagus. Sauté asparagus until tender and chops are cooked to your liking. Remove from heat, and add salt and black pepper to taste. Pour meat drippings over the asparagus and serve with the chops.

Yield: serves 2
Per serving: 27.5 g fat; 4 g net carbs; 29 g protein; 379 calories

Broiled Lamb Patties

These lamb patties make a novel accompaniment for eggs at breakfast or can serve as the main protein source at dinner along with your choice of vegetables.

8 ounces (225 g) ground lamb
1 tablespoon (6 g) dried granulated onion
1 tablespoon (1 g) snipped parsley
½ teaspoon salt
¼ teaspoon dried dill weed
Dash of garlic powder
4 strips sugar-free, nitrite-free bacon

Mix lamb, onion, parsley, salt, dill weed, and garlic powder. Shape mixture into 4 patties, each about 1 inch (2.5 cm) thick. Wrap a slice of bacon around the edge of each patty and secure with a wooden toothpick. Set oven control to broil or 550° F (250° C). Broil patties with tops about 3 inches (7 cm) from heat. Turn once, until done, about 6 to 8 minutes per side.

Yield: 4 patties
Per serving: 12 g fat; 0.5 g net carbs; 23 g protein; 202 calories

Lamb with Mustard Sauce

4 lamb chops, ½ inch (1 cm) thick
1 tablespoon (15 ml) Dijon mustard
1 teaspoon salt
½ teaspoon black pepper
4 strips uncooked sugar-free, nitrite-free bacon, finely chopped
¾ cup (175 ml) heavy cream
2 tablespoons (18 g) capers

Preheat oven to 350° F (180° C). While oven is heating, brush both sides of each lamb chop lightly with mustard and place them in an ungreased 9x9 x2-inch (22x22x5-cm) pan. Sprinkle chops with salt and black pepper. Sprinkle bacon over and around the chops. Bake uncovered for 60 minutes, or until the chops are cooked to your preference.

Remove chops to a warm platter and set aside. Keep drippings and bacon bits in the pan. Stir in cream and capers. Heat to boiling, stirring constantly; reduce heat. Simmer uncovered, stirring frequently, until thickened, about 8 minutes. Pour sauce over chops. The sauce also goes well poured over hot steamed vegetables.

Yield: 4 chops
Per serving: 16 g fat; 2 g net carbs; 31 g protein; 276 calories

Lamb with Sour Cream Sauce

2 tablespoons (30 ml) bacon drippings or coconut oil
1 medium onion, chopped
1 pound (450 g) lamb shoulder steak or chops
4 ounces (120 g) mushrooms, chopped
⅓ cup (80 ml) chicken or beef broth
½ teaspoon paprika

¼ teaspoon salt
¼ teaspoon dried dill weed
⅓ teaspoon black pepper
½ cup (115 g) sour cream

Heat oil in large skillet to medium heat. Add onion and cook until tender, then remove. In the same pan, cook lamb until each side is a golden brown, turning only once. Return the onion to the pan, then add mushrooms, broth, paprika, salt, dill weed, and black pepper. Cover and simmer until lamb is tender, about 40 minutes. Check liquid level occasionally, and add more broth or water if needed. Remove from heat and stir in sour cream until well blended. Serve lamb covered in the sour cream sauce.

Yield: 4 servings
Per serving: 21 g fat; 4 g net carbs; 33.5 g protein; 339 calories

Shepherd's Pie

Shepherd's Pie originated in England and is traditionally made with lamb. However, you can make a less expensive version using ground beef or pork. In the United States it is commonly made with ground beef. In England and Australia they call the beef dish a "cottage pie." Regardless of what you call it, Shepherd's Pie is basically a casserole with a layer of cooked meat and vegetables, topped with mashed potatoes, and baked in the oven. Of course, in our version we use cauliflower in place of the potatoes.

2 tablespoons (28 g) coconut oil or bacon drippings
12 ounces (340 g) ground lamb
1 cup (160 g) chopped onion
2 carrots, thinly sliced
1 cup (100 g) chopped green beans
1 cup (100 g) chopped celery
3 cloves garlic, minced
½ teaspoon salt
¼ teaspoon freshly ground black pepper
½ teaspoons dried rosemary
½ teaspoon dried thyme
¼ cup (60 ml) tomato sauce
1 teaspoon Worcestershire sauce
2 cups (200 g) chopped cauliflower
6 tablespoons (84 g) butter

½ teaspoon salt
¼ teaspoon onion powder
8 ounces (225 g) sharp cheddar cheese, shredded

Preheat oven to 375° F (190° C). Place oil in a skillet over medium heat. Add lamb, onion, carrots, green beans, and celery, and sauté until the meat is browned and vegetables are slightly tender, about 6 to 8 minutes. Add the garlic and cook another 1 to 2 minutes. Remove from heat and stir in salt, black pepper, rosemary, thyme, tomato sauce, and Worcestershire sauce. Pour into a casserole dish.

Put the cauliflower into a food processor and chop to rice-size pieces. Mix cauliflower with butter, ½ teaspoon salt, onion powder, and shredded cheese. Spoon the cauliflower mixture over the top of the filling in the casserole dish. Bake for 30 minutes.

Yield: 4 servings
Per serving: 45.5 g fat; 10 g net carbs; 40.5 g protein; 611 calories

Curried Lamb

You can use fresh or cooked lamb for this recipe. This is a good way to use leftover lamb roast. This dish consists of a curry sauce that is served over sautéed lamb and zucchini.

2 tablespoons (28 g) butter
1 medium onion, chopped
1 tablespoon (6 g) minced fresh ginger
2 cloves garlic, minced
¼ to ½ teaspoon red pepper flakes
2 medium tomatoes, diced
1 teaspoon ground cinnamon
½ teaspoon salt
¼ teaspoon black pepper
2 tablespoons (12 g) ground coriander
2 tablespoons (14 g) ground cumin
½ teaspoon ground turmeric
1 cup (240 ml) lamb, beef, or chicken broth
½ cup (8 g) chopped fresh cilantro
2 tablespoons (28 g) coconut oil
12 ounces (340 g) lamb, cut into bite-size pieces
2 medium zucchinis, sliced
1 cup (230 g) sour cream

Melt butter in a large skillet over medium heat. Add onion and sauté until it turns golden, about 10 to 15 minutes. Add ginger and garlic, and cook for another 2 minutes. Add red pepper flakes, tomatoes, cinnamon, salt, black pepper, coriander, cumin, turmeric, and broth, and simmer for 6 to 8 minutes to blend flavors.

Remove from heat and let cool slightly. Add cilantro and puree in a food processor until smooth. Set aside.

Heat coconut oil in skillet over medium heat. Sauté lamb (raw or cooked) and zucchini until meat is browned and zucchini is tender. Turn heat to medium-low, stir in the curry puree, and simmer for 3 to 4 minutes until hot. Stir in sour cream. Remove from heat and serve.

Yield: 4 servings
Per serving: 32.5 g fat; 11 g net carbs; 29.5 g protein; 454 calories

Rogan Josh

This is an aromatic lamb curry that originated in Persia. The Asian spices, like cardamom and coriander, give this dish it characteristic aroma and flavor.

2 tablespoons (28 g) coconut or red palm oil
1 pound (450 g) lamb, cut into bite-size pieces
1 large onion, chopped

2 stalks celery, chopped
2 carrots, chopped
¼ cup (56 g) butter
1 piece fresh ginger, 2 inches (5 cm) peeled and chopped
8 cloves garlic, chopped
¼ teaspoon ground cloves
¼ teaspoon black pepper
¼ teaspoon ground cinnamon
3 teaspoons ground cardamom
1 teaspoon ground coriander
2 teaspoons ground cumin
4 teaspoons paprika
⅓ teaspoon cayenne pepper
1 teaspoon salt
¾ cup (175 ml) water
½ cup (115 g) plain yogurt or sour cream
4 cups (480 g) Cauliflower Rice (page 112)
2 tablespoons (28 g) coconut oil

Heat oil in a large skillet over medium heat. Sauté lamb, onion, celery, and carrots until the meat is browned and vegetables are tender, about 12 to 15 minutes. Add butter, ginger, garlic, cloves, black pepper, cinnamon, cardamom, coriander, cumin, paprika, cayenne pepper, and salt, and continue cooking, stirring frequently, for about 2 minutes. Add water, reduce heat, cover, and simmer for 10 to 15 minutes to allow flavors to blend. Remove from heat and stir in yogurt.

Prepare Cauliflower Rice according to the directions on page 112. Heat oil in a separate skillet over medium heat. Cook Cauliflower Rice, stirring frequently, until tender, about 5 minutes.

Serve Cauliflower Rice topped with the lamb curry.

Yield: 4 servings
Per serving: 28 g fat; 11 g net carbs; 37 g protein; 426 calories

Lamb Ragout with Cauliflower

1 lamb shank (about 1 lb/450 g)
1 small head cauliflower (about 20 oz/560 g), cut into florets
¼ cup (56 g) coconut or red palm oil
2 stalks celery, chopped
1 carrot, chopped
1 medium onion, chopped
1 red bell pepper, chopped
4 cloves garlic, chopped
1 cup (240 ml) crushed tomatoes
1 tablespoon (2 g) finely chopped fresh rosemary or ½ teaspoon
    powdered rosemary
½ teaspoon Italian seasoning
2 teaspoons salt
½ teaspoon black pepper

Put the lamb shank in a pot and add enough water to cover it by about 1 inch (2.5 cm). Bring the water to a boil, reduce heat, cover, and simmer for 3 to 6 hours, or until the meat is tender. Check the meat occasionally to make sure that the water level does not drop below about 2 cups (470 ml). When done, remove the meat from the bone, cut into bite-size pieces, and set aside, but keep warm. Reserve 2 cups (470 ml) of the broth.

Put cauliflower into a steamer and cook until tender. Remove from heat, but keep warm.

Heat oil in a large skillet over medium heat. Sauté celery, carrot, onion, and bell pepper until tender, about 10 minutes. Add garlic and continue cooking for 3 to 4 minutes. Stir in the reserved broth, crushed tomatoes, rosemary, Italian seasoning, salt, and black pepper, and simmer for 15 minutes. Remove from heat. Puree vegetables in a blender or food processor until smooth. Stir lamb into the hot vegetable sauce. If needed, reheat sauce in the skillet until hot. Serve the sauce over steamed cauliflower. Garnish with parsley.

Yield: 4 servings
Per serving: 23 g fat; 12.5 g net carbs; 39 g protein; 413 calories

Poultry

Poultry refers to domesticated birds such as chickens, turkeys, ducks, and geese that are raised for their eggs and meat. Chicken is by far the most popular worldwide for both eggs and meat.

The chicken is a descendant of the Southeast Asian red jungle fowl first domesticated in India around 2,000 B.C. Broiler-fryers, roasters, stewing/ baking hens, capons, and Rock Cornish hens are all chickens. The following are definitions for each of these:

- Broiler-Fryer: a young, tender chicken about 7 weeks old; weighing 2½ to 4½ pounds (1 to 2 kg). Can be cooked by any method—fried, broiled, roasted, braised, grilled, or stewed.
- Rock Cornish Game Hen: a small broiler-fryer; weighing between 1 and 2 pounds (½ to 1 kg). Usually stuffed and roasted whole.
- Roaster: a young chicken between 8 and 12 weeks of age that is prepared ready-to-cook, weighing about 5 pounds (2.2 kg). It yields more meat per pound than a broiler-fryer. Usually roasted whole.
- Capon: a young castrated male chicken about 16 weeks to 8 months old. They weigh about 4 to 7 pounds (1.8 to 3 kg) and have generous quantities of tender, light meat, and are usually roasted.
- Stewing/Baking Hen: a mature laying hen 10 months to 1½ years old. Since the meat is less tender than young chickens, it's best when used in moist cooking such as stewing.
- Cock or Rooster: a mature male chicken with coarse skin and tough, dark meat. Requires long, moist cooking.

Storage Times		
Poultry Item	**Refrigerator Storage**	**Freezer Storage**
Fresh whole poultry	1 to 2 days	Fresh whole poultry
Fresh poultry parts	1 to 2 days	Fresh poultry parts
Ground poultry, giblets	1 to 2 days	Ground poultry, giblets
Cooked poultry	3 to 4 days	Cooked poultry
Cooked poultry dishes	3 to 4 days	Cooked poultry dishes
Poultry broth, gravy	3 to 4 days	Poultry broth, gravy
Lunch meat	unopened 2 weeks; opened 3 to 5 days	Lunch meat

Turkey is a large, widely domesticated North American bird with white plumage and a bare, wattled head and neck. The name *turkey* was originally applied to an African bird now known as the guinea fowl, which was believed to have originated in Turkey. When the Europeans came upon the American turkey, they thought it was the same bird as the African guinea fowl, and so they gave it the name "turkey," although the two species are quite distinct.

The sex designation of "hen" (female) or "tom" (male) turkey is optional on the label, and is an indication of size. Toms are larger but both toms and hens should be equally tender. Turkeys of either sex that are less than 8 months of age according to present regulations are considered "young" turkeys. Prepared turkeys are much larger than chickens and other poultry weighing between 4 to 20 pounds (1.8 to 13 kg) or more. Turkey can be purchased whole or cut in half or quartered or cut up into individual pieces—breast, legs, and such.

Other kinds of farm-raised poultry include ducks, geese, quail, pheasant, and guinea fowl. These birds are less commonly found in the market and are generally significantly more expensive. Broiler or fryer duckling is a very young duck weighing about 3 pounds (1.3 kg). Roaster duckling is slightly older (8 to 16 weeks) weighing 3 to 5 pounds (1.3 to 2.3 kg). Young geese weighing 4 to 14 pounds (1.8 to 6.3 kg) are best roasted. Most poultry has enough fat of their own to ensure succulence when roasted, but guinea fowl, pheasant, and some game birds may not. To improve succulence, cover or wrap the bird in sheets of fat back, bacon, or thinly sliced fresh pork side before roasting to keep the meat moist and juicy.

SAFE HANDLING
Storage
Store poultry products in a refrigerator that maintains 40° F (4° C) or below, or freeze at 0° F (-18° C) or below. Freezer storage times are for best quality. If frozen continuously, poultry products will be safe indefinitely.

Thawing

Poultry must be kept at a safe temperature during thawing. While frozen, poultry is safe indefinitely. However, as soon as it begins to thaw, any bacteria that may have been present before freezing can begin to grow again.

A package of frozen meat left thawing on the counter more than 2 hours is not at a safe temperature. Even though the center of the package may still be frozen, the outer layer of the food is in the danger zone between 40° and 140° F (4° and 60° C), the temperatures where foodborne bacteria multiply rapidly.

The two safest ways to thaw poultry are in the refrigerator and in a cold water bath. When thawing poultry in the refrigerator, plan ahead and allow approximately 24 hours for each 4 to 5 pounds (1.8 to 2.3 kg) in a refrigerator. Place the poultry in a container to prevent the juices from dripping on other foods.

Thawed poultry can remain in the refrigerator for 1 or 2 days before cooking. Foods thawed in the refrigerator can be refrozen without cooking, but there may be some loss of quality. When thawing poultry using a cold water bath, allow about 30 minutes per pound (0.5 kg). Be sure the meat is in a leak-proof plastic bag to prevent cross-contamination and to prevent the package from absorbing water. Submerge the wrapped meat in cold tap water. Cook it immediately after it is thawed. After cooking, poultry can be refrozen.

Poultry Thawing Chart		
Size	In the Refrigerator	In Cold Water
4 to 12 lb (2 to 5.5 kg)	1 to 3 days	2 to 6 hours
12 to 16 lb (5.5 to 7 kg)	3 to 4 days	6 to 8 hours
16 to 20 lb (7 to 9 kg)	4 to 5 days	8 to 10 hours
20 to 24 lb (9 to 11 kg)	5 to 6 days	10 to 12 hours
In the refrigerator approximately 24 hours for every 4-5 lb (1.8-2.3 kg). In cold water approximately 30 min per lb (½ kg).		

HOW TO ROAST POULTRY

Roasting Instructions for Whole Birds

Set the oven temperature no lower than 325° F (170° C). The oven should be preheated so that you have an accurate estimate of cooking time.

Be sure the bird is completely thawed. The cooking times in the roasting chart are based on fresh or completely thawed birds at refrigerator temperature.

Remove the paper wrapped giblets, and neck if present, from the body cavity. These will be cooked separately.

Place the bird breast-side up in a shallow roasting pan, 2 to 2½ inches (5 to 6.5 cm) deep.

If using stuffing (low-carb of course), fill the body cavity just before placing it in the oven. Tie or skewer the drumsticks to the tail if not already held in place with a nylon or metal hock lock.

Brush with melted butter, coconut oil, or other fat.

Insert a meat thermometer into the thickest part of the thigh or into the stuffing, not touching bone.

For large birds, 8 pounds (3.6 kg) or more, a tent of aluminum foil may be placed loosely over the breast of the bird to keep it from losing too much moisture and drying out. Remove the foil 1 to 2 hours before it is finished cooking to get a golden brown. If desired, for extra flavor and to keep the meat moist, you can baste every 30 minutes or so with meat drippings or oil during the final 1 to 2 hours.

Many older cookbooks and recipes, and even Internet sites, recommend cooking poultry until the internal temperature reaches 170° to 190° F (77° to 88° C) often resulting in a dry, tasteless product. The United States Department of Agriculture (USDA) has reevaluated the safe temperature for cooking poultry and now recommends an internal temperature of 165° F (74° C) as adequate to thoroughly cook poultry and make it safe to eat. The reduced cooking time produces a juicier, tastier product.

Use the times and temperatures given in the accompanying Poultry Roasting Chart as a guide. Monitor the internal temperature of the bird with the food thermometer. It is fully cooked when the temperature of the meat and the stuffing have reached a minimum of 165° F (74° C) regardless of cooking time. You can cook it longer if desired.

Poultry Roasting Chart

Bird	Oven Temperature		Cooking Time
	° F	° C	Hours
Chicken			
1½ to 2 pounds (0.7–0.9 kg)	375	190	¾ to 1
2½ to 4 lb (1–1.8 kg)	375	190	1¼ to 1¾
4½ to 7 lb (2–3.2 kg)	350	180	2 to 2½
Turkey (whole, unstuffed)			
4 to 8 lb (1.8–3.6 kg)	325	170	1¾ to 2¾
8 to 12 lb (3.6–5.5 kg)	325	170	2¾ to 3
12 to 16 lb (5.5–7.3 kg)	325	170	3 to 4
16 to 20 lb (7.3–9 kg)	325	170	4 to 4½
20 to 24 lb (9–11 kg)	325	170	4½ to 5
Turkey (halves or quarters)			
5 to 8 lb (2.3–3.6 kg)	325	170	2 to 2¾
8 to 10 lb (3.6–4.5 kg)	325	170	2¾ to 3¼
10 to 12 lb (4–5.5 kg)	325	170	3¼ to 3½
Boneless Turkey Rolls and Roasts (unstuffed)			
3 to 5 lb (1.3–2.3 kg)	325	170	1½ to 2
5 to 7 lb (2.3–3.2 kg)	325	170	2 to 2½
7 to 9 lb (3.2–4 kg)	325	170	2½ to 3
Turkey Breasts (unstuffed)			
3 to 6 lb (1.3–2.7 kg)	325	170	1½ to 2¼
6 to 8 lb (2.7–3.6 kg)	325	170	2¼ to 2¾
8 to 10 lb (3.6–4.5 kg)	325	170	2¾ to 3¼
10 to 12 lb (4.5–5.5 kg)	325	170	3¼ to 3½
12 to 14 lb (5.5–6.3 kg)	325	170	3½ to 4
Rock Cornish Game Hens			
1 to 1½ lb (0.5–0.7 kg)	375	190	¾ to 1
Guinea Fowl and Pheasant			
2 to 4 lb (0.9–2.7 kg)	350	180	1 to 2
Duck			
3 to 6 lb (1.3–2.7 kg)	375	190	1 to 2
Goose			
4 to 6 lb (1.8–2.7 kg)	325	170	1¾ to 2¼
6 to 8 lb (2.7 kg–3.6 kg)	325	170	2¼ to 2¾
8 to 12 lb (3.6–5.5 kg)	325	170	2¾ to 3¼
12 to 14 lb (5.5–6.3 kg)	325	170	3¼ to 3¾

Roasting Instructions for Halves, Quarters, or Breasts

Preheat oven to the temperature indicated on the Roasting Chart for the appropriate weight of the meat you are preparing. Place the meat skin side up in a lightly greased, shallow roasting pan. Brush with melted butter or coconut oil, and sprinkle with salt and pepper. Roast uncovered, without turning, until tender and browned, brushing, if needed to keep the meat moist, with additional butter or coconut oil. Use times in the roasting chart as a guide.

MARINATING, BRINING, AND BASTING

People are always on the lookout for new and interesting ways to prepare old standards like chicken and turkey. Several methods have become popular in recent years. These involve the use of a liquid to change or improve the flavor, taste, tenderness, or texture of poultry. Various liquids can be added to poultry by several methods, such as injection, marinating, brining, or basting. Consumers can purchase raw poultry products that have already been marinated, basted, or brined.

Marinating

To "marinate" means to steep food in a marinade. A marinade is a savory acidic sauce in which a food is soaked to enrich its flavor or to tenderize it.

According to *Woman's Day Encyclopedia of Cookery*, "Marinades began as simple brines for preserving fish. The word marinade stems from the same root as the word maritime. In modern usage, a marinade consists of a cooking oil, an acid (vinegar, lemon juice, wine), and spices. As the food stands in the mixture, the acid and the oil impart the savory flavors of the spices to the food. The acid also has a tenderizing action."

The acid in marinades causes poultry tissue to break down. This has a tenderizing effect. The breaking down of the tissue also causes the poultry to hold more liquid, making it juicier. Too much vinegar or hot sauce in a marinade can have the opposite effect, causing the meat to be stringy and tough.

Whole poultry or poultry parts may be marinated by completely immersing the poultry in the marinade. To help infuse the marinade into the poultry, you may use a fork to make random holes in the meat. A needle-like injector may also be used.

Poultry can be refrigerated for up to 24 hours in a marinade. Preferably use a stainless steel or glass container to marinate foods. Cover poultry while marinating it in the refrigerator. Don't use marinade from raw poultry as a sauce unless it is boiled first to destroy bacteria. If stuffing poultry, marinate the poultry first. Cook immediately after stuffing.

Brining

Brine is a strong solution of water and salt. The salt has two effects on poultry: it dissolves protein in muscle, and it reduces moisture loss during cooking. This makes the meat juicier and more tender, and it improves the flavor.

Dry brining is an easy alternative to traditional liquid brining methods. The technique seasons the meat with salt and spices without the use of a liquid salty solution.

This two-day process, completed in the refrigerator, drains moisture out of the poultry, creating a flavorful brine, which is then reabsorbed into the meat without adding additional water. Wet and dry brining are described below.

To prepare a brine solution for poultry, add ¾ cup (205 g) salt to 1 gallon (4 liters) of water, or 3 tablespoons (52 g) of salt per quart (liter) of water. Place brining solution in a container, preferably stainless steel or glass. Totally submerge poultry in solution and store covered in the refrigerator. For best results, refrigerate at least overnight. Poultry may be left in the refrigerator up to 2 days after it is thawed or purchased fresh. Remove poultry from brine. Discard brine after use. If stuffing a bird, brine the poultry first. Cook immediately after stuffing.

To prepare a dry brine, measure 1 tablespoon (17 g) of kosher salt, or seasoned salt for every 5 pounds (2.3 kg) of poultry. Additional aromatic ingredients may be added to the dry brine, such as herbs, spices, citrus, or garlic. Rub the dry brine mixture over the entire surface area of the poultry, place the poultry in a food-grade plastic bag, press out the air, and seal tightly. For best results, refrigerate for up to 2 days and massage the mixture into the skin of the poultry every 8 to 12 hours. Remove the poultry from the bag, pat dry with a paper towel, then cook.

Basting

Basting moistens meat during cooking. Melted butter or other fat, meat drippings, or liquid, such as a stock, is spooned or brushed on the meat as it cooks to moisten it. A bulb baster can also be used to drizzle the liquid over the meat. Basting adds flavor and color, and prevents poultry from drying out.

If basting poultry while it is roasting, remember that each time the oven door is opened, the oven temperature is lowered and additional cooking time may be needed. Always use clean utensils to avoid cross-contamination.

You can purchase raw poultry products that have been prepared for self basting. These products have been injected or marinated with a solution containing butter or other edible fat, broth, stock, or water, plus spices, flavor enhancers, colorings, or other approved ingredients. If you see terms such as "basted," "self basted," "marinated," or "for flavoring" on a raw poultry label, a solution has been added during processing—up to 3 percent by weight for bone-in poultry and up to 8 percent by weight for boneless poultry. The label must include a statement identifying the total quantity and common or usual name of all ingredients in the solution.

POULTRY RECIPES

Keto Vegetable Stuffing

The terms *stuffing* and *dressing* are often used to describe the same thing—a mixture of bread cubes, vegetables, and seasonings that are served with roasted poultry. There is no difference between the ingredients in a stuffing and dressing. The difference is that stuffing is cooked inside the cavity of the bird while dressing is cooked outside in a separate pan.

This stuffing recipe eliminates the bread and replaces it with vegetables, which are cooked inside the bird. You can use a variety of vegetables and add to or subtract from those listed here. This recipe makes enough stuffing to fill a medium-size turkey.

2 tablespoons (28 g) butter
3 ounces (85 g) ground pork or seasoned sausage
1 medium onion, chopped
1 carrot, chopped
2 stalks celery, chopped
1 cup (110 g) green beans, cut into 1-inch (0.5-cm) lengths
1 red bell pepper, chopped
4 ounces (110 g) mushrooms, coarsely sliced
½ teaspoon salt
¼ teaspoon freshly ground black pepper
½ teaspoon dried sage
½ teaspoon dried thyme
1 tablespoon (1.5 g) fresh rosemary or ½ teaspoon dried rosemary

Heat butter in a skillet over medium heat. Lightly sauté pork, onion, carrot, and celery until the meat just begins to turn brown, about 4 minutes. Remove from heat and place in a mixing bowl. Add green beans, bell pepper, mushrooms, salt, black pepper, sage, thyme, and rosemary, and mix together. Stuff the vegetable mixture inside the cavity of a turkey and roast as directed on the roasting chart on page 228 until the center of the stuffing reaches 165° F (74° C).

Yield: 6 servings
Per serving: 4.5 g fat; 4 g net carbs; 5 g protein; 76 calories

Low-Carb Turkey Dressing

Stuffing is always a favorite accompaniment to turkey, but it can also be served with chicken and other poultry. Traditionally, stuffing is made from dry bread crumbs or cubes and cooked inside the cavity of the bird. Stuffing, however, does not need to be made with bread or stuffed inside the bird. This low-carb, gluten-free dressing (stuffing) is cooked separately, but can accompany a roasted turkey or be used as the main dish itself. It is an excellent way to use leftover turkey or chicken.

4 eggs
⅓ cup (75 g) butter, melted
½ cup (32 g) coconut flour, sifted
2 cups (280 g) diced, cooked turkey or chicken
½ cup (80 g) finely chopped onion
½ cup (120 g) diced celery
1½ cup (120 g) chopped mushrooms
1 teaspoon salt
2 teaspoons ground sage
1 teaspoon thyme
¼ teaspoon black pepper

Preheat oven to 375° F (190° C). Whisk eggs and butter in a bowl until blended. Whisk in coconut flour until batter is smooth. Stir in remaining ingredients, coating the meat and vegetables evenly with the batter. Pour batter into a greased 11x7x1½-inch (28x18x4-cm) baking dish. Bake for 40 minutes. Serve smothered in turkey or chicken gravy.

Yield: 8 servings
Per serving: 12 g fat; 2 g net carbs; 14.5 g protein; 174 calories

Grilled Chicken Breasts with Cilantro Butter

2 tablespoons (28 g) butter, softened
1 tablespoons (1 g) fresh cilantro, finely chopped
½ teaspoon lime zest, finely grated
¼ teaspoon Tabasco or hot sauce
Salt
2 boneless chicken breasts
2 tablespoons (30 ml) fresh lime juice
1 tablespoon (14 g) coconut oil, melted

In small bowl, using a wooden spoon or rubber spatula, blend butter, cilantro, lime zest, hot sauce, and ¼ teaspoon salt. Scrape onto a piece of plastic wrap, then roll and twist to shape the butter into a short log. Set in the freezer for 10 minutes.

Butterfly the chicken breasts by slicing them in half lengthwise and opening them up like the wings of a butterfly. Season with ¾ teaspoon salt and drizzle with the lime juice and coconut oil. Let the chicken sit for 15 minutes.

Lay the chicken breasts on a hot grill. Turn the chicken breasts as necessary to get even grill marks. When done, immediately transfer the chicken to two warm serving plates. Quickly, thinly slice the chilled cilantro butter, and arrange butter slices all over the top of the chicken. Garnish with cilantro sprigs and serve with a keto side dish.

Yield: 2 servings
Per serving: 27 g fat; .5 g net carbs; 33 g protein; 377 calories

Toasted Turkey Burger

These bun-less burgers are not really toasted but baked. However, the cheese topping is cooked until it is almost crisp, giving it a toasted or broiled flavor. Although this recipe calls for ground turkey, you can use any type of ground meat. Serve with a side of vegetables of your choice.

8 ounces (225 g) ground turkey
1 egg, beaten
1 ounce (30 g) fresh spinach, finely chopped
¼ teaspoon salt
⅛ teaspoon black pepper
1 teaspoon chopped dried onion
2 teaspoons fresh lime juice
2 ounces (60 g) cheddar cheese, shredded

Preheat oven to 425° F (220° C). In a medium bowl, combine turkey, egg, spinach, salt, pepper, onion, lime juice, and half of the cheese. Thoroughly mix the ingredients, form two large patties, and place them in a baking dish. Sprinkle the tops with the remaining cheese. Bake for 30 minutes, until patties are cooked through and cheese begins to turn a toasty brown.

Yield: 2 servings
Per serving: 24 g fat; 4 g net carbs; 41 g protein; 396 calories

Chicken Casserole

6 ounces (170 g) uncooked chicken
½ medium onion, chopped
12 ounces (340 g) cauliflower, chopped
1 medium stalk celery, chopped
2 cloves garlic, chopped
2 tablespoons (18 g) jalapeño peppers, chopped
4 ounces (110 g) cream cheese, softened
4 ounces (110 g) sharp cheddar cheese, shredded
½ teaspoon salt
⅛ teaspoon black pepper
¼ cup (60 g) sour cream

Preheat oven to 350°F (180° C). In a large bowl, combine chicken, onion, cauliflower, celery, garlic, jalapeño peppers, cream cheese, cheddar cheese, salt, and pepper. Mix ingredients together and pour into an ungreased 9-inch (22-cm) baking dish or pie pan. Bake for 1 hour. Serve topped with sour cream.

Yield: 2 servings
Per serving: 46.5 g fat; 12 g net carbs; 48 g protein; 658 calories

Chicken Broccoli Casserole

6 ounces (170 g) uncooked chicken, cut into bite-size pieces
6 ounces (170 g) broccoli, chopped
2 stalks celery, chopped
½ medium onion, chopped
2 ounces (55 g) mushrooms, sliced
½ cup (115 g) mayonnaise (pages 37-40)

½ cup (115 g) sour cream
½ teaspoon salt
⅛ teaspoon freshly ground black pepper
4 ounces (110 g) Monterey Jack cheese, shredded

Preheat oven to 350°F (180° C). In a large bowl, combine chicken, broccoli, celery, onion, mushrooms, mayonnaise, sour cream, salt, pepper, and half (2 oz/55 g) of the cheese. Mix ingredients thoroughly, and pour into an ungreased 9-inch (22-cm) baking dish or pie pan. Top with the remaining cheese. Bake for 1 hour.

Yield: 2 servings
Per serving: 73 g fat; 10 g net carbs; 45 g protein; 877 calories

Chicken Chow Mein

Chow mein is traditionally made with noodles, either crispy or soft. In this version, the noodles are replaced with toasted almonds.

½ cup (75 g) whole almonds, toasted
2 tablespoons (28 g) coconut oil
½ medium onion, chopped
1 medium stalk celery, chopped
½ green bell pepper, chopped

8 ounces (225 g) raw chicken, cut into bite-size pieces
2 cloves garlic, finely chopped
3 ounces (85 g) bamboo shoots
2 ounces (60 g) mushrooms, sliced
4 ounces (120 g) bean sprouts
½ teaspoon salt
Soy sauce or coconut aminos to taste

Heat oven or toaster oven to 350° F (180° C). Put almonds in an oven safe dish and bake for about 7 minutes or until the almonds turn a light golden brown. Do not overcook. They can burn easily, so keep an eye on them as they cook. Remove from the oven and set aside.

Heat oil in a large skillet over medium-high heat. Add onion, celery, and bell pepper and sauté until vegetables are crisp tender, about 5 minutes. Add chicken, garlic, and bamboo shoots, and sauté until chicken turns white. Add mushrooms and bean sprouts, and cook until the mushrooms are limp, about 4 to 5 minutes. Stir in toasted almonds and salt, and remove from heat. Add soy sauce to taste.

Yield: 2 servings
Per serving: 36.5 g fat; 14 g net carbs; 47 g protein; 574 calories

Crispy Chicken Wings

You don't need a carb-rich batter to make crispy chicken wings. The secret to making crispy low-carb chicken wings is to keep the skins on and double-fry them. The initial frying at a low temperature thoroughly cooks the wings. The second frying, at a higher temperature, crisps them up. It is the fried chicken skin that gives the wings their crispness.

Coconut oil for frying
10 chicken wings, skin on
Salt to taste
Ranch Dressing (page 43) or Hot Dipping Sauce (see below)

Hot Dipping Sauce:
¼ cup (112 g) butter, melted
2 tablespoons (30 ml) hot sauce

Heat coconut oil in a deep fryer to 275° F (140° C). Add chicken wings and cook for about 12 to 15 minutes or until fully cooked. Remove the wings from the hot oil and set aside. Heat the oil to 350° F (180° C). Return the wings to the hot oil and cook until crisp, about 8 to 9 minutes. Remove from oil and let cool. Sprinkle a little salt on the wings and eat as is, or serve with Ranch Dressing or Hot Dipping Sauce.

To make the dipping sauce, melt the butter and mix with hot sauce.

Yield: 10 wings
Per wing: 2 g fat; 0 g net carbs; 4 g protein; 34 calories

Crisp Fried and Baked Chicken

This chicken is both fried and baked to bring out its crispiness. It is important that you leave the skin on the chicken, because that is what makes them crispy-delicious.

1 tablespoon (14 g) coconut oil
2 tablespoons (28 g) red palm oil
Salt and black pepper to taste
1 pound (450 g) chicken thighs or breasts, skin on
Spinach
Mushrooms and onions, sautéed

Preheat oven to 450° F (230° C). Heat oils in a large oven-safe skillet to medium-high heat. Sprinkle salt and pepper on each piece of chicken and place in the skillet, skin side down, making sure each piece lies flat. Cook until skin turns golden brown, about 5 to 7 minutes. Put the skillet into the hot oven and roast until juices from the thickest parts of the meat run clear when pierced with a knife, about 25 minutes. Serve crispy skin side up on a bed of cooked spinach and a side of sautéed mushrooms and onions. Spoon pan drippings over the chicken and vegetables.

Yield: about 4 servings
Per serving (meat only): 17 g fat; 0 g net carbs; 24.5 g protein; 251 calories

Chicken and Vegetables with Cream Sauce

2 chicken breasts
8 ounces (225 g) cream cheese, cut in chunks
2 tablespoons (28 g) butter
1 cup (235 ml) chicken broth
¾ cup (175 ml) heavy cream
¼ teaspoon curry powder
⅛ teaspoon ground rosemary
¼ teaspoon salt
2 cloves garlic, minced
1 stalk celery, chopped
1 cup (100 g) chopped fresh or frozen green beans
1 cup (70 g) sliced mushrooms
½ cup (50 g) chopped onion

Set oven to broil. Place chicken breasts in a pan, skin side up, in the oven about 6 inches below the heating element. Broil for about 6 to 8 minutes or until the skin is browned; you want to brown the skin, not completely cook the chicken. Remove the chicken from the oven and set aside.

Turn the oven down to 375° F (190° C). In a saucepan over medium-low heat, combine cream cheese, butter, chicken broth, and cream. Using a whisk, blend the ingredients together. Stir in curry powder, rosemary, salt, and garlic. Remove from heat and set aside.

Put the celery, green beans, mushrooms, and onion in a baking dish. Pour the cream mixture over the vegetables, making sure they are covered. Place the chicken breasts on top. Cover the dish and bake in the oven for 45 minutes. Remove the cover and continue to bake for another 15 minutes. Remove from the oven and let sit for 5 to 7 minutes to allow sauce to thicken.

Serve the chicken and vegetables covered in the cream sauce.

Yield: serves 2
Per serving: 54 g fat; 9 g net carbs; 30 g protein; 642 calories

Cheesy Cauliflower and Chicken Casserole

2 heads cauliflower (about 3 lb/1360 g), cut into bite-size pieces
10 ounces (280 g) cooked chicken, cut into bite-size pieces
4 ounces (110 g) cheddar cheese, shredded
8 ounces (225 g) Monterey Jack cheese, shredded

2 tablespoons (30 g) chopped jalapeño pepper (optional)
1 small onion, chopped
4 strips sugar-free, nitrite-free bacon, cooked crisp and crumbled
2 cloves garlic, minced
½ teaspoon salt
¼ teaspoon black pepper

Preheat oven to 350° F (180° C). Steam cauliflower until tender. In a large bowl, combine cooked cauliflower, chicken, half of the cheddar cheese, half of the Monterey Jack cheese, jalapeño pepper, onion, bacon, garlic, salt, and pepper. Mix ingredients and pour into a 9x13-inch (22x33-cm) glass baking dish. Sprinkle remaining cheese on top. Bake for 30 minutes or until the cheese on top is hot and bubbly.

Yield: serves 4
Per serving: 38 g fat; 12 g net carbs; 55 g protein; 610 calories

Parmesan Chicken Strips

¼ cup (56 g) coconut oil
1 cup (80 g) shredded Parmesan cheese
2 teaspoons (16 g) coconut flour
¾ teaspoon salt
½ teaspoon black pepper
1 teaspoon onion powder
16 ounces (450 g) chicken breasts, sliced lengthwise into
    1-inch (2.5-cm) wide strips
2 eggs, lightly beaten

Heat oil in a large skillet over medium heat. While the skillet is heating up, combine Parmesan cheese, coconut flour, salt, black pepper, and onion powder, and set aside. Dip chicken strips into beaten eggs, then place them in the cheese mixture and evenly coat. Place the chicken strips into the hot skillet and cook each side until browned and crisp. Serve with one or two keto vegetable side dishes.

Yield: serves 4
Per serving: 26 g fat; 1.5 g net carbs; 42.5 g protein; 410 calories

Chicken and Cauliflower in Velouté Sauce

    2 tablespoons (28 g) coconut oil
    6 chicken thighs
    6 cups (600 g) cauliflower, cut into bite-size pieces
    1 carrot, sliced
    Velouté Sauce (page 20)

Heat oil in a large skillet over medium heat. Add chicken, cover, and cook until bottom side is browned, about 12 to 15 minutes. Turn and cook the other side until browned. Remove the chicken and put in a bowl or plate and put in the oven to keep warm.

Add cauliflower and carrot to skillet and sauté, stirring occasionally, until slightly browned and tender, about 12 minutes. Remove from the skillet and combine with the chicken and keep in the oven.

Using the same skillet, prepare the Velouté Sauce as directed using chicken broth and ¼ teaspoon ground rosemary and ½ teaspoon thyme. After sauce thickens, return chicken and vegetables to the skillet. Cover chicken and vegetables with the sauce and cook, stirring occasionally, for 3 to 5 minutes, until the meat and vegetables are hot. Serve the chicken and vegetables covered with sauce.

Yield: 6 servings
Per serving: 20 g fat; 6 g net carbs; 29 g protein; 320 calories

Chicken Curry

    1 tablespoon (14 g) coconut oil
    2 tablespoons (28 g) butter
    6 ounces (170 g) uncooked chicken, cut into bite-size pieces
    ½ head medium cauliflower, cut into florets
    1 medium onion, chopped
    1 green bell pepper, chopped
    3 cloves garlic, minced
    3 teaspoons curry powder
    1 teaspoon ground coriander
    ⅛ teaspoon ground nutmeg
    ¼ teaspoon red pepper flakes
    ½ teaspoon salt
    1 teaspoon tapioca starch or arrowroot flour

1 cup (240 ml) chicken broth
1 cup (240 g) sour cream

Heat coconut oil and butter in a large skillet over medium heat. Add chicken, cauliflower, onion, and bell pepper, and cook, stirring occasionally, until meat is cooked and vegetables are tender, about 15 minutes.

Add garlic, curry, coriander, nutmeg, red pepper flakes, and salt, and cook about 3 to 4 minutes. Blend the tapioca starch with the broth, then stir it into the meat and vegetables, and simmer for about 10 minutes, until flavors blend. Remove from heat and stir in sour cream.

This dish tastes good as is, but you can also eat it over a bed of cooked Cauliflower Rice (page 112).

Yield: 2 servings
Per serving: 39.5 g fat; 12.5 g net carbs; 31 g protein; 529 calories

Lemon Chicken

This is a great meal you can prepare in advance. When you come home from work, all you have to do is pop it into the oven, and dinner is ready in less than an hour.

½ cup (120 ml) lemon juice (about 2 lemons' worth)
½ cup (120 ml) extra virgin olive oil
3 cloves garlic, minced
2 teaspoons dried thyme
1 teaspoon red pepper flakes (optional)
½ teaspoon salt
1 teaspoon lemon pepper
8 bone-in chicken drumsticks or thighs
1 large onion, cut into 8 wedges
2 medium carrots, sliced in ¼-inch (0.5-cm) rounds
16 ounces (450 g) cauliflower, cut into bite-size florets

Using a large, zip-close plastic bag, mix together lemon juice, olive oil, garlic, thyme, red pepper, salt, and lemon pepper. Add the chicken, onion, carrots, and cauliflower, then seal the bag and gently turn over several times to evenly coat the contents with the marinade. Refrigerate for at least 30 minutes or up to 12 hours, turning the bag occasionally.

When you are ready to cook, preheat the oven to 400°F (200° C). Dump the contents of the bag into a large baking dish, spread in an even layer, then bake uncovered for 45 to 60 minutes, until meat is cooked and vegetables are tender. If the vegetables brown too quickly on one side, turn them for more even cooking. Serve with the drippings poured over the meat and vegetables.

Yield: 4 servings
Per serving: 41 g fat; 9.5 g net carbs; 52.5 g protein; 617 calories

Chicken Pot Pie
This pot pie doesn't use a piecrust but is topped with creamed cauliflower and cheese.

Topping:
1 head cauliflower (about 18 oz/510 g)
3 eggs
1 teaspoon salt
2 tablespoons (28 g) butter, softened
4 ounces (110 g) Monterey Jack or Gouda cheese, shredded
4 ounces (110 g) Colby or cheddar cheese, shredded

Filling:
2 tablespoons (28 g) coconut or red palm oil

6 ounces (170 g) uncooked chicken, cut into small bite-size pieces
½ medium onion, chopped
2 stalks celery, chopped
2 medium carrots, chopped
4 ounces (110 g) green beans
6 ounces (170 g) mushrooms, sliced
1 teaspoon salt
½ teaspoon black pepper
1 teaspoon dried thyme
1 teaspoon dried sage
2 cups (470 ml) chicken broth
1½ cups (350 ml) heavy cream

To make the topping, cut cauliflower into florets and steam until tender. Put the cauliflower into a blender with eggs, salt, and butter. Blend until smooth. Stir in Monterey Jack cheese and set aside.

To make the filling, heat oil in a skillet over medium heat. Sauté chicken, onion, celery, carrots, and green beans for about 5 minutes, or until vegetables are tender. Add mushrooms, salt, black pepper, thyme, sage, chicken broth, and cream, and simmer for 5 minutes. Stir in ¾ cup of the cauliflower topping to thicken the filling.

Preheat oven to 400° F (200° C). Pour the filling into an 8x8-inch (20x20 -cm) casserole dish. Spoon the topping over the filling and sprinkle Colby cheese on top. Bake for 30 minutes.

Yield: 4 servings
Per serving: 65 g fat; 12 g net carbs; 39.5 g protein; 791 calories

Chicken Cacciatore

¼ cup (56 g) coconut oil
4 chicken breasts or 8 thighs and legs
4 cloves garlic, chopped
2 medium onions, sliced
4 ounces (110 g) daikon radish or turnip, cut into bite-size pieces
1 medium carrot, sliced
2 bell peppers, cut into bite-size pieces
3 stalks celery, cut into bite-size pieces
2 cups (450 g) crushed or stewed tomatoes
1 teaspoon salt

¼ teaspoon black pepper
1 teaspoon dried oregano
1 teaspoon dried basil
½ teaspoon celery seed

Heat oil in a large skillet over medium-high heat, then cook chicken until lightly browned on both sides, 6 to 8 minutes per side. Remove chicken from the skillet and set aside. Sauté garlic, onions, daikon radish, carrot, peppers, and celery until crisp tender. Return chicken to the skillet, then add crushed tomatoes, salt, and herbs, cover, and simmer for 30 minutes, or until the chicken is completely cooked. Serve chicken with the vegetables and sauce.

Yield: 4 servings
Per serving: 22.5 g fat; 14.5 g net carbs; 37.5 g protein; 410 calories

Chicken Fricassee

¼ cup (56 g) coconut oil
2 chicken breasts
1 cup chicken broth or water
1 medium onion, sliced

4 ounces (113 g) mushrooms, sliced
2 zucchini or yellow crookneck squash
½ cup (40 g) shredded Parmesan cheese
½ cup (120 ml) heavy cream
½ teaspoon salt
¼ teaspoon black pepper
½ teaspoon celery seed

Heat oil in large skillet over medium-high heat and brown each piece of chicken on both sides. Add chicken broth, reduce heat, and simmer for about 30 minutes or until chicken is cooked thoroughly. Add onion and simmer for 5 minutes, then add mushrooms, zucchini, Parmesan cheese, cream, salt, pepper, and celery seed. Simmer for another 8 to 10 minutes or until cream thickens. Serve each piece of chicken smothered in vegetables and creamy sauce.

Yield: 2 servings.
Per serving: 54 g fat; 11 g net carbs; 37 g protein; 678 calories

Seafood

FRESH SEAFOOD
How to Tell If the Fish Is Fresh

Nothing can be worse than buying and preparing seafood that is old or improperly handled. It tastes bad and can cause illness. When shopping for seafood, you want to select the freshest products available and avoid old and potentially harmful items.

Some refrigerated seafood may have time or temperature indicators on their packaging, which show if the product has been stored at the proper temperature. Always check the indicators when they are present, and only buy the seafood if the indicator shows that the product is safe to eat.

Here are some hints to help you tell if raw fish is fresh:

- Buy only fish that is refrigerated or displayed on a thick bed of fresh ice that is not melting (preferably in a case or under some type of cover).
- Fish should smell fresh and mild, not fishy, sour, or ammonia-like.
- A fish's eyes should be clear and bulge a little.
- Whole fish and fillets should have firm, shiny flesh and bright red gills free from milky slime.
- The flesh should spring back when pressed.
- Fish fillets should display no discoloration, darkening, or drying around the edges.

Selecting Shellfish

Follow these guidelines for safely selecting shellfish:

- Shrimp flesh should be translucent and shiny, with little or no odor.
- Throw away clams, oysters, and mussels if their shells are cracked or broken.
- Live clams, oysters, and mussels should close up when the shell is tapped. If they don't close when tapped, don't buy them.
- Live crabs and lobsters should show some leg movement. They spoil rapidly after death, so only live crabs and lobsters should be selected and prepared.

Frozen Seafood

Frozen seafood can spoil if the fish thaws during transport and is left at warm temperatures for too long. Follow these guidelines:

- Don't buy frozen seafood if its package is open, torn, or crushed on the edges.
- Avoid packages that are positioned above the "frost line" or are at top of the freezer case.
- Avoid packages with signs of frost or ice crystals, which may mean the fish has been stored a long time or thawed and refrozen.

Proper Handling, Storage, and Preparation

Put raw seafood on ice or in the refrigerator or freezer soon after buying it. If seafood will be used within two days after purchase, store it in the refrigerator. Otherwise, wrap it tightly in plastic, foil, or moisture-proof paper and store it in the freezer.

Any frozen fish or shellfish will be safe indefinitely, however, the flavor and texture will decrease after lengthy storage. For best quality, freeze (0° F/ -18° C) cooked fish for up to 3 months. Frozen raw fish is best used within 3 to 8 months, and shellfish within 3 to 12 months. You can store commercially canned fish, such as tuna, for up to five years in the pantry.

Seafood should never be left out of the refrigerator or the freezer for over two hours. To thaw frozen seafood safely, place it in the refrigerator overnight. If you have to thaw it quickly, seal it in a plastic bag and immerse it in cold water for an hour or two.

Most seafood should be cooked to an internal temperature of 145° F (63° C). If you don't have a food thermometer, there are other ways to determine whether seafood is done.

Fish: The flesh should be opaque and separate easily with a fork.

Shrimp and lobster: The flesh becomes pearly and opaque.

Scallops: The flesh turns opaque and firm.

Clams, mussels, and oysters: The shells open during cooking—throw out ones that don't open.

Uncooked spoiled seafood can have an ammonia odor. This odor becomes stronger after cooking. If you smell an ammonia odor in raw or cooked seafood, do not eat it.

After cooking, you can store any leftover seafood in the refrigerator up to 3 or 4 days.

Eating Raw Seafood: What You Need to Know

It's always best to cook seafood thoroughly to minimize the risk of foodborne illness. However, if you choose to eat raw fish anyway, one rule of

Freezer Storage Times for Seafood (0° F/-18° C)

4 to 6 months*	7 to 9 months	9 months or more
Bullhead	Bass, lake	Cod
Catfish	Bluegills	Blue pike
Herring, sea	Crappies	Haddock
Lake trout	Flounder	Hake
Mackerel	Halibut	Lingcod
Northern pike	Shellfish	Lutefisk
Pollock	Perch, ocean	Whiting
Rainbow trout	Rockfish	Yellow perch
Salmon, chum	Most salmon	Yellow pike
Shrimp	Sunfish	
Smelt	Whitefish	
Tuna		

*Do not store lake herring, crab meat, or cooked and peeled shrimp longer than 3 or 4 months.

Approximate Thawing Times for Fish

Thaw in unopened freezer wrappings; cook immediately and do not refreeze.

Fish	Refrigerator	Cold Water
Whole fish (4½ lb/2 kg)	20 hours	1¼ hours
Fish steaks, fillets (1 lb/450 g)	8 hours	½ hour
Shellfish (1 lb/450 g)	8 hours	½ hour

thumb is to eat fish that has been previously frozen. Some species of fish can contain parasites, and freezing will kill any parasites that may be present.

However, be aware that freezing doesn't kill all harmful microorganisms. Bacteria can survive and multiply rapidly at temperatures between 40° F and 140° C (4° and 60° C). That's why it is safest to cook your seafood.

Oysters are often eaten raw. Some oysters are treated for safety after they are harvested. That information may or may not be on the label. However, these oysters should still not be eaten raw by people who have a compromised immune system or health issues, or are pregnant or nursing. The post-harvest treatment eliminates some naturally occurring pathogens, but it does not remove all pathogens that can cause illness.

Storing Fish

Fish that is cleaned and frozen when very fresh will keep best. It is a good idea to package fish in meal-size units, cutting large fish into family-size steaks or fillets. Soak cut pieces in brine (except lake herring and pink salmon) for at least 20 seconds, using 1 cup (288 g) salt per gallon (4 liters) of water. This firms the fish and reduces leakage when thawed. Store in the coldest available temperature, near the bottom of a chest-type freezer or in contact with the refrigerated shelf in an upright model.

FISH RECIPES

Broiled Salmon

4 salmon fillets (4 oz/110 g each), skin on
1 teaspoon salt
1 teaspoon paprika
1 teaspoon ground ginger
2 tablespoons (28 g) butter

Preheat broiler. Rise salmon fillets under cold water and pat dry. Arrange on baking sheet, skin side down. Sprinkle seasonings on the top of each fillet. Broil for about 8 minutes or until cooked through. Remove from oven and let sit for 5 minutes before serving. Serve topped with a dollop of butter along with a keto side dish.

Yield: serves 4
Per serving: 14 g fat; 0 g net carbs; 22 g protein; 214 calories

Herbed Broiled Fish

1 pound (450 g) fish fillets
¼ cup (56 g) butter, softened
½ teaspoon salt
¼ teaspoon dried dill weed
⅛ teaspoon dried thyme
⅛ teaspoon onion powder

Preheat oven to broil or 550° F (280° C). If fish has not been skinned, place skin side up on rack in broiler pan. Mix butter, salt, dill, thyme, and onion powder. Brush the fish with half of the herb butter mixture. Broil with the top of the fish 2 to 3 inches (5 to 8 cm) from heating element until it turns a light brown, about 5 minutes. Turn carefully and brush other sides. Broil until fish flakes easily with fork, 5 to 6 minutes longer.

Yield: serves 4
Per serving: 7.5 g fat; 0 g net carbs; 27 g protein; 175.5 calories

Baked Fish

This is a basic recipe for any type of white fish.

2 tablespoons (28 g) butter, melted
½ teaspoon salt
⅛ teaspoon white pepper
1 tablespoon (15 ml) lemon juice
1 tablespoon (10 g) grated onion
1 pound (450 g) fish fillets

Preheat oven to 350° F (180° C). Mix together butter, salt, pepper, lemon juice, and grated onion. Coat both sides of the fillets with the butter mixture. Place the fillets in an ungreased baking dish. Pour any remaining butter mixture over fish. Bake uncovered for 25 to 30 minutes, or until fish flakes easily with a fork. Serve with keto vegetables or salad to boost total fat content of the meal.

Yield: serves 4
Per serving: 7.5 g fat; 0 g net carbs; 27 g protein; 175 calories

Baked Fish with Tomato

1 pound (450 g) fish fillets
8 ounces (220 g) tomato sauce
1 medium stalk celery, chopped
½ teaspoon dried oregano
½ teaspoon salt
1 medium onion, sliced
½ red bell pepper, sliced
2 tablespoons (30 ml) lemon juice
¼ cup (56 g) extra virgin olive oil
2 zucchini, sliced and steamed

Preheat oven to 350° F (180° C). Arrange fish in an ungreased baking dish. Mix together tomato sauce, celery, oregano, salt, onion, bell pepper, lemon juice, and olive oil, and pour over fillets. Bake uncovered for about 25 to 30 minutes, or until fish flakes easily with a fork. Serve the fillets alongside steamed zucchini with the sauce poured over top.

Yield: serves 4
Per serving: 14.5 g fat; 7 g net carbs; 28 g protein; 270 calories

Asian Baked Sea Bass

2 whole sea bass or trout (about 10 oz/280 g each)
4 cloves garlic, finely chopped
2-inch (5-cm) piece of fresh ginger, peeled and cut into matchsticks
3 tablespoons (45 ml) soy sauce or coconut aminos
2 tablespoons (30 ml) rice or coconut vinegar
2 tablespoons (28 g) coconut oil or bacon drippings, melted
1 tablespoon (9 g) chopped jalapeño pepper
4 scallions, cut into thin strips
1 cup (16 g) chopped fresh cilantro

Preheat oven to 400° F (200° C). Make a cut every 1 to 2 inches (2.5 to 5 cm) through both sides of the fish's rib cage, perpendicular to the backbone. Place the fish into a greased baking dish.

In a small bowl, combine garlic, ginger, soy sauce, vinegar, oil, jalapeño, scallions, and cilantro. Stuff a portion of the mixture into the cavity of each cut portion of the fish. Cover with plastic wrap or wax paper and let the fish sit at room temperature for 20 minutes, then bake for 20 to 25 minutes, or until the fish is just cooked through (can be easily pierced with a knife).

Remove from the oven and gently scrape off the skin using a small knife. Spoon some of the juices from the pan over the fish, and serve with a keto vegetable side dish.

Yield: serves 4
Per serving: 9.5 g fat; 2.5 g net carbs; 22 g protein; 183 calories

Crispy Baked Fish

This is a simple recipe that will give your baked fish a little crunch. The crunch comes from the crushed pork rinds used in the coating.

¼ cup (28 g) almond flour
1 ounce (28 g) pork rinds, crushed into pea-size pieces
¼ teaspoon salt
¼ teaspoon onion powder
⅛ teaspoon freshly ground black pepper
1 pound (450 g) fish fillets
2 tablespoons (28 g) coconut oil or butter, melted

Preheat oven to 350° F (180° C). In a bowl, combine almond flour, crushed pork rinds, salt, onion powder, and pepper. Dip the fish fillets in melted coconut oil or butter to moisten all sides. Press the fillets into the almond flour mixture to coat. Place the fillets in a baking dish. Sprinkle the remaining almond flour mixture on top of the fillets. Bake for 30 minutes.

Yield: serves 4
Per serving: 11.5 g fat; 0 g net carbs; 27 g protein; 211 calories

Fish Parmesan

1 pound (450 g) fish fillets
½ teaspoon salt
⅛ teaspoon black pepper
½ cup (115 g) sour cream
2 tablespoons (10 g) grated Parmesan cheese
¼ teaspoon paprika
⅛ teaspoon dried tarragon leaves
3 scallions, chopped
1 medium tomato, sliced

Preheat oven to 350° F (180° C). Roll up fish fillets and place seam side down on ungreased square baking dish, 8x8x2-inches (20x20x5-cm). Sprinkle with salt and black pepper. Mix sour cream, Parmesan cheese, paprika, and tarragon, and spread over fish. Bake uncovered for 25 to 30 minutes, or until fish flakes easily with a fork. Remove from oven and serve garnished with chopped scallion and tomato slices.

Yield: serves 4
Per serving: 8.5 g fat; 2.5 g net carbs; 29 g protein; 202 calories

Cheese-Encrusted Baked Fish

1 pound (450 g) fish fillets
1 egg, lightly beaten
½ cup (50 g) grated Parmesan cheese
¼ cup (30 g) shredded sharp cheddar cheese
2 tablespoons (14 g) almond flour
¼ teaspoon salt
⅛ teaspoon (or to taste) cayenne pepper
2 tablespoons (30 g) sour cream

Preheat oven to 350° F (180° C). Place fillets in a greased square baking dish, 8x8x2-inches (20x20x5-cm). Mix together egg, Parmesan cheese, cheddar cheese, almond flour, salt, and cayenne pepper. Spoon an equal amount of the mixture over each fillet. Bake for 25 to 30 minutes, or until fish flakes easily with a fork. Serve with a dollop of sour cream along with a keto side dish.

Yield: serves 4
Per serving: 9 g fat; 1 g net carbs; 28 g protein; 197 calories

Fish Creole

1 pound (450 g) fish fillets
1 medium tomato, chopped
½ green pepper, chopped
3 tablespoons (45 ml) lemon juice
2 tablespoons (28 g) coconut oil
1 teaspoon salt
1 tablespoon (10 g) finely chopped onion
½ teaspoon dried basil leaves
¼ teaspoon coarsely ground black pepper
1 teaspoon hot sauce

Preheat oven to 400° F (200° C). Place fillets an ungreased baking dish. Mix tomato, green pepper, lemon juice, oil, salt, onion, basil, black pepper, and hot sauce, and pour over the fillets. Bake about 15 minutes, or until the fish flakes easily with a fork.

Yield: serves 4
Per serving: 9 g fat; 2 g net carbs; 27 g protein; 197 calories

Shrimp Creole

  2 tablespoons (28 g) coconut or red palm oil
  4 ounces (110 g) sausage
  ½ medium onion, chopped
  1 medium stalk celery, chopped
  ½ green bell pepper, chopped
  4 ounces (110 g) shrimp
  2 cloves garlic, finely chopped
  2 cups (240 g) Cauliflower Rice (page 112)
  ¼ cup (60 ml) tomato sauce
  2 teaspoons fish sauce
  ½ teaspoon paprika
  ½ teaspoon salt
  ½ teaspoon hot sauce
  1 teaspoon prepared horseradish

Heat oil in a large skillet over medium heat. Sauté sausage, onion, celery, and bell pepper until tender, about 6 to 7 minutes. Add shrimp and garlic, and cook 4 to 5 minutes, until shrimp is cooked. Stir in Cauliflower Rice, tomato sauce, fish sauce, paprika, salt, hot sauce, and horseradish, and cook, stirring often, until cauliflower is tender, about 5 minutes.

  Yield: 2 servings
  Per serving: 30.5 g fat; 9.5 g net carbs; 27 g protein; 420 calories

Asparagus Shrimp

  2 tablespoons (28 g) butter
  8 ounces (225 g) asparagus
  1 cloves garlic, chopped
  1 teaspoon finely chopped ginger
  6 ounces (170 g) shrimp
  2 tablespoons (30 ml) fresh lemon juice
  2 tablespoons (2 g) chopped cilantro
  Salt and black pepper to taste

Heat butter in a skillet over medium heat. Sauté asparagus, garlic, and ginger for about 5 minutes. Add shrimp and sauté until cooked, about 5 minutes.

Remove from heat and stir in lemon juice and cilantro. Add salt and pepper to taste. Serve with a side of keto vegetables of your choice.

Yield: serves 2
Per serving: 13 g fat; 3.5 g net carbs; 22 g protein; 219 calories

Halibut in Coconut Cream Sauce

2 tablespoons (28 g) coconut oil
½ small yellow onion, sliced
2 medium zucchini, sliced
2 halibut fillets (4 oz/110 g each)
½ cup (120 ml) coconut milk
½ teaspoon salt
½ teaspoon curry powder
2 tablespoons (2 g) cilantro, chopped

Heat oil in a large skillet over medium heat. Sauté onion and zucchini until tender, about 6 minutes. Add fish, cover, and cook until it turns white, about 5 minutes. Stir in coconut milk, salt, and curry powder. Simmer for 3 to 4 minutes to blend flavors. Serve fish and vegetables with coconut sauce topped with cilantro.

Yield: serves 2
Per serving: 20.5 g fat; 6.5 g net carbs; 23.5 g protein; 304 calories

Spicy Jumbo Shrimp

3 tablespoons (42 g) coconut oil
5 cloves garlic, crushed
1 teaspoon chopped jalapeño pepper
1 teaspoon cumin
½ teaspoon black pepper
½ teaspoon salt
2 tablespoons (30 ml) tomato sauce
2 tablespoon (30 ml) soy sauce or coconut aminos
1½-inch (4-cm) piece of fresh ginger, cut into matchsticks
8 scallions, finely chopped
1½ pounds (680 g) raw jumbo shrimp, shells removed

Heat oil in a large skillet over medium heat. Add garlic, jalapeño pepper, cumin, black pepper, and salt. Cook for 2 minutes, then add the tomato sauce, soy sauce, ginger, and about three-quarters of the scallions; cook for another 2 minutes. Add the shrimp and cook, stirring occasionally, until the shrimp turn pink, about 3 to 4 minutes. Remove from heat and serve topped with the remaining scallions along with a keto side dish.

Yield: serves 4
Per serving: 10.5 g fat; 3.5 g net carbs; 32 g protein; 236 calories

Coconut-Crusted Fish Fillets with Broccoli

You can use any type of white fish for this dish—sea bass, halibut, sole, mahi-mahi, etc. The fish goes well with broccoli, but you can use any vegetable of your choice.

¾ cup (84 g) almond flour
¼ cup (20 g) finely shredded coconut (unsweetened)
¾ teaspoon salt
½ teaspoon black pepper
¼ cup (56 g) coconut oil
½ medium onion, chopped
20 ounces (568 g) broccoli (about 8 cups), chopped
2 small cloves garlic, minced
16 ounces (450 g) fish fillets
1 egg, lightly beaten

Combine almond flour, coconut, salt, and pepper, and set aside. Heat oil in a large skillet over medium heat. Sauté onion and broccoli until the vegetables begin to caramelize, about 10 to 12 minutes. Stir in garlic and cook another 3 or 4 minutes. Remove the vegetables, put into a warm bowl, and set aside.

Dip fish fillets into beaten egg and then into the almond flour mixture, evenly coating both sides. Place into the hot skillet and cook, turning once, until golden brown, about 5 minutes per side. Remove from skillet. Return vegetables to the skillet and reheat until hot. Serve the hot vegetables with the fish.

Yield: serves 4
Per serving (made with sea bass): 30.5 g fat; 9.5 g net carbs; 36.5 g protein; 458 calories

Pecan-Breaded Fish Fillets with Dijon Mustard Sauce

2 tablespoons (28 g) plus 2 teaspoons Dijon mustard
⅔ cup (150 g) sour cream
¼ teaspoon salt
¼ teaspoon freshly ground black pepper
1 egg
½ cup (56 g) pecan or almond meal
¼ cup (60 g) butter, melted
16 ounces (450 g) fish fillets

To make the sauce, use a small saucepan over medium-low heat. Add 2 teaspoons of Dijon mustard, sour cream, salt, and black pepper. Heat and stir until warm and well blended, but do not boil. Remove from heat and set aside.

In a small bowl, whisk together egg and 2 tablespoons Dijon mustard until well blended. Place the pecan meal in a shallow dish.

Heat butter in a large skillet over medium heat. Cut the fish fillet(s) into four equal pieces. One at a time, dip the fish fillets into the egg mixture and then into pecans to coat. Place fillets into the hot skillet and cook for about 4 minutes or until lightly browned. Turn and cook the other side.

Serve the fish smothered in mustard sauce along with a side or two of keto vegetables.

Yield: serves 4
Per serving: 19 g fat; 2 g net carbs; 28 g protein; 291 calories

Salmon Cakes

These are delicious tasting fish patties that make a great main dish. Complement with a side of vegetables of your choice. You can use fresh or canned salmon. Tastes incredible using smoked salmon. This recipe can also be made using other types of fish.

¼ cup (56 g) cooking oil
2 eggs, lightly beaten
1 tablespoon (8 g) coconut flour
¼ teaspoon fish sauce (optional)

¼ cup (40 g) red onion, finely chopped
6 ounces (170 g) cooked salmon
¼ teaspoon salt
⅛ teaspoon black pepper
¼ teaspoon celery seed
¼ teaspoon dill weed
¼ teaspoon onion powder
¼ teaspoon dried parsley

Heat the oil in a skillet over medium heat. Put eggs into a small bowl and whisk in coconut flour. Add fish sauce, onion, salmon, salt, black pepper, celery seed, dill weed, onion powder, and parsley, and blend together into a batter. Spoon the batter into the hot skillet making 12 evenly sized patties. Cover and cook for about 4 to 5 minutes or until the underside of the patties are browned. Turn the patties over and cook, uncovered, for another 4 to 5 minutes, or until the bottoms are browned. Remove from heat and serve with sliced tomatoes or avocado.

Yield: 12 fish cakes (serves 2)
Per serving: 40 g fat; 2 g net carbs; 22.5 g protein; 458 calories

Variation:
Add 2 ounces of shredded sharp cheddar cheese to the batter. Omit dill and parsley, and add 1 teaspoon minced cilantro.

Breakfast and Eggs

USING AND STORING EGGS

Identifying Fresh Eggs

Eggs are among the most nutritious foods on the planet and can be an important part of a healthy diet. However, they are perishable just like raw meat, poultry, and fish. Egg processors typically print "code dates" on cartons for purposes of rotating stock or controlling inventory. "Sell By," "Use By," and "Use Before" are examples of terminology used for code dating. When buying eggs, look at the date to make sure it hasn't passed. Also, choose clean, uncracked shells. Make sure they've been refrigerated in the store. Bacteria can enter eggs through cracks in the shell. Never purchase cracked eggs. However, if eggs crack on the way home from the store, you may break them into a clean container, cover them tightly, keep refrigerated, and use within 2 days.

Although you may purchase eggs that have not passed the "Sell By" date, you really don't know how fresh the eggs are. There are ways you can spot older eggs. When chicken eggs are laid they are at a temperature of 105° F (41° C), and normally have no air pockets inside. As the egg cools, a small air cell forms, usually in the larger end of the egg, and develops between the two shell membranes. In a fertilized egg, this air pocket provides the chick with its first few breaths of air just before hatching. Whether fertilized or not, all eggs have an air pocket.

As the egg ages, the air cell increases in size. An egg can float in water when its air cell has enlarged sufficiently to keep it buoyant. This means the egg is old, but it may be perfectly safe to eat. Aging can make peeling a hard-boiled eggs easier. The fresher the egg, the more difficult it is to peel after hard cooking. That's because air infiltrates the shell over time, loosening the junction between the shell membrane and the egg white.

If you want to hard- or soft-cook an egg, it is best to use an older one. The way to test this is to submerge the egg in water. Fresh eggs will sink below the surface. Older eggs will tilt on end and very old eggs may float to the surface.

As an egg ages, the white and yolk lose quality. The yolk absorbs water from the white. Moisture and carbon dioxide in the white evaporate through the pores, allowing more air to penetrate the shell, and the air cell becomes larger. If broken, the contents of older eggs are more liquid and will spread out over a wider area. The white becomes thinner, losing some of its thickening and leavening powers. The yolk becomes flatter, larger, and more easily broken. The chalazae (kah-LAY-zuh), the twisted cordlike strands of egg white that anchor the yolk in the center of the white, become less prominent and weaker, allowing the yolk to move off center.

Cloudy egg whites may be a sign of contamination. Pink or iridescent egg whites indicate spoilage due to bacteria. Some of these microorganisms, which produce a greenish, fluorescent, water-soluble pigment, are harmful to humans. Refrigeration slows the loss of quality over time. Crack the egg into a bowl and examine it for an off-odor or unusual appearance before deciding to use or discard it. A spoiled egg will have an unpleasant odor when you break open the shell. The odor will persist even when cooked.

Occasionally when you break open an egg, you will see a tiny dark speck or spot of blood. These are caused by a rupture of one or more small blood vessels in the yolk at the time of ovulation. It does not indicate the egg is unsafe.

Egg Storage Chart		
Product	**Refrigerator**	**Freezer**
Raw eggs in shell	3 to 5 weeks	Do not freeze
Raw egg whites	2 to 4 days	12 months
Raw egg yolks	2 to 4 days	Yolks do not freeze well
Hard-boiled eggs	1 week	Do not freeze
Raw egg accidentally frozen in shell	Use immediately after thawing	Keep frozen; then refrigerate to thaw

The color of yolk varies in shades of yellow depending upon the diet of the hen. If she eats plenty of yellow-orange plant pigments, such as from marigold petals and yellow corn, the yolk will be a darker yellow than if she eats a colorless diet, such as white cornmeal. Artificial color additives are not permitted in commercially produced eggs.

A green ring on a hard-cooked yolk can be a result of overcooking, and is caused by sulfur and iron compounds in the egg reacting on the yolk's surface. The green color can also be caused by a high amount of iron in the cooking water. Eggs with a green color are safe to eat.

Sizing of Eggs

Although large eggs are the most commonly sold, you can get eggs in various sizes. Size tells you the minimum required net weight per dozen eggs. It does not refer to the dimensions of an egg or how big it looks. While some eggs in the carton may look slightly larger or smaller than the rest, it is the total weight of the dozen eggs that puts them in one of the following classes:

Are Organic or Free-Range Eggs More Nutritious?

Organic eggs are produced from chickens that are given only GMO-free, organic feed and that are allowed to roam around and eat bugs and weeds. Free-range chickens are allowed a portion of time to roam outside and eat naturally, but their feed can be the same given to any other commercially produced chicken. The advantage of being able to walk around freely, even if only for a limited time, is that exercise is provided, along with the opportunity to diversify their diet with bugs and grass, and this results in a healthier chicken and a more nutritious egg. The eggs will be enriched with beta-carotene, lutein, omega-3 fatty acids, and other nutrients obtained from the foods the chickens hunt and gather themselves. This is reflected in the color of the egg yolk. A darker yellow or orange yolk indicates a diet richer in nutrients.

Chickens, by their very nature, are not vegetarian. They love meat and prefer eating worms and bugs over grass or grains. Some eggs are advertised as being from chickens that were fed a vegetarian diet. This is unnatural and unhealthy. If their diet is truly vegetarian, it means they were fed exclusively on commercial feed consisting of grains and plant matter and were locked up in cages without access to bugs, worms, or sunshine.

Another very important aspect to organic and free-range eggs is that they are raised in more humane and healthier conditions so their eggs are perfectly safe to eat raw or cooked as long as the shell is not damaged or broken. Large commercial chicken farms where the animals are kept locked in overcrowded cages often breeds disease. Consequently, eggs from these sources can potentially harbor bacteria, primarily salmonella. Unhealthy chickens can be infected with salmonella and pass the bacteria to the developing egg, so that even an unbroken egg can be contaminated from the inside. Large egg production facilities often feed their chickens antibiotics in order to reduce this problem. For this reason, it is not generally recommended that you eat commercially produced eggs raw. The general recommendation is to cook the eggs until the yolk is firm. This is not necessary with organic and free-range eggs or eggs from small farms. People have been enjoying foods with raw and partially cooked eggs, such as eggnog, mayonnaise, soft-boiled eggs, and fried eggs with a soft yolk, for generations without harm. You can, too, if you choose your source of eggs properly.

Egg Products

The term "egg products" refers to eggs that have been removed from their shells for processing at facilities called "breaker plants." The processing of egg products includes breaking eggs, filtering, mixing, stabilizing, blending, pasteurizing, cooling, freezing or drying, and packaging. Basic egg products include whole eggs, whites, yolks, and various blends—with or without non-egg ingredients. They may be available in liquid, frozen, and dried forms. All egg products are pasteurized. They are rapidly heated and held at a minimum required temperature for a specified time. This destroys bacteria, but it does not cook the eggs or significantly affect their color, flavor, nutritional value, or use. However, there is some concern that processing may increase the rate of oxidation of the fats and cholesterol in the egg.

Some of these products, such as egg whites or cholesterol-free egg substitutes, are available in supermarkets. Most, however, are used in the food service industry and the commercial food industry because of their convenience and ease in handling and storing. Restaurants use them to make scrambled eggs, omelets, quiches, and other egg-based products. Food manufacturers use them as ingredients in making noodles, mayonnaise, ice cream, and baked goods.

Egg white powder is dried egg white. It can be reconstituted by mixing the powder with water. The reconstituted powder whips like fresh egg white. The product is usually sold along with supplies for cake baking and decorating.

When given the choice, it is best to use fresh eggs.

How to Separate an Egg and Beat Egg Whites

Many delicious egg recipes require the egg yolks and whites to be separated and the whites to be whipped. For best results, the eggs should be at room temperature. Start by striking the egg sharply against the countertop or other flat surface to create a slight depression in the shell, then carefully pull the halves apart forming two relatively equal halves. Let the egg white fall into a bowl but catch the yolk in one half of the shell, then transfer the yolk to the other shell half, letting the remaining egg white drain into the bowl. Place the yolk into a separate bowl.

Be very careful not to allow *any* of the yolk to mix with the whites; even the tiniest speck of yolk in the whites will keep them from whipping properly.

If some shell fragments get into the whites, it can be difficult trying to remove them using a spoon or knife. Your best tool for this job is a larger piece of the shell itself.

Egg whites should be beaten just before using, as they tend to lose volume the longer they sit. Using an electric hand mixer or whisk, beat the whites until they thicken and stiff peaks form. The peaks will still be soft, but they will be

Whip egg whites until stiff peaks form. Transfer a portion of the egg whites into the lightly beaten yolks.

Mix the portion of egg white with the yolks until blended. Add the egg white-yolk mixture to the rest of the egg whites and carefully fold in.

able to stand up when the beater is removed. The purpose for beating the whites is to create volume. During the beating process, air is whipped into the whites, giving the cooked product a soft, spongy texture. This is what makes sponge cakes spongy and what makes soufflés puffy and delicious.

Although not required, adding a pinch of cream of tartar or a drop of lemon juice or vinegar to the egg whites will give them greater volume and stability when whipped.

The yolks are usually combined with the whipped whites. Often, seasonings and other ingredients are mixed into the yolks prior to mixing them with the whites.

Whipped whites quickly break down when mixed with other food ingredients. To prevent rapid breakdown, mix about a fourth of the whipped whites with the egg yolks. Once mixed, using a rubber spatula or large spoon, carefully fold the egg yolk mixture into the remaining egg whites. Fold just enough to marble the two, you do not need to completely mix the ingredients. Immediately cook as directed by the recipe.

EGG RECIPES

How to Cook the Perfect Soft-Boiled Egg

Opinions of the perfect soft-boiled egg vary due to people's personal preferences. Some like the yolk runny with the white perfectly set, others prefer a creamy, custard-like white, and still others like their yolks partially set. Whichever you prefer is the perfect soft-boiled egg for you. However, achieving this goal can be tricky using the traditional egg-in-boiling-water method.

One of the challenges with achieving this is the difference in temperatures needed to cook the yolk and the white. Egg whites must reach 180° F (82° C) in order to set, while the yolks set at a lower temperature of 158° F (70° C). This is why it is best to use chilled eggs straight from the refrigerator to cook soft-boiled eggs than ones at room temperature.

There are just too many variables in the traditional boiling method that can affect your final result. Do you put the egg in the water before heating or after? Many cooks heat the water and eggs together to avoid cracking the shells, but when you do this, you cannot accurately calculate cooking time. If you wait until the water comes to a boil, you must turn down the heat before adding the eggs. If you turn it down too much, however, the eggs will require more time to cook. If you don't turn it down enough, you run the risk of cracking the shell. If you cook multiple eggs, you must increase the cooking time proportionally for each added egg. Far too much guesswork is involved to achieve consistent results every time.

However, there is a method that is faster and easier, reduces the risk of cracking, and produces perfect results each and every time. The secret is steam. Instead of boiling the egg, you steam it in a vegetable steamer. Inside the steamer, the temperature remains relatively constant at 212° F (100° C) the entire time. The temperature is the same no matter how many eggs you cook, so you can cook a half-dozen eggs for

the same period of time you would cook just one. Also, the small amount of water you put in the steamer heats up much faster than water in a saucepan, which can cut about 5 minutes off your wait time before you begin cooking the eggs.

The following directions are for standard large eggs. Extra-large, jumbo, medium, and small eggs will require slight adjustments in cooking times. Start

by heating ½ inch (1 cm) water in a vegetable steamer on high setting. When the water begins to boil, turn the heat down to a gentle boil. Put *chilled* eggs straight from the refrigerator into the steamer and cover. Begin timing. Depending on your preference, you will steam the eggs for 5, 7, or 9 minutes.

St. Jude Children's
Research Hospital

ALSAC • Danny Thomas, Founder

Finding cures. Saving children.

stjude.org

St. Jude Children's Research Hospital

ALSAC • Danny Thomas, Founder

Finding cures. Saving children.

stjude.org

If you like your yolk runny with a creamy, custard-like egg white, cook for 5 minutes, then remove with a slotted spoon.

If you like your yolk runny with the egg white set, cook for 7 minutes and remove.

If you like your yolk partially set but still very soft, with the egg white fully set, cook for 9 minutes and remove.

Immediately put the eggs in cold water and let them rest for 3 to 4 minutes. This stops the cooking process and quickly cools them off so you can handle them.

Serve in an egg cup. If you don't have an egg cup, you can make an improvised cup by filling a small cup or bowl half-full of uncooked rice or wheat and push the cooked egg partially into the grain, which will hold it in place.

To eat, remove the top portion of the egg by tapping it with a table knife all the way around the top. Pull off the top to expose the white and yolk. Enjoy!

One large egg: 5 g fat; 0.5 g net carbs; 6 g protein; 70 calories

How to Cook the Perfect Hard-Boiled Egg

The perfect hard-boiled egg is not actually boiled, as is traditionally done, but steamed in a vegetable steamer. Follow the directions above for cooking soft-boiled eggs, but increase the cooking time to 12 minutes.

Remember to reduce the heat on the steamer to a gentle boil before adding the eggs. This method reduces the risk of cracking the shells during cooking. Although this sometimes still happens, the occurrence is less often.

Besides getting a perfectly cooked egg each time, the shell comes off a little easier than from the traditional boiling method. I've cooked fresh eggs straight from the henhouse that are less than a day old using this method and the shells peel off almost as easily as a more mature egg.

Peeling an egg is easier if you crack the shell all around and roll the egg between your hands to loosen the shell. Hold the egg under running cold water to help ease the shell off. Gently dry with a paper towel before serving.

One large egg: 5 g fat; 0.5 g net carbs; 6 g protein; 70 calories

Deviled Eggs

6 eggs, hard-boiled and peeled
¼ cup (60 g) mayonnaise
   (pages 37-40)
1 teaspoon apple cider vinegar
1 teaspoon prepared mustard
⅛ teaspoon salt
Freshly ground black pepper
Paprika

Slice the eggs in half lengthwise and remove the yolks. Put the yolks in a bowl, and with a fork mash them into fine pieces. Add mayonnaise, vinegar, mustard, salt, and pepper, and mix until smooth. Spoon an equal amount of the mixture into each of the egg whites. Garnish with paprika and serve.

Yield: 12
Per serving: 6 g fat; 0 g net carbs; 3 g protein; 66 calories

Spicy Deviled Eggs

6 eggs, hard-boiled and peeled
¼ cup (60 g) mayonnaise
1 teaspoon Dijon mustard
2 teaspoons minced onion
⅛ teaspoon hot sauce
Salt and pepper to taste

Slice the eggs in half lengthwise and remove the yolks. Put the yolks in a bowl, and with a fork mash them into fine pieces. Add mayonnaise, mustard, onion, hot sauce, salt, and pepper, and mix until smooth. Spoon an equal amount of the mixture into each of the egg whites. Garnish with paprika, and chill in the refrigerator for 1 to 2 hours before serving.

Yield: 12
Per serving: 6 g fat; 0 g net carbs; 3 g protein; 66 calories

Rosemary Deviled Eggs

6 hard-boiled eggs, chilled
2 tablespoons (30 g) mayonnaise
1 tablespoon (15 ml) cream
1 teaspoon white wine vinegar
2 scallions, chopped
½ teaspoon fresh rosemary or ¼ teaspoon of powdered rosemary
⅛ teaspoon dry mustard
½ teaspoon salt
Dash pepper

Peel eggs and cut in half lengthwise. Spoon yolks into a small mixing bowl and mash with a fork. Add mayonnaise, cream, vinegar, scallions, rosemary, mustard, salt, and pepper, and beat with the fork until creamy. Stuff egg whites with filling, and chill at least 1 hour before serving.

Yield: 12
Per serving: 9 g fat; 1 g net carbs; 5.5 g protein; 107 calories

Guacamole Deviled Eggs

6 eggs, hard-boiled and peeled
2 ripe avocados
1 tablespoon (15 ml) lime juice
1 tablespoon (28 g) sour cream
¼ teaspoon ground cumin
½ teaspoon salt
1 tablespoon (1 g) chopped cilantro

2 teaspoons chopped jalapeño pepper
1 tablespoon (3 g) chopped chives

Slice the eggs in half lengthwise, remove the yolks, and place in a bowl. With a fork, mash the egg yolks into fine pieces. Remove the pits from the avocados, scoop out the flesh, and add to the bowl. Add lime juice, sour cream, cumin, and salt, and mash the ingredients together with the fork. Stir in cilantro and jalapeño pepper. Mound a generous and equal amount of the mixture into each of the egg whites. Garnish with chives and serve.

Yield: 12
Per serving: 9 g fat; 1 g net carbs; 3.5 g protein; 99 calories

Poached Eggs

Poaching eggs is extraordinarily easy, yet surprisingly difficult to accomplish with perfection each time. However, if you follow a few simple guidelines, your poached eggs will come out winners consistently.

Put water (or broth) in a skillet up to about 1½ to 2 inches (3.5 to 5 cm). Heat the water to boiling, then reduce it to a simmer. Break an egg into a measuring cup or saucer. Hold the cup close to the surface of the simmering

liquid and slide the egg in. For multiple eggs, follow this procedure 1 egg at a time. Simmer until the desired doneness, between 3 to 5 minutes. Remove with a slotted spoon.

Yield: 1 egg per serving
One large egg: 5 g fat; 0.5 g net carbs; 6 g protein; 70 calories

Poached Eggs Espagnole
Poached eggs taste great covered in the French classic Espagnole Sauce.

Espagnole Sauce (page 27)
2 or more poached eggs

Prepare Espagnole Sauce according to directions. Poach 2 or more eggs following the directions above. Serve each poached egg covered in ½ cup of Espagnole Sauce.

Yield: 1 egg per serving
Per serving: 15 g fat; 4 g net carbs; 13 g protein; 203 calories

Baked Eggs
Baking is an easy way to prepare eggs for breakfast or at any time of the day. The recipe is for one egg, but you can cook as many eggs as you like with the same cooking time and temperature.

1 tablespoon (28 g) butter, softened
1 egg
Salt and black pepper to taste
¼ ounce (7 g) shredded cheese (optional)
Paprika (optional)

Preheat oven to 325° F (170° C). Use half of the butter to coat a 6 ounce (170 g) custard cup. Break 1 egg and carefully drop it into the custard cup. Place the remaining butter on top and sprinkle with salt and pepper. Add shredded cheese, if desired. Bake for 16 to 20 minutes until desired doneness. The white should be set but the yolk soft. Garnish with paprika before serving.

Yield: 1 egg
Per serving: 29 g fat; 0.5 g net carbs; 7.5 g protein; 293 calories

Ham, eggs, carrot sticks, and fermented daikon radish (page 120).

Fried Eggs

Frying, without breaking the yolk, is one of the most popular ways of serving eggs. There are different ways to fry eggs. Some people like to flip their eggs, but this often breaks the yolk or overcooks it. If you like your yolk thoroughly cooked, you can use this method, but you don't have to. You can cook an egg to any degree you prefer, without flipping it.

You can use butter, coconut oil, bacon drippings, or red palm oil. Each oil will give the eggs a slightly different flavor. You can even combine two or more oils. I like to combine bacon drippings with red palm oil or coconut oil.

Heat 1 to 2 tablespoons of oil in a skillet over medium heat. The oil is hot and ready for the egg when a few drops of water sizzle when dropped into the pan. Break an egg and carefully drop it into the hot pan. To avoid getting burned by spattering oil, you can break the egg into a measuring cup first and slide it into the hot oil. Follow this procedure with each egg.

Place a lid on the skillet and cook until desired doneness, checking periodically, about 2 to 4 minutes. I love glass lids that allow you to see the eggs while they're cooking so you know exactly how long to cook them. If you want the tops of the yolks to cook faster, you can spoon hot oil on top of the eggs as they are cooking; or you can add a little water to the pan and cover, which will create steam that will cook the tops of the eggs.

Yield: 1 egg per serving
Per serving: 5 g fat; 0.5 g net carbs; 6 g protein; 70 calories

Ham and Eggs with Cheese Sauce

Cheese Sauce (page 24)
1 tablespoon (14 g) coconut oil or bacon drippings
3 ounces (85 g) sliced sugar-free, nitrite-free ham
1 fried or poached egg

Prepare Cheese Sauce as directed. Heat coconut oil in a skillet and cook ham alongside egg to desired doneness. Place ham on serving dish, add the fried or poached egg on top of the ham, and cover with Cheese Sauce.

Yield: 1 egg and slice of ham per serving
Per serving with ½ cup (120 ml) the Cheese Sauce: 67 g fat; 4.5 g net carbs; 28 g protein; 729 calories

Scrambled Eggs

Scrambled eggs are a classic breakfast favorite. They are incredibly simple to make and taste great. The only ingredients you need are oil, eggs, and salt, however, other ingredients can be added at your discretion. The flavor of the dish is strongly affected by the type of oil you use. Bacon drippings are a favorite, but also try coconut oil, red palm oil, butter, beef tallow, and even chicken or duck fat. You might even try mixing two or more oils.

2 tablespoons (28 g) coconut oil or bacon drippings
2 eggs
Salt and black pepper to taste

Heat the oil in the skillet until hot, crack open each egg, and drop it into the hot skillet. Using a fork, immediately stir or scramble the eggs, and then let them cook, uncovered, for about 4 to 5 minutes. Using a spatula, turn and cook the eggs until the desired doneness is achieved. Add salt and black pepper to taste, and it's ready to eat. Goes well with a side of bacon, ham, or other breakfast meat. May also be served topped with salsa or sliced avocado.

The method you use to cook the eggs influences the flavor and texture of the finished product. Scrambling the eggs in the hot skillet produces a different result in comparison to beating the raw eggs together before adding them to the skillet, as you would an omelet. Scrambling the eggs in the pan allows the eggs to partially cook before they are completely mixed, giving them a marbled appearance, and lets you taste both the egg white and yolk. In contrast, mixing the egg before cooking produces a more uniform texture and taste.

Yield: serves 1
Per serving: 36 g fat; 1 g net carbs; 11 g protein; 372 calories

Scrambled Egg Variations:

Prepare scrambled eggs as described above, but add to the eggs any of the following: minced chicken livers or paté, chopped cooked breakfast sausage, minced ham; minced cooked fish, shellfish, chicken, or turkey; sautéed mushrooms, onions, garlic, or green peppers; cooked asparagus tips; minced cooked cauliflower or broccoli; crisp, crumbled bacon; cooked artichoke hearts; chopped tomatoes; fresh minced herbs (basil, parsley, chives, dill, tarragon, chervil, marjoram, cilantro, or sage); ground spices (chili powder, coriander, cumin, curry powder, dry mustard, oregano, paprika, red pepper flakes, ground rosemary, thyme, turmeric); and chopped jalapeño or other chili peppers.

Fiesta Scramble

This is a simple way to spice up your scrambled eggs. Make scrambled eggs following the recipe above. Before serving, top the eggs with 1 tablespoon (16 g) salsa, ¼ avocado (sliced), and 1 tablespoon (1 g) chopped cilantro.

Yield: serves 1
Per serving: 43 g fat; 2 g net carbs; 12 g protein; 443 calories

Sour Cream and Chives Scramble

Make the Scrambled Eggs recipe on page 275 and serve topped with a dollop of sour cream and a teaspoon of minced chives.

Yield: serves 1
Per serving: 39 g fat; 1.5 g net carbs; 11.5 g protein; 403 calories

Cottage Cheese Scramble

This is a great variation to ordinary scrambled eggs. The cottage cheese gives the eggs a slight, pleasant-sour taste that is sweetened by the addition of dehydrated onions. If you don't have dehydrated onions on hand, onion power will do.

2 tablespoons (28 g) coconut oil or bacon drippings
2 eggs, beaten
¼ cup (55 g) cottage cheese
1 teaspoon dehydrated chopped or granulated onion
¼ teaspoon salt

Heat oil in a skillet over medium heat. Beat together eggs, cottage cheese, onion, and salt. Pour mixture into hot skillet, cover, and cook until the egg sets, about 5 minutes.

Yield: serves 1
Per serving: 37 g fat; 3.5 g net carbs; 19 g protein; 423 calories

Three-Pepper Scramble

This dish uses three types of garden peppers, two mild (green and red bell peppers) and one hot (jalapeño).

1 medium yellow onion, sliced very thin
1 green pepper, cut in ¼-inch (0.5-cm) wide strips
1 red pepper, cut in ¼-inch (0.5-cm) wide strips
2 tablespoons (28 g) coconut oil or lard
1 clove garlic, minced
2 medium tomatoes, cored, seeded, and coarsely chopped
½ cup (75 g) cooked sugar-free, nitrite-free ham, cut into strips
   ¼ inch (0.5 cm) wide and 2 inches (5 cm) long
½ teaspoon salt
⅛ teaspoon black pepper
2 tablespoons (28 g) butter
1 tablespoon (9 g) chopped jalapeño pepper or other hot pepper
4 eggs, lightly beaten

In a large skillet over medium-low heat, sauté onion, green pepper, and red pepper in coconut oil until limp, not brown, about 10 minutes. Add garlic, tomatoes, ham, salt, and black pepper. Cook until most of the liquid has evaporated, about 6 minutes. Push the vegetables to the edge of the skillet. Add butter to the center of the skillet. Mix the chopped jalapeño with the eggs and pour into the center of the skillet. Cook without stirring until eggs are just barely set. Mix the eggs with the vegetables, remove from heat, and serve.

Yield: serves 4
Per serving: 20 g fat; 5.5 g net carbs; 10 g protein; 242 calories

Variation:

Follow the directions above, but stir in ½ cup (75 g) feta cheese just before removing the skillet from the heat.

The egg mixture is poured over the Canadian bacon to prevent the cream cheese in the eggs from burning.

Cream Cheese Scramble

    1 tablespoon (14 g) coconut oil, bacon drippings, or red palm oil
    2 ounces (56 g) sugar-free, nitrite-free Canadian bacon or ham
    2 eggs, lightly beaten
    2 teaspoons dehydrated onion
    ⅛ teaspoon salt
    3 ounces (85 g) cream cheese, softened

Heat the oil in a skillet over medium-low heat. Place the Canadian bacon in hot pan and cook one side for about 2 minutes. While the meat is cooking, combine eggs, dehydrated onion, salt, and cream cheese, and mix until well blended. Flip Canadian bacon over and pour egg mixture over the top, cover, and cook until the top of the egg is just set. Do not overcook, as the bottom burns easily because of the cream cheese. Cooking the egg mixture on top of the Canadian bacon helps prevent burning.

Yield: serves 1
Per serving: 56.5 g fat; 6 g net carbs; 29.5 g protein; 650 calories

Scrambled Eggs and Shrimp

Cocktail Sauce (page 33)
2 eggs, lightly beaten
2 ounces (56 g) baby shrimp
¼ teaspoon fish sauce
2 tablespoons (28 g) bacon drippings

Prepare Cocktail Sauce as directed. In a small bowl, mix eggs, shrimp, and fish sauce. Heat bacon drippings in a skillet, and when hot, pour in egg mixture. Cook, stirring occasionally, until the eggs set. Place eggs on serving plate and top with Cocktail Sauce. Garnish with fresh cilantro or parsley if desired.

Yield: serves 1
Per serving with ¼ cup (60 ml) Cocktail Sauce: 39.5 g fat; 1.5 g net carbs; 24 g protein; 457 calories

Salmon-Asparagus Scramble

1 tablespoon (14 g) coconut oil
3 large spears asparagus, cut into bite-size pieces
2 eggs, beaten
2 teaspoons dehydrated onion
1 ounce (28 g) smoked or cooked salmon, separated into bite-size pieces
1 ounce (28 g) Asiago or Parmesan cheese, shredded
Salt and black pepper

Heat the oil in a skillet over medium heat. Sauté asparagus until just tender, about 5 minutes. Combine eggs and onion and pour into skillet with the asparagus, cover, and cook for about 2 minutes, or until the egg is only partially set. Add salmon and cheese on top, cover, and continue cooking until the egg is set, about 5 minutes. Remove from heat, add salt and black pepper to taste and serve.

Yield: serves 1
Per serving: 34 g fat; 5 g net carbs; 25.5 g protein; 428 calories

Red Pepper Scramble

This is a great way to liven up your eggs in the morning.

Red Pepper Sauce (page 29)
2 tablespoons (28 g) coconut oil or bacon drippings
2 eggs, lightly beaten
Salt

Prepare Red Pepper Sauce as directed. Heat the oil a skillet, then cook eggs until set. Salt to taste. Serve covered in about ½ cup (120 ml) sauce.

Yield: serves 1
Per serving with ½ cup (120 ml) Red Pepper Sauce: 49 g fat; 4.5 g net carbs; 24 g protein; 555 calories

Easy Omelet

Omelets are easy to make and, with different ingredients, can be made into many variations. Omelets made in the traditional French manner can be a bit complicated. This recipe is a simplified version that tastes just as good and allows for multiple variations. The following directions are for a plain omelet.

2 tablespoons (28 g) coconut oil or bacon drippings
4 eggs
¼ teaspoon salt
⅛ teaspoon black pepper

Melt oil in skillet over medium heat. Whisk together eggs, salt, and pepper in a bowl until bubbly. Pour mixture into the hot skillet, cover, and cook without stirring until the top of the omelet is set, about 5 minutes. Remove omelet from pan and serve hot.

Yield: 2 servings
Per serving: 22.5 g fat; 0.5 g net carbs; 11 g protein; 248 calories

Variations:

A variety of omelets can be made using many different ingredients, including ham, bacon, chicken, sausage, ground beef, ground lamb, shrimp, crab, onions, eggplant, zucchini, garlic, sweet or hot peppers, tomatoes, avocado, asparagus, broccoli, cauliflower, spinach, and mushrooms. The meats and most of the vegetables are cooked before combining with the egg mixture. Tomatoes, avocados, and garnishes such as cilantro and chives are best used raw and added after cooking. Sour cream can be used as a garnish, as well. Cheese can be melted on top during the cooking of the eggs. Any one or more of these ingredients can be combined. You should make note of the quantities of each ingredient used so that you can calculate the net carbs and fat content.

Herb Omelet

Make the Easy Omelet as described above, but add 1 teaspoon minced chives, ½ teaspoon minced fresh chervil, and ¼ teaspoon minced fresh tarragon to eggs before whisking.

Yield and nutritional values are the same as the Easy Omelet.

Cheese Omelet

Follow the directions for making the Easy Omelet, but after pouring the egg mixture into the hot skillet, sprinkle ¾ cup (84 g) of shredded cheese over the top. Cover and cook without stirring until the omelet is set and the cheese is melted.

Yield: 2 servings
Per serving: 35.6 g fat; 1.2 g net carbs; 21.6 g protein; 414 calories

Lorraine Omelet

Make the Easy Omelet as described above. Midway through cooking, sprinkle ¼ cup (30 g) shredded Gruyere cheese on top of the omelet, then cover and finish cooking. When the omelet is set, turn off the heat and sprinkle with 1 tablespoon minced parsley and 2 slices of crumbled crisp bacon. Using a spatula, fold half of the omelet over onto the other half and remove from the skillet.

Yield: 2 servings
Per serving: 36.5 g fat; 0.5 g net carbs; 19.5 g protein; 408 calories

Spanish Omelet

2 tablespoons (30 g) butter
1 pimiento, slivered
1 small tomato, peeled, cored, seeded, and coarsely chopped
1 garlic clove, crushed
1 tablespoon (4 g) minced parsley

Heat butter in a skillet over medium heat. Stir-fry pimiento, tomato, garlic, and parsley for about 3 minutes until softened. Remove from heat and set aside. Make the Easy Omelet as directed above. When the omelet is set, add the vegetables to the top. Using a spatula, fold half of the omelet over the other half and remove from the skillet.

Yield: 2 servings
Per serving: 34 g fat; 4.5 g net carbs; 12.5 g protein; 374 calories

Greek Omelet

2 tablespoons (28 g) olive oil
2 bay leaves
1 clove garlic, chopped
4 eggs
¼ teaspoon salt
⅛ teaspoon black pepper
1 tablespoon (3 g) minced chives
¼ cup (40 g) crumbled feta cheese

Heat olive oil in a skillet over medium heat. Add bay leaves and garlic, and cook for 3 to 4 minutes to infuse flavors into the oil, then remove the bay leaves. Whisk together eggs, salt, and pepper in a bowl until bubbly. Pour eggs into the hot skillet, cover, and cook without stirring until the top of the omelet is set, about five minutes. Sprinkle chives and feta cheese over the top. Using a spatula, fold half of the omelet over onto the other half and remove from the skillet. Serve hot.

Yield: 2 servings
Per serving: 26 g fat; 2 g net carbs; 14 g protein; 298 calories

Sausage, Mushroom, and Tomato Omelet

This is a good example of how to prepare an omelet that is combined with meats and vegetables. See the many variations below.

2 tablespoons (28 g) coconut oil or bacon drippings
¼ pound (120 g) sausage
2 mushrooms, sliced
3 eggs
¼ teaspoon salt
½ cup (90 g) chopped tomato

Heat coconut oil in a skillet. Add sausage and mushrooms, and cook until sausage is browned. Whisk together eggs and salt in a bowl. Pour mixture into the hot skillet over the sausage and mushrooms, cover, and cook without stirring until the top of the omelet is set, about 5 minutes. Add tomato, cover, and cook 1 minute. Remove omelet from pan and serve hot.

Yield: 2 servings
Per serving: 37.7 g fat; 1.9 g net carbs; 20.9 g protein; 429 calories

Bacon Zucchini Omelet

4 slices sugar-free, nitrite-free bacon
1 small zucchini (about 6 ounces/170 g), chopped
3 eggs
2 teaspoons jalapeño pepper, chopped
Salt
2 ounces (55 g) cheese, shredded

Cook bacon in a skillet over medium heat until crisp, remove from pan, and set aside. Sauté zucchini in bacon grease, turning occasionally, until browned, about 10 minutes. Whisk together eggs, jalapeño pepper, and salt, and pour evenly over the zucchini. Sprinkle cheese over the eggs. Crumble the bacon and sprinkle on top. Cover and cook until the egg sets, about 7 minutes.

Yield: 2 servings
Per serving: 31.5 g fat; 3 g net carbs; 30 g protein; 415 calories

Onion Frittata

This is an omelet for onion lovers. It is of Italian origin and is browned on both sides.

1 medium Bermuda onion, peeled and sliced very thin
3 tablespoons (42 g) coconut or olive oil
1 clove garlic, minced
4 eggs, lightly beaten
¾ teaspoon salt
⅛ teaspoon black pepper
1 teaspoon dried basil
¼ cup (80 g) shredded Parmesan cheese

In a skillet, sauté onion in half of the oil over medium-low heat for 5 to 8 minutes until limp, not brown. Add garlic and sauté for about 1 minute. Place in a bowl and mix the onion and garlic with eggs, salt, black pepper, basil, and cheese. Add the remaining oil to the skillet, let it heat for about 1 or 2 minutes, then add the egg mixture. Cover and cook without stirring for about 3 to 4 minutes, until the bottom is browned and the top is just set. Cut in quarters, flip, and brown the other side.

Yield: 2 servings
Per serving: 38.5 g fat; 6.5 g net carbs; 24.5 g protein; 470 calories

Fluffy Soufflé

Soufflés have a distinctively different taste and texture to omelets even though they may contain the same ingredients. This version starts on the stovetop like an omelet but is finished off in the oven, giving it a fluffy taste and texture. The secret to a fluffy soufflé is to cook the eggs slowly. Use eggs at room temperature; this will give them better volume. It is important to use a skillet that is both stovetop and oven safe.

4 eggs, separated
¼ teaspoon salt
⅛ teaspoon black pepper
3 tablespoons (42 g) coconut oil, butter, or bacon drippings

Preheat oven to 325 degrees F (170 C). Using an electric beater, beat egg whites until stiff peaks form. In a separate bowl, mix egg yolks, salt, and pepper until creamy. Gently mix one-fourth of the egg whites into the yolks until well blended. Fold the yolk mixture into the remaining whites. Do not over mix.

At medium heat, heat oil in an oven safe skillet on the stovetop. Pour egg mixture into the hot skillet, gently smooth out the top, reduce heat to medium-low, and cook uncovered for about 5 minutes, or until the bottom of the soufflé starts to brown. Transfer the skillet to the preheated oven and cook uncovered for 18 to 20 minutes, or until soufflé is puffy and delicately browned. Remove from the oven, divide in half with a spatula, and serve.

As with all of the recipes in this chapter, you can add more oil to increase the fat content. You can also increase fat content by adding cheese, sausage, and other high-fat ingredients.

Yield: 2 servings
Per serving: 30 g fat; 0.5 g net carbs; 11 g protein; 316 calories

Cheese Soufflé

In this recipe, you first make a cheese sauce, which is then mixed into the egg whites. Use a skillet that is both stovetop and oven safe.

2 tablespoons (28 g) butter
½ cup (120 ml) heavy cream
1¼ cups (150 g) sharp cheddar cheese, shredded
3 eggs, separated
¼ teaspoon salt
⅛ teaspoon black pepper
1 tablespoon (14 g) coconut oil

Melt butter in a saucepan over moderate heat. Add cream and cheese, stirring until cheese is melted. Mix egg yolks, salt, and pepper lightly with a fork. Blend about ¼ cup (60 ml) of hot cheese sauce into the yolks, then immediately stir the yolk mixture into the cheese sauce. Cook the sauce over low heat, stirring constantly, for 1 to 2 minutes. Remove from heat and let cool to room temperature.

Meanwhile, preheat oven to 325 degrees F (170 C). In a separate bowl, beat egg whites until stiff peaks form. Gently mix one-fourth of the egg whites into the cheese sauce. Fold the remaining whites into the sauce. Do not over mix or your soufflé will become flat. At medium heat, heat coconut oil in an oven safe skillet on the stovetop. Pour egg mixture into the hot skillet, reduce heat to medium-low, and cook for about 5 minutes, or until the bottom of the soufflé begins to brown. Transfer pan to oven and cook uncovered for 18 to 20 minutes, or until soufflé is puffy and delicately browned. Remove from oven, divide in half with a spatula, and serve.

Yield: 2 servings
Per serving: 72.5 g fat; 3 g net carbs; 28.5 g protein; 778 calories

Variations:
Prepare Cheese Soufflé as directed, but before cooling cheese sauce, mix in ¼ to ½ cup (25 to 50 g) of any of the following: cooked ham or sausage, crisp crumbled bacon, minced sautéed chicken livers, deviled ham, minced sautéed mushrooms, minced cooked fish or shellfish, or minced cooked vegetables (pimiento, asparagus, spinach, broccoli, cauliflower, cabbage, Brussels sprouts, or onions). Adjust net carbs to account for additional ingredients.

Cinnamon Peach Soufflé

Although the name of this soufflé sounds like it is a sweet dessert, it is only very mildly sweet and completely keto friendly. The cinnamon and fruit give this soufflé a flavor that differs from the typical savory egg dishes.

4 eggs, separated
⅛ teaspoon salt
¼ teaspoon almond extract
¼ teaspoon cinnamon
⅛ teaspoon ground cloves
¾ cup (128 g) finely chopped peaches
¼ cup (30 g) chopped pecans
1 tablespoon (8 g) coconut flour
2 tablespoons (28 g) coconut oil

Preheat oven to 350 degrees F (180 C). With an electric hand mixer, beat egg whites until stiff peaks form. In a separate bowl, mix egg yolks, salt, almond extract, cinnamon, cloves, peaches, pecans, and coconut flour. Gently add one-third of the egg whites into the yolk mixture and mix until well blended. Fold the yolk mixture into the remaining whites. Do not over mix.

At medium heat, heat oil in an oven safe skillet on the stovetop. Pour egg mixture into the hot skillet, gently smooth out the top for even thickness, reduce heat to medium-low, and cook uncovered for about 4 minutes or until the bottom of the soufflé just starts to brown. Transfer the skillet to the preheated oven and cook uncovered for 18 to 20 minutes, or until soufflé is puffy and delicately browned. Remove from oven, divide in half with a spatula, and serve.

Yield: 2 servings
Per serving: 34.5 g fat; 7 g net carbs; 14 g protein; 394 calories

Pineapple Soufflé

This recipe makes a mildly sweet, ketogenic soufflé. The sweetness comes from the small amount of pineapple used. Use fresh or canned pineapple. If canned, use sliced pineapple or pineapple chunks, not crushed pineapple.

4 eggs, separated
⅛ teaspoon salt
¼ teaspoon orange extract
¼ teaspoon ground nutmeg or allspice
¾ cup (130 g) finely chopped pineapple
¼ cup (30 g) chopped pecans
1 tablespoon (8 g) coconut flour
2 tablespoons (28 g) coconut oil

Preheat oven to 350 degrees F (180 C). With an electric hand mixer, beat egg whites until stiff peaks form. In a separate bowl, mix egg yolks, salt, orange extract, nutmeg, pineapple, pecans, and coconut flour. Gently add one-third of the egg whites into the yolk mixture and mix until well blended. Fold the yolk mixture into the remaining whites. Do not over mix.

At medium heat, heat oil in an oven safe skillet on the stovetop. Pour egg mixture into the hot skillet, gently smooth out the top for even thickness, reduce heat to medium-low, and cook uncovered for about 4 minutes, or until the bottom of the soufflé just starts to brown. Transfer the skillet to the preheated oven and cook uncovered for 18 to 20 minutes, or until soufflé is puffy and delicately browned. Remove from oven, divide in half with a spatula, and serve.

Yield: 2 servings
Per serving: 34 g fat; 9.5 g net carbs; 14 g protein; 400 calories

Apple Soufflé

You can use any variety of apple to give this recipe a mild sweetness. Use a medium-size apple weighing about 5 ounces (150 g) after it has been peeled and cored.

4 eggs, separated
⅛ teaspoon salt
¼ teaspoon almond extract
¼ teaspoon cinnamon
⅛ teaspoon ground nutmeg
1 medium apple, peeled, cored, and diced
¼ cup (30 g) chopped pecans
1 tablespoon (8 g) coconut flour
2 tablespoons (28 g) coconut oil

Preheat oven to 350 degrees F (180 C). With an electric hand mixer, beat egg whites until stiff peaks form. In a separate bowl, mix egg yolks, salt, almond extract, cinnamon, nutmeg, apple, pecans, and coconut flour. Gently add one-third of the egg whites into the yolk mixture and mix until well blended. Fold the yolk mixture into the remaining whites. Do not over mix.

On the stovetop, heat oil to medium heat in an oven safe skillet. Pour egg mixture into the hot skillet, gently smooth out the top for even thickness, reduce heat to medium-low, and cook uncovered for about 4 minutes, or until the bottom of the soufflé just starts to brown. Transfer the skillet to the preheated oven and cook uncovered for 18 to 20 minutes, or until soufflé is puffy and delicately browned. Remove from oven, divide in half with a spatula, and serve.

Yield: 2 servings
Per serving: 34 g fat; 10.5 g net carbs; 13.5 g protein; 402 calories

Blueberry Soufflé

This recipe calls for blueberries, but you can use raspberries, blackberries, boysenberries, or a combination of mixed berries.

4 eggs, separated
⅛ teaspoon salt
¼ teaspoon almond extract
1 cup (145 g) blueberries
¼ cup (30 g) chopped pecans
1 tablespoon (8 g) coconut flour
2 tablespoons (28 g) coconut oil

Preheat oven to 350 degree F (180 C). With an electric hand mixer, beat egg whites until stiff peaks form. In a separate bowl, mix egg yolks, salt, almond extract, blueberries, pecans, and coconut flour. Gently add one-third of the egg whites into the yolk mixture and mix until well blended. Fold the yolk mixture into the remaining whites. Do not over mix.

Heat oil in an oven safe skillet on the stovetop over medium heat. Pour egg mixture into the hot skillet, gently smooth out the top for uniform thickness, reduce heat to medium-low, and cook uncovered for about 4 minutes, or until the bottom of the soufflé just starts to brown. Transfer the skillet to the preheated oven and cook uncovered for 18 to 20 minutes, or until soufflé is puffy and delicately browned. Remove from oven, divide in half with a spatula, and serve.

Yield: 2 servings
Per serving: 34.5 g fat; 10.5 g net carbs; 14 g protein; 408 calories

Cauliflower Cups

This recipe is actually a soufflé cooked in muffin cups. The cups are light and soft, are best eaten with a fork, and are very delicious.

16 ounces (450 g) cauliflower, chopped
1 medium shallot, peeled and cut in half
¼ cup (60 g) sour cream
4 ounces (110 g) sharp cheddar cheese, shredded
1 tablespoon (4 g) minced parsley
¼ teaspoon salt
⅛ teaspoon black pepper
4 eggs, separated
¼ cup (38 g) diced sugar-free, nitrite-free ham

Preheat oven to 375° F (190° C). Grease a 12-cup muffin tin. Steam cauliflower and shallot until tender, about 15 minutes. Remove vegetables from the steamer and let set a few minutes to allow excess moisture to evaporate. Puree in a food processor until smooth. Combine with sour cream, cheese, parsley, salt, and black pepper. Stir in egg yolks. In a separate bowl, beat egg whites until stiff peaks form. Gently fold egg whites into cauliflower mixture just until combined. Spoon into muffin cups and bake for 25 to 30 minutes, until browned. Serve hot.

Yield: 12 cups
Per cup: 6 g fat; 1.5 g net carbs; 5.5 g protein; 82 calories

Eggs Benedict

Classic Eggs Benedict is made by layering a poached egg and a slice of ham on an English muffin and covering it with Hollandaise sauce. In this version, a ham soufflé serves the purpose of the egg, ham, and muffin. Like the original, Hollandaise sauce is poured over the top.

Make the Fluffy Soufflé according to directions on page 284. However, add ½ cup (75 g) chopped ham to the hot skillet and cook for about 5 minutes before adding the whipped egg mixture.

Top with Hollandaise Sauce (page 30).

Yield: 2 servings
Per serving: 33 g fat; 1.5 g net carbs; 17 g protein; 371 calories

Keto Bread

One of the things most people miss when they go keto is bread. Here is a delicious low-carb, no-grain keto version. The recipe below makes enough for 4 "slices" of bread; if you want more, just double or triple the recipe. The bread tastes best fresh out of the oven, so it is preferable to make the bread whenever you want it, rather than make a lot at one time and keep it around for several days.

Each piece of bread is about the same size as a regular slice of bread and looks more like a large round cookie than a slice of bread. Two slices can be used to make a sandwich or function as a hamburger bun. One slice folded

Keto bread made with eggs, almond flour, and cheese.

in half can hold a hot dog or be used like a taco shell or a wrap. Since Keto Bread already has cheese in it, you don't need to add any more cheese to your sandwich, unless you want to.

2 eggs, beaten
¼ cup (30 g) almond flour
1 cup (115 g) shredded Monterey Jack or other mild cheese

Preheat the oven to 350° F (180° C). Lay a piece of parchment paper over a baking sheet and spray it with non-stick cooking spray. I like to use a coconut oil–based cooking spray. In a small bowl, mix together eggs and almond flour until smooth. Stir in cheese until the cheese is well coated. Spoon 4 equal portions of the batter onto the parchment paper. With the back of the spoon, spread the batter out so it is 4 to 5 inches (10 to 12 cm) in diameter. Bake for 20 minutes, until lightly browned. Remove from the parchment paper and let cool.

Yield: 4 slices
Per slice: 12 g fat; 0 g net carbs; 10 g protein; 148 calories

Use Keto Bread like you would a hot dog bun, taco shell, or wrap stuffed with your favorite fillings.

Sausage and Cheese Pancakes

This is a type of egg dish made with coconut flour, sausage, and cheese. Coconut flour is a low-carb flour that can be used to make low-carb baked goods.

    6 ounces (170 g) pork sausage
    4 eggs
    ¼ teaspoon onion powder
    ¼ teaspoon salt
    2 tablespoons (16 g) coconut flour
    2 teaspoons finely chopped jalapeño pepper
    2 ounces (56 g) shredded cheddar cheese
    3 tablespoons (42 g) coconut oil

Brown sausage in a skillet, remove from heat, and let cool. In a bowl, whisk together eggs, onion powder, and salt. Add coconut flour and whisk until smooth. Stir in jalapeño pepper, sausage, and cheese. Melt coconut oil in skillet. Spoon batter into the hot skillet, making a dozen 2½-inch (6-cm) diameter pancakes. Cook until the undersides of the pancakes are browned, then turn and cook the other side (about 5 minutes each side, depending on the temperature of the skillet).

Eat as is, or top with sour cream, avocado, salsa, or other topping of your choice.

Yield: 12 pancakes
Per pancake: 10 g fat; 0.8 g net carbs; 6 g protein; 125 calories

Breakfast Pizza

You have breakfast burritos, so why not breakfast pizza? If you want a keto pizza experience, this is it! The crust is light, not too crunchy, much like a thick crust pizza. It is not quit stiff enough to eat by hand as you do a conventional pizza, so you will want to use a fork. The taste of this keto pizza is as close as I have found to a conventional pizza and still be truly ketogenic. No flours are used to make this pizza, the crust is made from eggs and cheese. Of course, you don't need to restrict this pizza to just breakfast, it can be eaten for lunch or dinner, as well.

    1 tablespoon coconut oil or bacon drippings
    2 eggs, separated
    ⅛ teaspoon salt
    ½ cup (58 g) shredded cheese

Preheat oven to 350° F (180° C). Put 1 tablespoon of coconut oil or bacon drippings in a 9-inch (22-cm) pie dish and place it in the oven as it is preheating.

Beat egg whites until stiff peaks form and set aside. Combine egg yolks, salt, and cheese, and mix well. Add about a fourth of the whipped egg whites to the egg yolk mixture and blend in with a spoon. Fold the egg yolk mixture into the whipped egg whites, do not over mix.

Once the oven is heated and pie dish is hot, remove the dish from the oven. Tilt the dish from side to side to evenly coat the bottom and sides of the dish with the melted oil. Add the egg mixture and gently smooth out the top. Place the dish back into the oven and cook for 18 to 20 minutes or until the egg crust is fluffy and beginning to turn a light brown.

Remove the pizza crust from the oven. Turn the oven on to broil or to 450° F (230° C). While the oven is heating up, add pizza sauce, shredded cheese, sausage, onions, bell peppers, or any topping you desire. The meat and vegetables should be thoroughly cooked just before adding them onto the pizza crust. Place the loaded pizza crust into the broiler and cook for another 3 to 4 minutes until the cheese topping is completely melted. At this point, you are not cooking the pizza but simply melting the cheese. Remove from the oven and enjoy.

This recipe makes a hearty dish for one or a moderate dish for two. If you go lightly on the pizza toppings, it makes a great single serving pizza.

Yield: 1 pizza crust
Per pizza crust: 42 g fat; 1.5 g net carbs; 25 g protein; 484 calories

Breakfast pizza.

Vegetable Chakchoukah

Chakchoukah is a hot, spicy Tunisian pepper stew with eggs poached in it. In this version, some of the peppers are replaced with cabbage and the spiciness is toned down a bit.

2 tablespoons (28 g) coconut oil
½ cup (50 g) chopped onion
½ cup (60 g) chopped red bell pepper
2 cloves garlic, diced
2 medium tomatoes, chopped
1 cup (85 g) chopped cabbage
½ teaspoon ground coriander
½ teaspoon cumin powder
½ teaspoon chili powder
4 eggs
Salt and pepper
Cayenne pepper (optional)

Heat coconut oil in a skillet over medium heat, then cook onion for 2 minutes. Add red bell pepper and garlic, then cook for 5 minutes, stirring occasionally. Add tomatoes, cabbage, coriander, cumin, and chili powder, then cook for another 10 minutes, or until all the vegetables are tender. Make four depressions in the mixture with the back of a large spoon, and crack one egg into each. Cover and simmer until eggs whites are set, but yolks still soft. Season with salt and black pepper to taste. If you like your foods with a little kick, add a couple of dashes of cayenne.

Yield: Serves 2
Per serving: 15.9 g fat; 9.3 g net carbs; 13.4 g protein; 242 calories

Vegetable Chakchoukah.

Eggs and Cauliflower Hash

The cauliflower hash is made using Cauliflower Rice. This is one of those dishes where you can load up on as much fat as you like because the Cauliflower Rice absorbs the oil. Although the recipe only calls for 2 tablespoons of oil, you can easily add ¼ cup (60 ml) or more.

2 tablespoons (28 g) coconut oil
6 ounces (170 g) sausage
½ cup (2 oz/60 g) chopped onion
¼ cup (1 oz/30 g) chopped red bell pepper
8 ounces (226 g) Cauliflower Rice (page 112)
Salt and pepper, to taste
Eggs

Egg and Cauliflower Hash.

Heat the oil in a large skillet over medium heat. Sauté sausage, onion, and bell pepper until the meat is lightly browned. Add Cauliflower Rice and continue to cook, uncovered, for about 10 minutes, stirring occasionally, or until the cauliflower is tender. Add salt and pepper to taste. Remove from heat. Serve with fried or scrambled eggs.

Yield: serves 2
Per serving without eggs: 38 g fat; 6 g net carbs; 19 g protein; 442 calories
Per egg: 4 g fat; 0.5 g net carbs; 6 g protein; 62 calories.

Sausage and Eggs Stir-Fry

This is one of my favorite breakfasts and adds a nice variety to morning eggs.

2 tablespoons (28 g) coconut oil
6 ounces (170 g) pork sausage
½ cup (80 g) chopped onion
½ green bell pepper, chopped
3 eggs, lightly beaten
2 cups (180 g) chopped cabbage
Salt and black pepper

Heat the oil in a large skillet, and sauté sausage, onion, and bell pepper until the meat is lightly browned. Push the meat and vegetables to one side of the skillet and add the eggs to the other side, cover and cook until the eggs are set (about 4 to 5 minutes). Chop cooked eggs into bite-size pieces and stir in cabbage, cover and cook another 4 to 5 minutes, or until the cabbage is limp. Add salt and pepper to taste. Remove from heat and serve.

Yield: serves 2
Per serving: 44.5 g fat; 7.5 g net carbs; 26.5 g protein; 536 calories

Breakfast Brats and Kraut

Who needs a bun to enjoy brats and kraut? This is a tasty dish where eggs make up for the bun.

3 tablespoons (42 g) coconut oil
2 bratwursts (3 oz/85 g each)
4 eggs, lightly beaten
Dash salt
Dash black pepper
½ cup (70 g) sauerkraut
Dill pickle relish
Dijon mustard

Heat the oil in a skillet and cook bratwursts until lightly browned on all sides and thoroughly cooked. Push the bratwursts to the edge of the pan and pour in eggs. Cover and cook until the eggs have set. Add salt and pepper to taste, and cover the eggs with sauerkraut, cover and cook 1 minute to warm the sauerkraut. You are not cooking the sauerkraut, just warming it up. Remove from heat. Serve garnished with dill pickle relish and mustard, if desired.

Yield: serves 2
Per serving: 54 g fat; 5 g net carbs; 23 g protein; 598 calories

Egg Stack

This dish is served with the meat and vegetables topped with a fried egg. The name of this dish comes from the stacking of the fried egg on top of the meat and veggies.

1 tablespoon (14 g) cooking oil
3 ounces (85 g) ground or chopped beef
1 ounce (28 g) onion, chopped
1 ounce (28 g) bell pepper, chopped
1 egg
Salt and black pepper to taste
1 tablespoon (14 g) salsa or hot sauce

Heat the oil in a skillet over medium heat. Sauté meat, onion, and bell pepper, stirring together, for about 5 to 6 minutes, or until meat is cooked and vegetables are crisp tender. Push the mixture to one side of the pan and add the egg to the cleared side. Cover and fry the egg for 4 to 5 minutes or until the egg has turned white but the yolk is still a little runny. Remove the egg from the pan and add salt and pepper to taste. Pile the meat mixture in the center of a plate and top with the egg. Serve with salsa or hot sauce over the egg.

Yield: serves 1
Per serving: 23.5 g fat; 4.5 g net carbs; 32 g protein; 358 calories

Variations:
Cook along with the meat mixture 1 ounce (28 g) of any of the following: chopped spinach, kale, mushrooms, zucchini, turnip, or sweet potato.
Top with shredded cheese or sour cream.

Egg Stack.

Portobello mushrooms.

Egg Scramble Portobello

This is a great change of pace to the ordinary ham and eggs for breakfast.

2 tablespoons (28 g) cooking oil
6 ounces (170 g) sugar-free, nitrite-free ham, cut in small cubes
2 eggs, beaten
4 slices (1 oz/28 g each) cheddar cheese
2 large (2.8 oz/80 g each) Portobello mushrooms
Salt and black pepper to taste
1 tablespoon sour cream

Heat the oil in a skillet over medium heat. Combine the ham with the eggs, pour into the hot pan, cover, and cook for 4 to 5 minutes, or until the eggs are firm. Put 1 slice of cheese into each of the mushroom caps, add the scrambled egg mixture, and top with a second slice of cheese. Place the mushrooms into the hot pan, pour ¼ cup (60 ml) water into the pan, cover immediately, and steam for about 3 minutes, or until the cheese is melted. Remove from heat, add salt and pepper to taste, and place on serving dish. Top with sour cream.

Yield: serves 2
Per serving: 27 g fat; 5.5 g net carbs; 24.5 g protein; 361 calories

Eggs Foo Young (Chinese Pancakes)

This is a Chinese-inspired egg and vegetable dish that can be made with a variety of ingredients. Eggs Foo Young is basically a vegetable pancake made without flour. Meat is optional, but in our recipe it is included.

6 eggs
1 cup (50 g) bean sprouts
¼ cup (24 g) minced scallions
¼ cup (38 g) chopped bamboo shoots
½ cup (45 g) shredded Chinese cabbage
½ cup (70 g) chopped cooked chicken, pork, or shrimp
1 teaspoon soy sauce or coconut aminos
3 tablespoons (42 g) coconut oil or lard

Mix eggs, all vegetables, meat, and soy sauce. Heat coconut oil in a skillet over medium heat. Spoon egg mixture into hot skillet as if you were making pancakes. Cook until lightly browned on the bottom, then turn and brown the other side. Keep warm, but do not stack, while you are frying the remaining pancakes.

Eggs Foo Young is often topped with a gravy or sauce. If you like, you can cover it with Sausage Gravy (page 18), Chunky Chicken Gravy (page 19), or Brown Gravy (page 16), or one of its variations.

Yield: 4 pancakes
Per serving without gravy: 17.5 g fat; 2.5 g net carbs; 14.5 g protein; 225 calories

Ham and Egg Portobello

This is a very quick and simple but delicious egg dish.

2 tablespoons (28 g) cooking oil
2 eggs
6 ounces (170 g) sliced sugar-free, nitrite-free ham or pastrami
4 slices (1 oz/28 g each) Monterey Jack cheese
2 large (2.8 oz/80 g each) Portobello mushrooms
1 tablespoon (9 g) jalapeño pepper, chopped (optional)
Salt and black pepper to taste

Heat the oil in a skillet over medium heat. Open and drop each egg into the hot pan, cover, and cook until egg white is firm but yolk is still runny.

Remove the eggs and set aside. Add the ham and heat both sides 1 to 2 minutes per side. Remove the meat and set aside. Place 2 slices of cheese in each mushroom cap, cover with the chopped jalapeño pepper, top with the ham, and place the mushrooms into the hot pan. Pour ¼ cup (60 ml) of water into the pan and immediately cover. Steam the mushrooms for about 3 minutes or until the cheese is

melted and mushrooms are cooked. Remove from heat, place the mushrooms on serving plates, top each with a fried egg, and add salt and pepper to taste. Serve immediately.

Yield: serves 2
Per serving: 26 g fat; 5.5 g net carbs; 24.5 g protein; 352 calories

Broccoli Quiche Cups

These little serving-size crust-less quiches are baked in muffin cups.

1 tablespoon (14 g) butter
3 eggs
¼ cup (60 ml) heavy cream
1 cup (120 g) shredded cheddar cheese
1 ounce (28 g) onion, diced
1 teaspoon Dijon mustard
½ teaspoon salt
⅛ teaspoon black pepper
5 ounces (140 g) broccoli, cut into bite-size pieces

Preheat oven to 400° F (200° C). Apply butter generously to a 6-cup muffin pan. Whisk the eggs and cream together. Stir in ½ cup (60 g) cheese, onion, mustard, salt, and black pepper. Pour the mixture evenly into 6 muffin cups. Add broccoli pieces and top with the remaining cheese. Bake for 20 to 24 minutes, or until the edges begin to turn brown.

Yield: 6 quiche cups
Per serving: 11 g fat; 2 g net carbs; 8.5 g protein; 141 calories

Quiche Stuffed Bell Pepper

Quiche is traditionally made in a pastry shell. This low-carb version uses a bell pepper as the "crust." I think it tastes better than conventional quiche.

2 bell peppers
4 eggs
3 ounces (85 g) sugar-free, nitrite-free ham, finely chopped
½ cup (80 g) diced onion
½ teaspoon salt
⅛ teaspoon black pepper
¼ teaspoon red pepper flakes (optional)
¼ teaspoon dried thyme
3 ounces (85 g) Colby, Monterey Jack, or cheddar cheese, shredded

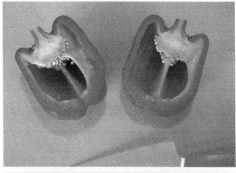

Preheat oven to 350° F (180° C). Cut each bell pepper in half lengthwise, do not remove the stem, but carefully remove the seeds and membranes. Fill a large pot with enough water to cover the peppers. Heat to boiling, add peppers, and cook for 5 minutes. Using a slotted spoon, remove the peppers from the water and set aside to cool and allow moisture to evaporate.

Stir together eggs, ham, onion, salt, black pepper, red pepper flakes, thyme, and half of the cheese. Place the bell peppers on a baking sheet or dish. Spoon an equal amount of filling into each bell pepper and sprinkle the rest of the cheese on the top. Don't overfill, as the filling will expand slightly while cooking. Bake for 40 minutes or until filling has set.

Yield: 4 stuffed peppers (halves)
Per serving: 13.5 g fat; 4.5 g net carbs; 15 g protein; 199 calories

Sausage and Mushroom Quiche Stuffed Bell Peppers

2 bell peppers
1 tablespoon (14 g) coconut oil
6 ounces (170 g) ground pork, turkey, or lamb
½ cup (80 g) onion, chopped
2 ounces (60 g) mushrooms, chopped
4 eggs
1 teaspoon salt
1 tablespoon (9 g) chopped jalapeño pepper (optional)
2 ounces (60 g) Colby, Monterey Jack, or cheddar cheese

Preheat oven to 350° F (180° C). Cut each bell pepper in half lengthwise, do not remove the stem, but carefully remove the seeds and membranes. Fill a large pot with enough water to cover the peppers. Heat to boiling, add peppers, and cook for 4 to 5 minutes. Using a slotted spoon, remove the peppers from the water and set aside to cool and allow moisture to evaporate.

Heat the oil in a skillet, and sauté sausage and onion, just until the sausage turns brown. Add the mushrooms and cook 1 to 2 more minutes, remove from heat, and allow to cool slightly. Stir together eggs, salt, jalapeño pepper, and sausage mixture. Place the bell peppers on a baking sheet or dish. Spoon an equal amount of filling into each bell pepper and sprinkle the cheese on the top. Don't overfill as the filling will expand slightly while cooking. Bake for 40 minutes, or until filling has set.

Yield: 4 stuffed peppers (halves)
Per serving: 14.5 g fat; 4.5 g net carbs; 21.5 g protein; 234 calories

Cauliflower and Egg Stuffed Bell Pepper

2 bell peppers
1 tablespoon (14 g) butter
3 ounces (85 g) ground pork
¼ cup (40 g) finely chopped onion
6 ounces (170 g) cauliflower
2 ounces (56 g) cream cheese, softened
2 eggs
½ teaspoon salt
2 teaspoons jalapeño pepper, diced (optional)
4 ounces (110 g) Monterey Jack or cheddar cheese, shredded

Preheat oven to 350° F (180° C). Cut each bell pepper in half lengthwise, do not remove the stem, but carefully remove the seeds and membranes. Fill a large pot with enough water to cover the peppers. Heat to boiling, add peppers, and cook for 4 to 5 minutes. Using a slotted spoon, remove the peppers from the water and set aside to cool and allow moisture to evaporate.

Heat butter in a small skillet over medium heat. Sauté ground pork and onion until the meat turns brown and onion is tender, about 5 minutes. Remove from heat and set aside.

Cut cauliflower into florets and steam until tender. Put into a food processor along with cream cheese, eggs, and salt. Blend until smooth. Stir in cooked sausage and onion and jalapeño pepper.

Place the bell peppers on a baking sheet or dish. Spoon an equal amount of the filling into each bell pepper and sprinkle the cheese on the top. Bake for 45 minutes.

Yield: 4 stuffed peppers (halves)
Per serving: 20 g fat; 5 g net carbs; 17.5 g protein; 270 calories

Portuguese Baked Eggs

This recipe makes a hearty breakfast or dinner for 2 or a light meal for 4.

¼ cup (56 g) extra virgin olive oil
1 red bell pepper, thinly sliced
1 cup (82 g) peeled and cubed eggplant
½ medium red onion, thinly sliced
1 medium tomato, cut into wedges
2 cloves garlic, thinly sliced
2 tablespoons (5 g) fresh basil leaves
2 tablespoons (8 g) fresh oregano leaves
1 teaspoon chili powder
½ teaspoon paprika
¼ teaspoon salt
5 to 8 drops liquid hot sauce
¾ cup (188 g) ricotta cheese
4 eggs
½ cup (58 g) shredded sharp cheddar cheese
¼ cup (20 g) grated Parmesan cheese

Preheat oven to 400° F (200° C). While oven is heating, heat oil in an oven-safe skillet over medium heat. Add bell pepper, eggplant, and onion, cook, stirring occasionally, until softened and just beginning to brown, about 10 to 12 minutes. Add tomatoes, garlic, basil, oregano, chili powder, and paprika. Reduce heat to medium-low and cook until vegetables are very soft and liquid begins to thicken, about 20 minutes. Season with salt and liquid hot sauce.

Using the back of a large spoon, make 4 evenly spaced depressions in the mixture. Spoon a dollop of ricotta cheese into each depression, then crack 1 egg into each. Top with cheddar and Parmesan cheese. Place the skillet into the oven and bake for about 15 to 18 minutes, until cheese is melted and egg whites are almost set but yolks are still runny.

After removing the skillet from the oven, the eggs will continue to cook in the hot mixture. If you like the eggs soft, serve immediately. If you want them cooked a little more, let them rest a few minutes on the stovetop or counter before serving.

Yield: serves 2
Per serving: 54 g fat; 14 g net carbs; 34 g protein; 678 calories

Eggs Florentine

8 strips sugar-free, nitrite-free bacon
1 small onion, finely chopped
3 cloves garlic, minced
5 cups (140 g) baby spinach
¼ teaspoon ground nutmeg
¾ cup (60 ml) heavy cream
⅔ cup (66 g) grated Pecorino Romano or Parmesan cheese
¼ teaspoon salt
⅛ teaspoon freshly ground black pepper
4 eggs, poached
2 large tomatoes, cut into 1-inch (2.5-cm) thick slices

In a skillet over medium heat, cook bacon until crisp, remove, crumble, and set aside. Keep bacon drippings in the skillet, add onion, and cook, stirring frequently, until soft, about 5 minutes. Add the garlic and cook until fragrant, about 1 minute. Add the spinach and nutmeg, and cook until the spinach has wilted, about 2 to 3 minutes. Stir in cream and bring to a simmer. Cook, stirring occasionally, until the mixture thickens slightly, about 5 minutes. Remove the skillet from the heat and stir in the Romano cheese, salt, and black pepper. Cooking one egg at a time, poach eggs according to the directions on page 272.

Place one tomato slice on each of four salad plates. Spoon one-fourth of the hot spinach sauce over the tomato slice. Add a poached egg onto the sauce, and sprinkle crumbled bacon over the top.

Yield: 4 servings
Per serving: 39 g fat; 6.5 g net carbs; 26.5 g protein; 483 calories

Asparagus and Scrambled Eggs with Cheese Sauce

This is a great way to dress up otherwise ordinary scrambled eggs and give variety to your breakfast. The Cheese Sauce gives the total fat content a real boost.

Cheese Sauce (page 24)*
3 strips sugar-free, nitrite-free bacon, cooked crisp
4 ounces (110 g) asparagus spears
2 eggs, lightly beaten
Salt
Black pepper

Prepare Cheese Sauce as directed. Cook bacon in a skillet until crisp and remove and set aside. Sauté asparagus spears in the bacon drippings, turning occasionally, until tender and slightly browned. At the same time you are cooking the asparagus, push them to one side of the pan and pour in the eggs and let them cook on the opposite side. Add salt and black pepper to taste. Once done, put asparagus and scrambled eggs on a serving plate, pour about ½ cup (120 ml) or so of hot Cheese Sauce over the top, add bacon strips, and enjoy!

*For variety, you can make this dish using the Basic White Sauce and any of its variations (page 21).

Yield: serves 1
Per serving: 72.5 g fat; 6.5 g net carbs; 42.5 g protein; 848 calories

Ham and Eggs Espagnole

Espagnole Sauce (page 27)
1 tablespoon (14 g) coconut oil or bacon drippings
3 ounces (85 g) sugar-free, nitrite-free ham
2 eggs

Prepare Espagnole Sauce as directed. Heat the oil in a large skillet over medium heat. Add ham and eggs. You can make fried or scrambled eggs. When done to your preference, place the ham and eggs on a serving plate and cover the eggs with hot Espagnole Sauce.

Yield: serves 1
Per serving with ½ cup (120 ml) Espagnole Sauce: 41 g fat; 7 g net carbs; 32 g protein; 525 calories

Cauliflower Muffins

This recipe uses a combination of mashed cauliflower and eggs and is baked in a muffin tin to produce the "muffins." These cauliflower cups are a little softer than regular muffins and best eaten with a fork.

8 ounces (225 g) cauliflower
2 ounces (56 g) cream cheese, softened
3 eggs
½ teaspoon salt
2 ounces (56 g) cheese, shredded

Preheat oven to 400° F (200° C). Cut cauliflower into florets and steam until tender. Remove from heat and let cool slightly. Put into a food processor along with cream cheese, eggs, and salt. Blend until smooth.

Apply a generous amount of butter to a muffin tin. Pour an equal amount of creamed cauliflower into each muffin cup. Top with cheese. Bake for 30 minutes.

Yield: 6 cauliflower muffins
Per serving: 9 g fat; 1.5 g net carbs; 6.5 g protein; 113 calories

Snacks and Appetizers

When you are on a ketogenic diet, even your snacks need to maintain the low-carb, high-fat percentages that define the diet as ketogenic. These recipes can be used as an accompaniment to a regular meal, be added as appetizers or desserts, or be eaten by themselves as a light snack in place of a full meal.

Some foods and meals may be very low-carb, but not have enough fat to actually be ketogenic. I refer to these foods as keto-friendly, meaning that they can easily become ketogenic if a little more fat is added. For example, a 3 ounce (85 g) fish fillet can be keto-friendly but not necessarily ketogenic. Adding an accompanying high-fat dish or condiment, however, can make it ketogenic. These snacks and appetizers can help accomplish this.

SNACK RECIPES

Bacon-Guacamole Stuffed Baby Peppers

Baby sweet peppers range from deep red to bright yellow in color and are only about a quarter the size of regular bell peppers. Being sweet, these peppers have no heat of their own. The little kick this recipe has is from the hot sauce in the guacamole. Of course, if you don't have baby sweet peppers on hand, you can make do by cutting and dividing a regular bell pepper.

6 sweet baby peppers
1 avocado

1 tablespoon (15 ml) lime juice
2 tablespoons (2 g) chopped cilantro
½ teaspoon (or to taste) hot sauce
Salt to taste
12 strips sugar-free, nitrite-free bacon, cooked crisp

Cut peppers in half lengthwise; remove membrane, seeds, and stem, and set aside. To make the filling, combine avocado, lime juice, cilantro, hot sauce, and salt, and mash together. Fill the peppers with the avocado mixture and top with a strip of bacon.

Yield: 12 stuffed pepper halves
Per serving: 11 g fat; 2 g net carbs; 7.5 g protein; 137 calories

Jalapeño Poppers

This is a delicious way to increase your daily fat intake. Each popper delivers hefty 7.5 grams of fat.

12 jalapeño peppers
4 ounces (110 g) cream cheese, softened
4 ounces (110 g) cheddar cheese, shredded
12 strips bacon, cut in half

Preheat oven to 425° F (220° C). Cut jalapeño peppers in half lengthwise and remove seeds and membrane. Mix cream cheese with cheddar cheese until evenly blended. Fill each pepper with the cheese mixture. Layer on a half slice of bacon. Set onto a jelly-roll pan. A jelly-roll pan, as opposed to a cookie sheet,

has a rim around the outside edge that prevents grease from dripping off the pan and into the oven. While the poppers are cooking, the bacon will release a lot of grease, so do not use a cookie sheet unless you have some way to contain the grease.

Bake for 18 to 20 minutes, until bacon is cooked crisp. Serve fresh and hot. Save the bacon drippings for another recipe. Poppers can be stored, in a sealed container, in the refrigerator for a couple of days. Just reheat to serve.

Yield: 24 poppers
Per popper: 7.5 g fat; 0.5 g net carbs; 5 g protein; 89 calories

Bacon-Wrapped Mozzarella Sticks

Bacon-wrapped mozzarella sticks may sound decadent, but they look and taste delicious!

6 mozzarella cheese sticks, frozen
Coconut oil for frying
12 strips sugar-free, nitrite-free bacon

Freeze the mozzarella sticks at least 2 hours beforehand. Preheat coconut oil in a deep fryer to 350° F (180° C). Wrap each cheese stick in 2 slices of bacon, overlapping as you wrap to hold the bacon on, and secure it with a toothpick. Do not worry about not covering the ends of the cheese sticks with

bacon; when frying, the cheese will not leak out unless you cook it too long. The key to preventing leaking is to make sure the cheese is completely frozen before you start and make sure the temperature of the oil is at least 350° F (180° C).

Place the bacon-wrapped cheese sticks into the hot oil and cook until the bacon is crispy brown, about 2 to 3 minutes. Watch closely because they cook quickly and can burn easily. Remove from the hot oil and let cool before eating.

Yield: 6 wrapped cheese sticks
Per cheese stick: 21 g fat; 0.5 g net carbs; 22 g protein; 279 calories

Cottage Cheese and Berry Pudding

This isn't a pudding in the tradition sense, as it contains no added sugar and is made primarily from blending coconut oil with cottage cheese, which produces a near pudding–like texture. The berries (any combination of raspberries, boysenberries, or blackberries) give it added flavor and a mild sweetness. This makes a great high-fat snack. I often eat this in place of a full meal as it is very satisfying.

¼ cup (120 g) coconut oil, melted
½ cup (65 g) berries
½ cup (115 g) cottage cheese
⅛ teaspoon almond extract

Put the coconut oil in a small stovetop safe bowl or small saucepan. I use a 1 cup (240 ml) glass bowl. Heat the oil and the berries in the bowl on the stove over medium to low heat until the oil is melted or mildly hot (about 150° F/65° C). Heating the berries brings out their flavor. Remove the bowl from the heat, scoop in the cottage cheese and almond extract, and mix together with a spoon until the mixture is well blended but speckled with curds and berries.

Yield: 2 servings
Per serving: 28.5 g fat; 3.5 g net carbs; 8 g protein; 302 calories

Keto Peach Custard

Keto custards make a pleasant, mildly sweet, high-fat treat that is fully compatible with a ketogenic diet without any added sugar or artificial sweeteners. The sweetness comes completely from the small amount of fruit used.

Each serving supplies about 6 grams of carbs. These are not meant to be eaten as meals in themselves but snacks or treats, so don't eat more than one at a time, as the carb count can climb quickly. Custards can be kept refrigerated for up to 5 days.

3 eggs, lightly beaten
2 cups (470 ml) heavy cream or coconut milk
1 teaspoon almond extract
⅛ teaspoon salt
1½ cups (255 g) finely chopped peaches
Cinnamon
1 tablespoon (7 g) sliced almonds

Preheat oven to 350° F (180° C). Whisk together eggs, cream, almond extract, and salt. Stir in peaches. Pour mixture into six 5-ounce (140 g) custard cups. Sprinkle the top of each with cinnamon. Place the cups into a large pan with a 2-inch (5-cm) rim. Pour hot water into the pan to a depth of 1 inch (2.5 cm). Bake for 40 to 45 minutes until a knife inserted in the center of the custard comes out clean. Remove the custard cups from the water bath and let cool. Eat warm or refrigerate and eat chilled. Serve topped with sliced almonds.

Yield: 6 servings
Per serving: 32 g fat; 6 g net carbs; 5 g protein; 332 calories

Keto Berry Custard

3 eggs, lightly beaten
2 cups (470 ml) heavy cream or coconut milk
1½ teaspoon vanilla extract
⅛ teaspoon salt
3 cups (440 g) mixed raspberries, boysenberries, blackberries, and blueberries

Preheat oven to 350° F (180° C). Whisk together eggs, cream, vanilla extract, and salt. Stir in berries. Pour mixture into six 5-ounce (140 g) custard cups. Place the cups into a large pan with a 2-inch (5-cm) rim. Pour hot water into the pan to a depth of 1 inch (2.5 cm). Bake for 40 to 45 minutes until a knife inserted in the center of the custard comes out clean. Remove the custard cups from the water bath and let cool. Eat warm or refrigerate and eat chilled.

Yield: 6 servings
Per serving: 32 g fat; 6.5 g net carbs; 5.5 g protein; 336 calories

Keto Pineapple Custard

3 eggs, lightly beaten
2 cups (470 ml) heavy cream or coconut milk
1 teaspoon vanilla extract
1½ teaspoons orange extract
⅛ teaspoon salt
1 cup (155 g) diced pineapple
Cinnamon
6 tablespoons (30 g) unsweetened shredded coconut, toasted

Preheat oven to 350° F (180° C). Whisk together eggs, cream, vanilla extract, orange extract, and salt. Stir in pineapple. Pour mixture into six 5 ounce (140 g) custard cups. Sprinkle the top of each generously with cinnamon. Place the cups into a large pan with a 2-inch (5-cm) rim. Pour hot water into the pan to a depth of 1 inch (2.5 cm). Bake for 40 to 45 minutes until a knife inserted in the center of the custard comes out clean. Remove the custard cups from the water bath and let cool. Eat warm or refrigerate and eat chilled. Top with toasted shredded coconut.

Yield: 6 servings
Per serving: 33.5 g fat; 6 g net carbs; 5 g protein; 345 calories

Rollups

Rollups are simple to make, and when prepared in advance, make an excellent mini-lunch you can take with you when you are out and about. They also make a quick snack when you are at home. You can change up the recipe and use whatever condiments or fillings suit your tastes. Other possible filling ingredients include avocado, julienne cut bell peppers, jalapeño peppers, coleslaw, scallions, sliced tomatoes, etc.

1 slice (1 oz/28 g) deli meat (without sugar or nitrites)
1 slice (1 oz/28 g) cheese
1 tablespoon (14 g) mayonnaise
½ ounce (14 g) sliced pickle
½ ounce (14 g) mixed sprouts

You can use most any type of thinly sliced meat (ham, beef, chicken, turkey) and thinly sliced hard cheese (cheddar, Colby, Edam, Monterey Jack, Swiss, mozzarella, Munster). To make the basic rollup, layer one thinly sliced piece of cheese on top of a thinly sliced piece of meat, followed by the mayonnaise, pickle, and sprouts. Roll it into a log with the meat on the outside and sprouts on the inside. Eat and enjoy.

Yield: 1 serving
Per slice: 15.5 g fat; 4 g net carbs; 16 g protein; 219 calories

Eggnog

This is a mildly sweet, low-carb, high-fat ketogenic beverage. This is an excellent addition to any meal that needs a boost in fat content, as each serving delivers a whopping 53 grams of fat (87 percent of total calories from fat). You can use MCT oil or coconut oil in this recipe. I prefer the MCT oil, as it will remain liquid even in a cold beverage. Coconut oil begins to solidify at temperatures below 76° F (24° C), so it is best when consumed warm or hot. The recipe calls for 1 tablespoon (14 g) of oil, but you can boost the oil content even higher by increasing it to 2 or 3 tablespoons (28 to 42 g).

1 cup (240 ml) heavy cream or coconut milk
½ cup (120 ml) water
¼ teaspoon cinnamon
⅛ teaspoon nutmeg
1 egg, lightly beaten
1 tablespoons (14 g) MCT or coconut oil, melted
¼ teaspoon vanilla extract
⅛ teaspoon almond extract
2 tablespoons (18 g) crushed pineapple

In a small saucepan, bring cream and water to a low simmer. Add cinnamon and nutmeg, and simmer, but do not boil, for 1 minute. The heat brings out the flavor of the spices. Remove from heat and let cool. Stir in all remaining ingredients. Drink warm or chilled.

Yield: 2 servings
Per serving: 53 g fat; 4.5 g net carbs; 4 g protein; 511 calories

Tomato Juice Cocktail

This drink is good served hot and tastes much like a light tomato soup. Goes well with coconut oil, making a convenient way of adding this health-promoting oil into the diet and increase your daily fat intake.

1 can (8 oz/240 ml) tomato sauce
1½ cups (355 ml) water
¼ teaspoons onion powder
1½ teaspoons lemon juice
2 tablespoons (28 g) coconut oil
¼ teaspoon salt
Pepper to taste

Combine tomato sauce, water, and onion powder in a small saucepan and heat until hot. Remove from heat, and stir in lemon juice and coconut oil. Add salt and pepper to taste. Stir and enjoy.

Yield: 2 servings
Per serving: 14 g fat; 8 g net carbs; 2 g protein; 166 calories

Creamy Tomato Juice Cocktail

This is a creamy, higher-fat version of the Tomato Juice Cocktail. Make the Tomato Juice Cocktail as described above, but add ½ cup (120 ml) heavy cream to the saucepan with the tomato sauce and water.

Yield: 2 servings
Per serving: 36 g fat; 8.5 g net carbs; 2 g protein; 366 calories

Coco Fries

I love toasted coconut—shredded coconut that is cooked to a golden brown. Coco Fries are larger, French fry–size, pieces of fresh coconut kernel that are deep fried in coconut oil. They are far healthier than potato fries, contain far less carbs, and deliver a healthy ketogenic dose of coconut oil. The flavor is more savory than sweet and provides a nice chewy keto snack.

1 mature coconut
Coconut oil for frying
Salt

Remove the coconut meat from a fresh coconut. Cut the meat into ¼-inch (0.5-cm) wide strips; lengths will vary. You do not need to shave off the brown membrane attached to the white meat, the membrane is perfectly safe to eat, and

a lot of trouble to peel off. Place the coconut into a container and put into the freezer until fully frozen, at least 3 hours. The coconut can remain frozen for up to 6 months. The freezing stage is very important, as it softens the coconut fibers, which allows more moisture to escape while cooking, producing better browning, and allows a slight absorption of the cooking oil, increasing the amount of coconut oil consumed.

When you are ready to cook the coconut, remove it from the freezer and let it thaw, about 30 to 60 minutes, at room temperature. Dry the defrosted coconut off with a paper towel before frying. Preheat coconut oil in a deep fryer to 340° F (170° C). Place a handful of sliced coconut into the hot oil; do not try to cook too much at one time, cook them in batches. The oil will bubble slightly as moisture in the coconut is converted into water vapor and evaporates. Cook until the coconut strips turn a golden brown, about 6 to 8 minutes. Remove the coconut and place on a plate, a paper towel is not necessary to absorb excess oil, because as the coconut cools, the oil on the surface is absorbed, leaving the strips with a dry surface. Sprinkle with salt and enjoy.

Uneaten Coco Fries can be kept for several days if stored in a paper bag to allow air circulation. A plastic bag or sealed container will cause the remaining moisture inside the fries to make its way to the surface and make them damp.

Yield: about 10 servings of 8 strips ¼ x 2 inches (0.5 x 5 cm) each
Per serving: 15 g fat; 2 g net carbs; 2 g protein; 151 calories

Cheese Puffs

These cookie-shaped snacks taste much like fluffy, mild cheese-flavored crepes. The texture is thick and spongy, much like a sponge cake. The great thing about them is that you can eat them like a slice of bread or a flat biscuit. These Cheese Puffs are delicate and tear easily, so handle gently. Sharp cheddar cheese is used in this recipe, but you can use Monterey Jack, Pepper Jack, Swiss, and others.

    2 eggs, separated
    ⅛ teaspoon cream of tartar
    1 tablespoon (14 g) butter, softened
    1 cup (115 g) shredded sharp cheddar cheese

Preheat oven to 325° (170° C). Combine egg whites and cream of tartar, and beat with an electric hand mixer until stiff peaks form. In a separate bowl, blend together egg yolks and butter. Add the cheese and thoroughly mix. Take about one-third of the beaten egg whites and mix it into the yolks until well blended. Fold the yolk mixture into the remaining whites. Do not over mix.

Place a sheet of parchment paper on a baking sheet. Spoon 4 even mounds of the whipped egg mixture onto the parchment paper. The cheese puffs will flatten while baking Bake for 18 to 20 minutes or until lightly browned. Remove the puffs from the oven and let cool, then remove with a spatula. Be very careful as you remove the cheese puffs, as they are very tender and deform easily.

Yield: 4 cheese puffs
Per cheese puff: 15 g fat; 0.5 g net carbs; 10 g protein; 177 calories

Cheese Crackers

This recipe makes great tasting keto cheese crackers. There is only one ingredient—cheese. Use a mild flavored cheese, as the flavor is enhanced as the cheese bakes. Sharp cheddar cheese produces a cracker with a very strong flavor, so stick with mild cheddar, Monterey Jack, Pepper Jack, Munster, or something similar. Pepper Jack cheese contains spicy peppers, and unless you really like hot foods, you might want to combine it with another type of cheese to mellow out the heat.

Use ½ cup (55 g) of shredded cheese for each 5-inch (12-cm) cracker or ¼ cup (28 g) for a smaller cracker. Preheat oven to 350° F (180° C). Lay a sheet of parchment paper over a cookie sheet and spray it with non-stick cooking spray. I prefer cooking spray over simply spreading oil or butter on the parchment paper because the spray has more anti-stick ability, and melted cheese tends to get sticky. Put ½ cup (55 g) of cheese on the parchment paper and spread it out evenly to 5 inches (12 cm). Make as many mounds as you like. Bake for 25 to 30 minutes, or until the cheese is hot and bubbly and beginning to turn a golden brown. Remove from the oven and let cool. Crackers can be stored in an airtight container for several days.

Yield: 1 serving per half cup (55 g) of cheese
Per serving: 18 g fat; 0.5 g net carbs; 13.5 g protein; 218 calories

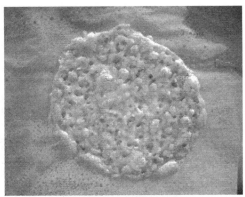
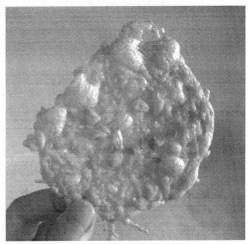

Variations:

Add any one or more of the following items to the cheese before cooking: jalapeño pepper, chopped onion, sesame seeds, caraway seeds, chopped raw bacon, sliced turkey, Canadian bacon. If you add sliced turkey or Canadian bacon, place them down on the parchment paper first and sprinkle the cheese on top. All of the other ingredients can be placed on top of the cheese.

A delicious combination is 2 tablespoons (20 g) of chopped onion and 1 teaspoon chopped jalapeño pepper on top of ½ cup (55 g) shredded cheese.

Stuffed Celery Sticks

A quick and easy snack is a celery stick layered with a high-fat filling. All of the following celery stick filling recipes follow the same basic steps:

Mix the filling ingredients. Cut celery stick in thirds. Dry each piece with a paper towel. Using a knife, spread the filling down the center indentation of each celery stick and enjoy. Store extra filling in the refrigerator, and prepare the celery sticks fresh every time you want to eat them.

Nut Butter Fillings

Celery is a very low-carb vegetable. A stalk of celery contains only 0.5 grams of carbohydrate and essentially no fat or protein. So the filling will determine how much fat, protein, and carbohydrate each stuffed celery stick delivers. One stalk of celery will hold about 2 tablespoons of filling. Nut butters make simple, tasty fillings.

Stuffed Celery Sticks make a great snack.

Each serving listed below gives approximate values for 1 stalk of celery and 2 tablespoons of nut butter.

Macadamia nut butter
Per serving: 22 g fat; 2 g net carbs; 2 g protein; 214 calories

Coconut spread
Per serving: 9.5 g fat; 2 g net carbs; 1 g protein; 97 calories

Almond butter
Per serving: 14 g fat; 4.5 g net carbs; 5 g protein; 164 calories

Peanut butter
Per serving: 14 g fat; 4.5 g net carbs; 7 g protein; 172 calories

Crab Stuffing

1 package (8 oz/225 g) cream cheese, softened
½ cup (60 g) crabmeat, drained, or imitation crabmeat
1 tablespoon (14 g) mayonnaise
½ teaspoon lemon juice
2 scallions, finely chopped
⅛ teaspoon onion salt

⅛ teaspoon garlic salt
8 stalks celery

Yield: 8 stuffed celery stalks
Per serving: 11 g fat; 2.5 g net carbs; 3 g protein; 121 calories

Cheese Pimiento

½ cups (115 g) mayonnaise
2 ounces (56 g) diced pimiento
½ teaspoon Worcestershire sauce
1 teaspoon, minced onion
⅛ teaspoon cayenne pepper
8 ounces (225 g) sharp cheddar cheese, shredded
8 stalks celery
Paprika for garnish

Yield: 8 stuffed celery stalks
Per serving: 20 g fat; 1.5 g net carbs; 7.5 g protein; 216 calories

Cream Cheese and Green Olives

1 package (8oz/225 g) cream cheese, softened
⅓ cup (55 g) chopped pimento-stuffed green olives
1 clove garlic, minced
Dash of salt and black pepper
8 stalks celery

Yield: 8 stuffed celery stalks
Per serving: 10 g fat; 2 g net carbs; 2 g protein; 106 calories

Cream Cheese and Pineapple

1 package (8oz/225 g) cream cheese, softened
8 ounces (225 g) crushed pineapple
8 stalks celery

Yield: 8 stuffed celery stalks
Per serving: 10 g fat; 4.5 g net carbs; 2.5 g protein; 118 calories

DIPS

Dips can make great high-fat, keto friendly appetizers and snacks. In place of high-carb crackers and chips for dipping, use carrot sticks, celery, cauliflower, broccoli, sliced daikon radish, celeriac (celery root), and other low-carb vegetables. While vegetables go well with dips, you are not limited to them. Also try crispy bacon (see following page), pork rinds, Cheese Crackers (page 321), and Keto Bread (page 290).

Bacon Guacamole Bites

4 strips bacon
8 tablespoons Cilantro Lime Guacamole Dip (below)

Cut bacon strips in half and cook until crisp. Use the bacon like a cracker and put a scoop of guacamole on each half strip (or full strip) and enjoy.

Yield: 8 half strips of bacon (8 servings)
Per serving (with 1 tablespoon/14 g of guacamole): 22 g fat; 1.5 g net carbs; 5.5 g protein; 226 calories

Cilantro Lime Guacamole Dip

This recipe can be used as a dip or, salad dressing, or as an accompaniment to meats and vegetables.

2 avocados
2 tablespoons (30 ml) fresh lime juice
¾ teaspoon salt, more as needed
½ teaspoon ground coriander
¼ teaspoon ground cumin

Bacon with Cilantro Lime Guacamole Dip.

4 tablespoons (4 g) chopped cilantro
1 scallion, minced
2 teaspoons minced garlic
1 teaspoon minced jalapeño pepper
¼ cup (45 g) finely chopped Roma tomatoes

Cut the avocados in half, remove the pits, and scoop the flesh, putting it into a small mixing bowl. Add lime juice, salt, coriander, and cumin, and mash them together with a spoon or fork. Stir in cilantro, scallion, garlic, jalapeño, and tomatoes. Salt to taste.

Yield: 1 ½ cups (230 g)
Per serving (¼ cup/38 g): 13 g fat; 1.5 g net carbs; 1.5 g protein; 129 calories

Hot Bacon and Cheese Dip

This dip is great as an appetizer when you have company. Provides 4 grams of fat for each tablespoon (14 g) serving. Tastes so good you can end up eating several tablespoons in no time.

4 ounces (110 g) cream cheese, room temperature
1 cup (230 g) sour cream
¾ cup (90 g) shredded cheddar cheese
6 strips sugar-free, nitrite-free bacon, cooked crisp and crumbled
3 scallions, chopped

Preheat oven to 375° F (190° C). In a bowl, combine all ingredients and mix together until well blended. Transfer to a small baking dish and bake for 30 to 35 minutes or until cheese is totally melted and bubbly.

Yield: about 2½ cups (590 g)
Per 1 tablespoon (14 g) serving: 4 g fat; 0.5 g net carbs; 2 g protein; 46 calories

Spinach Dip

1 tablespoon (15 ml) extra virgin olive oil
1 teaspoon minced garlic
9 ounce (255 g) package frozen chopped spinach, thawed and squeezed
    to remove excess liquid
8 ounce (225 g) package cream cheese
¾ cup (90 g) shredded Monterey Jack cheese
¼ cup (20 g) shredded Parmesan cheese
¼ cup (60 ml) heavy cream
¼ cup (10 g) minced fresh basil
Salt and black pepper

Preheat oven to 350° F (180° C). Heat the oil in a skillet over medium heat. Add the garlic and stir for 30 seconds. Add the spinach and cook, stirring frequently, until spinach is cooked and no liquid remains in the pan, about 4 minutes. Remove from heat and let cool.

In a medium bowl, combine the cream cheese, Monterey Jack, Parmesan, cream, basil, and a pinch of salt and black pepper. Using an electric mixer, blend the ingredients together. Add the cooked spinach mixture and mix again until blended. Pour the mixture into a casserole dish and bake for 20 minutes or until hot and bubbly. Serve with chopped vegetables, pork rinds, or Keto Bread (page 290).

Yield: about 2¾ cups (670 g)
Per 1 tablespoon (14 g) serving: 3 g fat; 0.5 g net carbs; 1 g protein; 33 calories

Avocado Egg Dip
This dip is basically guacamole with hard-boiled eggs. You can use it as a dip for vegetables or pork rinds, or as a filling for a wrap.

1 avocado
2 hard-boiled eggs, diced
¼ cup (16 g) minced fresh parsley or cilantro
2 scallions, chopped
1 tablespoon (15 ml) lemon juice
2 teaspoons lemon zest
¼ cup (60 g) mayonnaise
¼ cup (60 g) sour cream
¼ teaspoon ground cumin
1 teaspoon diced jalapeño pepper
Salt and fresh ground black pepper to taste
Several drops of hot sauce (optional)

Peel avocado and remove the pit. Chop the avocado and put it into a bowl and mash with a fork. Add diced eggs, parsley, scallions, lemon juice, lemon zest, mayonnaise, sour cream, cumin, jalapeño pepper, salt, pepper, and a few drops of hot sauce. Mix well and serve.

Yield: about 2¼ cups (500 g)
Per 1 tablespoon (14 g) serving: 2 g fat; 0.5 g net carbs; 0.5 g protein; 22 calories

Sour Cream Anchovy Dip

1 cup (230 g) sour cream
3 tablespoons (45 g) anchovy paste
1 tablespoon (15 ml) lemon juice

Mix sour cream with anchovy paste and lemon juice. Use as a dip for raw vegetables or as an accompaniment with fish.

Yield: about 1¼ cups (280 g)
Per tablespoon (14 g): 5 g fat; 0.5 g net carbs; 0.5 g protein; 49 calories

Sour Cream and Chives Dip

1 cup (230 g) sour cream
¼ cup (12 g) minced chives
1 teaspoon salt
⅛ teaspoon black pepper

Mix sour cream and chives. Taste, and if desired, add salt and pepper to your preference.

Yield: about 1 cup (224 g)
Per tablespoon (14 g): 3 g fat; 0.5 g net carbs; 0.5 g protein; 29 calories

Ranch Dip

¼ cup (30 g) plain yogurt
¼ cup (30 g) sour cream
¼ cup (4 g) diced fresh cilantro
1 scallion, finely chopped
½ teaspoon onion powder
¼ teaspoon garlic powder
½ teaspoon salt

Mix all the ingredients together. Store in an airtight container in the refrigerator. Use within 2 days.

Yield: about ½ cup (110 g)
Per tablespoon (14 g): 1 g fat; 0.5 g net carbs; 0.5 g protein; 13 calories

Salmon Dip

1 can (6 oz/170 g) salmon
½ cup (115 g) mayonnaise
1 tablespoon (14 g) extra virgin olive oil
2 ounces (56 g) sharp cheddar cheese, shredded
1 scallion, finely chopped
¼ cup (60 g) finely chopped dill pickle
⅛ teaspoon paprika
Salt and black pepper to taste

Mix salmon, mayonnaise, and olive oil until well blended. Stir in cheese, scallion, pickle, paprika, salt, and pepper. Can be stored in the refrigerator for up to a week.

Yield: about 1 cup (224 g)
Per tablespoon (14 g): 9.5 g fat; 0 g net carbs; 3 g protein; 97 calories

Index

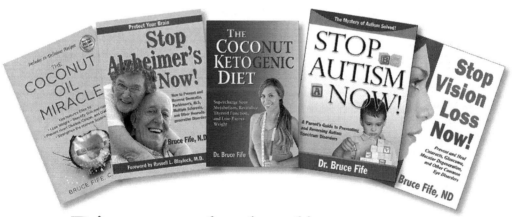

Made in the USA
Middletown, DE
02 January 2017